A STATE OF SIEGE
Politics and Policing of the Coalfields:
Miners' Strike 1984

Jim Coulter, Susan Miller & Martin Walker

GW00481132

Canary Press

A State Of Siege

© Jim Coulter, Susan Miller and Martin Walker

ISBN 0 9509967 0 X

Published by Canary Press
With the assistance of Housmans Bookshop,
Greenwich Branch NALGO and Islington Branch NALGO.

First Edition in this form, November 1984

Vols I and II published separately as 'A State of Seige' and 'The Iron Fist'

Printed in Great Britain by Grassroots, London.

Cover designed by Len Breen

Trade Distribution by Housman's
5 Caledonian Road, London N1.
01 837 4473
Mail Order and bulk Trade Union copies:
Greenwich Branch NALGO
Staffside office, Basement,
Borough Treasurer, Wellington St.
Woowich, London S.E. 18

JIM COULTER: is electrician at Woolley Colliery in the Barnsley Area. He is an NUM member who has been active in the strike since it began.

SUSAN MILLER: is a worker in the London Borough of Islington Police Committee Support Unit. She is an active NALGO member.

MARTIN WALKER: is Advisor to the London Borough of Greenwich Police Sub-Committee and a NALGO member. He is also co-author, with Geoff Coggan, of 'Frightened For My Life: an account of deaths in British prisons' (*Fontana paperback* 1982).

The work on this book undertaken by Susan Miller and Martin Walker was carried out not as local government officers but as trade unionists. The views expressed are those of the authors and do not represent the views of either Greenwich or Islington Councils or any of their members.

Acknowledgements:

We would like to thank: Mr Owen Briscoe, Yorkshire Area General Secretary and NUM National Executive Committee member, who gave us the chance to carry out the research for these volumes in the fifth week of the strike. Stephen Gallagher and James MacBride, Legal officers for Yorkshire NUM who made us feel at home in the Barnsley offices. Other Yorkshire Area officers and employees who were friendly and supportive to us. All those mineworkers from Yorkshire and Nottinghamshire who with their wives and families shared their time, knowledge and hospitality. We would also like to thank everyone who played some part in making this book and the first two volumes: for typing, Helen O'Keefe and Marion McCarthy. For reading, correcting and distribution: Chris Shurety, Lesley Sutcliffe, Prathema Mahabir, Paul Holmes, Franky Smeeth, Jill O'Brien, Brian Hill, Dave Brewer and Sue Bray. For help with organising the printing and production Andrew Burgin, Tan, Peter Webb, Craig Liddle and everyone at Grassroots.

For personal support we would like to thank Hilary Potter, Dave Brewer, Debbie Allen, Ian Cameron and Peggy Eagle. we would especially like to thank Bernard Greenbank for the editorial help and support he has given us. Finally we would like to thank those Labour councillors of Islington and Greenwich Boroughs who gave us reassurance and the officers and members of Greenwich and Islington NALGO who have given us financial support.

CONTENTS

VOLUME III Agitate! Educate! Organise!

Preface

This book is the result of nine weeks' work in the coalfields during the miners' strike. When we began, we did not intend to produce a book; we went to Yorkshire originally to offer help on legal strategies and police powers to the Yorkshire Area NUM. When we arrived in Yorkshire, and when we first went to Nottinghamshire, we found many miners confused by the tactics of the police and the courts. Then, at the beginning of the strike, it seemed important to record and relay the experience of these miners to a broader public and also to give them and their families a voice.

We wrote 'A State of Siege', the first volume in this book, covering the period March to April, and published it ourselves. Over the next five months we spent another eight weeks in Yorkshire and Nottinghamshire and wrote, 'The Iron Fist'—May to June, and 'Agitate! Educate! Organise!'—June to July. During the writing of the third volume, we decided to publish all the materials together as a book.

We realise that the book is not a coherent whole; at best, it is a chronology of the police tactics in the first five months of the strike and the strikers' reactions to them. There are changes which could have been made in each volume but increasingly we felt that publishing the material quickly was more important than creating a well ordered or 'perfect' book. Now, in the seventh month of the strike, the biggest propaganda campaign mounted by the Government and its allies centres upon violence. The media reflects an ahistorical view of the world which fails to give a background to the present struggle. We hope that this book will bring to the attention of many people the way in which the strike has developed and explain the way in which the state has escalated its use of organised and institutional violence against the members of the NUM and their families.

Of the things which we would have changed if we had the time, two things stand out; the book would undoubtedly be better with more detailed information about the immediate history of the NUM, the mining industry and other industries which have come under threat.

However, we chose to concentrate on policing, and we believed from the beginning that in this strike, policing would be at the very centre of the government's strategy to crush the NUM.

A second change would involve the way in which we recorded the role of women in the strike. Concentrating as we did upon the pickets, after their arrest, we missed interviewing and talking to women about the strike. Also, their role developed, extended, and became more organized while we were writing up areas of work which we had planned. The section of the book in which women speak of their role, holding up half the sky, comes at the end, not as it were, tucked away or as an afterthought, but placed there so that readers will be left with the strongest impression of the womens' role in the strike.

Since the separate publication of the first two volumes, a number of criticisms have been made of our work. One consistent criticism has been suggestion that we have described a working class cowed in the face of an all-powerful state. We accept that the story which the book unfolds is in some respects depressing. Because the writing dwells upon the most organized and powerful institution of the state police, it records some of the most depressing news of the strike. However, we believe that it is important to inform everyone of the powers which the state is organizing against the working class, not so that we might weaken and give up, but so that we fight with a real understanding of what is ahead of us. Although the story within the book is depressing at times, it is not demoralizing; the determination and the strength of the miners and their families to win and defeat policies which damage us all is self-evident.

To some, our account of the police actions during the strike will appear simplistic and lacking in polemical argument or analysis; perhaps some will consider that we have strayed too far into the realm of sociology. We were from the beginning determined to let as many people as possible speak for themselves. Not only is the voice of the striking miner stifled in most reflections on the strike but the radical voice of the working class, their life and their history is constantly avoided by organizations and individuals even on the left.

All three of the authors have a profound belief that the miners' strike is not just another strike and those on the left who portray it as such are doing a tragic disservice to the working class. We believe that the National Union of Mineworkers presently holds within its grasp the fate of the whole organized working class. That is not to say that if they are defeated the class will be defeated, but it is essential for working people to know what a defeat will entail.

During the early seventies, in a period of high employment, the defeat of the dock workers striking to resist containerisation, passed with little notice. There were even those who said, as they say now about print workers, that the defence of obviously redundant jobs by unions is an anachronism in a period of rapid technological change. The defeat of the car workers at British Leyland also passed without the collective voice of the Trade Union movement making itself heard. There the state isolated and divided off the activists within the union using exactly the same strategies which are now being used against the miners. And, as in the case of the miners, the same voices could be heard informing us that after all, car workers were like dockers: overpaid, lazy and all too eager to strike. Nothing of course, could be further from the truth. It was only with the defeat of the steel workers and the rationalisation of that industry in a period of high unemployment that it became clearly evident what was at stake.

It is not new technology which determines employment patterns, the number of the unemployed or the poverty which they are doomed to in our society. The advance and the consolidation of new technology has an ideological master: the politics of capitalism. Capitalism has but one objective, to ensure that the rate of profit stays high. To this end all its functions are directed: ideology, culture and the apparatus of repression.

When the Conservatives talk about using monetarism to balance the books, they are trying to deceive us. Capitalism has never had the slightest interest in balancing the books; the expression implies a sense of equal distribution. The books can't balance when the capitalists are walking away with wealth by the sack-load. Even within the petty and tyranical terms of monetarism itself, the books will not balance; never has such a shallow theory been so dishonestly embellished. Every country that has employed monetarism as an economic practice has suffered and still suffers from inflation; more seriously still, unemployment has become endemic and the repressive apparatus of the state has been strengthened to deal with the resistance of those unemployed.

In the present crisis, the state will develop and use all its most brutal forms of repression based upon its new technology. The police system, which has been undergoing modification since the end of the economic boom in late sixties has now entered its most repressive cycle. It could be termed 'siege policing'. Whether it be by infiltrating or containing, the police are concerned to curtail the movements of, and to hem in, all those who wish to manifest their collective power on the streets, in the community, or at public gatherings. Siege policing is not simply the 'crisis policing' which has been used against the working class in strikes for a hundred years, it is *continuous* crisis policing, even in times of apparent order. Whether it be at Greenham, during anti-nuclear demonstrations, anti-apartheid pickets, 'Stop the City', or in the coalfields, its aim is to control and criminalise, separate and keep separate those who own nothing from those who own capital.

Out of the ruins of de-industrialisation, from the ghost towns populated by the growing unemployed, in the north of England, in Scotland and in the six counties of the north of Ireland, a class will begin to coalesce which considers itself not only forgotten by the Labour Party and the Trade Union bureaucracy, but victims *of capitalism itself*. It will be absolutely clear to this underclass that capitalism, however it is reformed or amended, can never afford them participation in their own lives or the regeneration of their communities. This class, at the one moment thrown on the scrap heap, will in the next moment provide the base for the coming struggle against the state.

The miners' strike, even when it is won, will not be the end of the struggle in that industry; redundancies, pit closures and sackings will appear on the agenda again and again. Capitalism has to create unemployment in order to survive.

But after this strike, those organised within work and in the community, will have their class resolve sharpened and those whose labour is dispensed with will not allow themselves to 'die' discretely. There will be an army of the conscious unemployed and a workforce which puts politics first; they will find their class sisters and brothers amongst those who have become politically marginalised in the urban areas, in black struggles and womens' struggles. Allies will appear amongst those who have seen and felt the gathering power of the state, amongst the Irish and the working class youth who are increasingly branded as criminal.

The miners' strike, is not *just another strike*, neither it nor the factors which provoked it will go away. It represents the first mass, organised working class opposition in England, Scotland and Wales to the restructuring of capitalism and the state. In this present period, cut off from an earlier history, the miners and other working class groups have been shown the way by black movements and the womens' movement, particularly the women of Greenham. These women, more than any other group have shown that real change has now got to be total change; real opposition, total opposition. A committment to struggle now means a committment to new values, a new understanding and new forms of organisation.

A DEFEAT FOR THE MINERS IS A DEFEAT FOR US ALL!
VICTORY TO THE MINING COMMUNITIES!

Jim Coulter
Susan Miller
Martin Walker
October 1984

The first British police were public order police, tested in Ireland and then established on the mainland in 1829 by Sir Robert Peel's Police Act. Not only did they harass thieves and criminals but they were used against the nascent working-class movement. The police were later used physically to restrain the growing power of organised labour. The British political genius was to make this police force, clearly taking sides in a class struggle, appear to be an independent, non-partisan agency simply enforcing the law.

Tom Bowden
Beyond the Limits of the Law, Pelican 1978.

The nature of an authoritarian regime is determined by the balance of forces within the system. The first stage in the development of a modern police state is the centralisation of all police services, if hitherto they have been on a local footing.

Finally, the police apparatus detaches itself from its dependence on the army for armed force, and either a riot police section is reinforced with armoured vehicles or a standing gendarmerie becomes a para-military force subordinate to the police authorities. When the police apparatus is immune to control by the civil service, the judiciary and the army, and is an independent leading state institution in its own right, a modern police state has been formed.

Brain Chapman
Police State,
Key Concepts in Political Science 1970.

VOLUME I
A State of Siege

PART ONE
The Context

Introduction

When the strike of the National Union of Mineworkers began in Yorkshire in March 1984, no doubt many workers imagined that it would be a strike much like any other, an uneven but winnable struggle.

The miners' strike was, however, from its beginning unlike many strikes which have taken place in Britain since the second world war. It was not a strike over a demarcation dispute, nor were its demands economistic; simply demands for higher wages. The miners' strike was a strike in favour of community, in favour of working class culture, a class strike against capital and its power to move families and workers about or throw them into poverty.

The dispute is not a struggle between two strong men, Ian McGregor and Arthur Scargill, as the media likes to portray it; behind these symbols, two classes are locked in battle. The miners and Ian McGregor are speaking different languages; while McGregor and his class are talking about profitability, the miners and their families are talking about the survival of their class and community.

Neither the working class as a whole nor the miners in particular have chosen the time for this present struggle. The miners' strike has come about because of the brutal economic policies of a Conservative Government. The radical right of the present Conservative Government believe in monetarism, an economic philosophy which depends upon the idea of the 'free market' of the eighteenth and nineteenth centuries, periods when organised labour was badly formed or non-existent. In order to return to a 'free market' economy the government will have to destroy the organisations of the working class, principally the trade unions and the political parties of the left.

Monetarism is a philosophy which believes that the books can be balanced entirely in monetary terms. The present government is a government of profit and loss, and if welfare and community do not pay dividends then they will go to the wall.

The state's weapons in this uneven battle against the unions and working class communities are varied, from the media to the civil law, but most essentially they include a national and well equipped para-military police force in close collaboration with the armed forces.

It is within this framework that we have to understand 'civil liberties' or 'rights'. Civil liberties are a luxury which only survive at times of economic growth. When there is a crisis of profitability or when the owners of capital decide to re-locate labour or abandon it, civil liberties become dead letters. The freedom to move about the country, for example, is only a right as long as there is work and capital needs labour.

While the state has a number of weapons at its disposal to divide the miners and keep pits open, the working class only has the power of its withdrawn labour, the weapon of its class solidarity.

Conservatism: The Politics of Civil War

'Under a future Conservative government confrontation is inevitable. What remains to be determined is the timing, the ground of battle, the balance of forces, all the factors which will in short, spell defeat or victory'.

'It is not confrontation, after all, which would be the ultimate tragedy: the ultimate tragedy would be to have confrontation and to lose'.

Editorial: *The Free Nation* paper of NAFF

'What of human rights? The quick answer is that in a war, human rights are unfortunately likely to suffer'.

Brian Crozier, on class struggle.

As the mineworkers strike continues it becomes evident that what motivates the government is nothing to do with the economic viability of the mining industry. This particular government would see the whole industry in complete ruin if they could win a final victory over the Trade Union movement.

As in many matters the right wing politics of Margaret Thatcher dictate that a major part of the motivation for any conflict is political and ideological. While there may be economic reasons for the struggles which this government has pressed upon the working class these are obscure to the general population and clear only to right wing academics and American monetarists. What remains upon the surface, and is the motivating factor, is an obsession with breaking the Trade Union movement and pauperising the working class.

A portion of the following report deals with the politics behind policing the coalfields rather than the strategy on the ground. It is important to understand the politics behind the policing because through the politics we can see that what the Conservative government are pursuing is not the 'rule of law' but the 'law of rule'; brute force and violence.

Rather than policing being an incidental spin off from the dispute it is at the very heart of it. The dispute is no longer a trade dispute between workers and their employers but a life or death struggle between those who produce coal and therefore wealth, and the state which demands autocratic control over that labour and wealth.

With their response to the picketing of Orgreave Coking Depot in the last weeks of May the government showed what was really at stake. Orgreave was from the beginning both a cabinet decision and an experimental battle ground for the National Riot Force, it was intended to be a set piece battle of historic proportions. The venue, the provocation of some 6,000 police, the highly paid scab lorry drivers with their police escort, had all been theatrically managed in order to publicly teach the miners a lesson.

By the second day Orgreave was turned into an embattled camp. Upwards of six thousand police were stationed in its environs. They marched in serials up and down the long straight road past the coking plant. They brought with them a retinue of cavalry, dogs and vans laden with armour and weaponry. Office blocks were taken over as police headquarters, marquees set up in the backs of buildings to feed the troops. Only a quagmire was needed to turn the scene to that of war rather than an industrial dispute. It had become a war in all but appearance.

The Yorkshire NUM instructed its pickets only to fall back on Orgreave if pits in Nottinghamshire could not be reached. To make sure that men *did* fall back on Orgreave the police tightened their road blocks on the Yorkshire/Nottinghamshire border. For Thatcher and McGregor Orgreave was to be the miners' Waterloo. They counted not just upon physical force and media management but on thirty years of post war working class socialisation. They believed that this socialisation would deter workers from physically fighting with the police. Their assumptions were wrong; despite the injuries, despite even the horses and the unleashed dogs, the miners came back time and again, each time better prepared and better organised. What began for the government as an excercise for the National Riot Force ended in ignominy for the police when British Steel suspended the lorry convoys in the middle of June.

At Orgreave the true political intentions of the government became clear, they had nothing to do with the coal industry, nothing to do with reconciliation or a settlement to the industrial dispute. The sole object of the Cabinet was ideological, to mortally wound the National Union of Mineworkers, to defeat it with military force and naked violence. But the miners had known from the beginning that what was at stake was their very future, the future of their families, their communities and class.

The present Conservative government sees as its historic task the crushing of the organised working class. Wherever the collective working class are powerful the government has made cuts. Its economic designs go hand in hand with a philosophy which will brook no opposition from the Trade Union movement or left political parties. After the fall of the Heath government in 1974, the extreme right within the Conservative Party began to organise. For years they believed that they had seen the party and the country betrayed by Conservative politicians who had flirted with socialism, whose policies gave little or no support to full blooded capitalism.

The heritage of the radical right which began to form the Conservative Party after 1974, drew upon obscure early capitalist thinkers, unheard of in the mainstream of intellectual development, men like Ludwig Von Mises. It bolstered its philosophy with individualist propagandists like Friedrich Hayek (given a knighthood in 1984) who believes that the working class should not be allowed any collective organisation and who wrote in 'The Road to Serfdom', "there has often been more cultural and spiritual freedom under an autocratic rule than under some democracies".

They found a contemporary guru in Milton Friedman who believes that Hong Kong with its slave labour and almost totally corrupt and violent police force represents the prize of market economies. A man whose economic philosophies underpinned the bloody overthrow of the democratically elected government of Salvadore Allende in Chile in 1974.

There was no group too right wing to be embraced by the radical right and though it made slighting asides about fascism it gathered into itself religious movements financed by South Africa. Its contacts inhabited para-military fascist groups like the British Movement and Column 88. At its heart were men for whom the war against the working class had become a game for old, and not so old soldiers, men who had collected money from unknown Foreign Office sources to run private armies and reaped harvests from the CIA. Private armies abounded and were grant aided. Beyond this lunatic fringe were men and women of the lower middle class who could have been fascists in another age, who now used the language of the right, morality, thrift, will and power, in planning the butchery of the Health Service, the Education system and Nationalised industries.

There were those on the left and even within the Labour Party who could see what was coming; few raised their voices because the prospect seemed too alarming. By the late seventies these figures from the shadows were represented in government and Britain was ruled by a consortium of right wingers whose true political hue was so horrifying that even some of its adherents were frightened to claim membership.

As some realised after Thatcher came to power the Conservative Party was no longer Conservative. It was a classical Liberal party drawing upon a variety of economic and personal philosophies united by the theme of 'freedom' for the lower middle class. It was though an odd kind of freedom, the freedom of those in employment, the freedom to exploit, the freedom to make private profit out of collective labour and the freedom to rule without criticism or genuine debate. The freedom of those frustrated by lack of power.

The new Conservative party was rabidly anti-communist and grotesquely anti-working class. While it proclaimed a desire to 'roll back the frontiers of the state', it only did this in those situations when private capital held the upper hand over labour, in other areas the balance would have to be righted by the intervention of a state controlled police force wading in on the employers' side. Although it professed a belief in the free play of market forces its first aim was to dismantle the Trade Union movement leaving labour without any bargaining power. With a massive reserve of unemployed, capital would be able to determine wage rates and still make profits during a world crisis.

The first Conservative government under Thatcher in 1979 owed much of its success to the National Association For Freedom (NAFF), now called the Freedom Association NAFF gained an almost mystical potency amongst left observers and activists. Essentially it was an umbrella organisation beneath which all the Conservative dissidents gathered after the fall of Heath. NAFF came into being after Ross McWhirter was assassinated by the Irish Republican Army in

December 1975. Before his death McWhirter set up a group called 'Self Help' with Lady Birdwood, and in June 1975, still stinging from the collapse of the Conservative government they placed large advertisements in the press asking industrialists and bankers to fight the power of the unions. The Trade Unions, they considered, were the gravest of all menaces to the prosperity and well-being of Great Britain. The advertisement was entitled 'Time to stand up to the Unions'.

Self Help was an organisation which inhabited the extreme right wing fringe; nevertheless, it teamed up with NAFF and added its resources and philosophy to the campaign for Thatcher and a Conservative government. The original council of NAFF was made up of industrialists, individualists, counter-insurgency experts and right wing M.P.'s, amongst others, John Gouriet, Robert Moss, Peregrine Worsthorne, Rhodes Boyson, Stephen Hastings M.P., Norman Tebbit M.P., Sir Robert Thompson, Winston Churchill M.P., John Gorst M.P., and Jill Knight M.P.

From 1975 until 1979 NAFF was involved in many anti-trade union and anti-working class activities. With 'Self Help' and other right wing pressure groups they organised against SLADE and other print unions who they saw as a threat to the 'free press'; they took out an injunction against the crew of the Eagle Ferry who had refused to unload the boat in England after the business was sold during the Ferry's voyage, making the crew redundant; they fought the Labour government's plan to bring in comprehensive schools in Thameside; they provided scab labour for the Randolf Hotel in Oxford when the employees struck; they tried to take out an injunction against post office workers when they threatened a boycott of South Africa and finally they fought by the side of the Grunwick management. There they organised a strike breaking mail delivery of films to be processed.

NAFF selected, tutored and then exploited to the full those with grievances against Trade Unions. They took legal action a number of times. Their case was always that of the misrepresented and downtrodden employer, the small business person and the individual worker crying for the freedom to work without responsibility to the rest of the work force. They took up a number of cases against the closed shop. Behind this pretence of defending the weak individual against collective coercion was the strength and money of the bosses and the multinational corporations. NAFF obtained funds and support from large industrial concerns.

The intelligence system of the radical right, based upon official Government sources and industry financed information services, was extensive. Through groups and associations like the Institute for the Study of Conflict, the Royal Institute for International Affairs, the Economist 'Foreign Report' and even the Foreign Office itself, they were able to influence the emerging foreign policy of the new Conservative Party. Through secret international organisations like the 'Bilderburgh Group' and the 'Trilateral Commission', meetings of leading industrialists, academics and Government ministers, they were able to influence foreign policy perhaps more powerfully than any democratically elected western government. At home through organisations like IRIS the anti-marxist information service, the 'Economic League' and 'Common Cause', many of which organisations had right wing trade unionists on them, they were able to provide employers with information on trade unionists who applied for jobs or who worked in 'vulnerable' industries.

NAFF spawned and took under its wing a series of smaller pressure groups whose aims coincided with its own. It became a popularist campaigning organisation which drew marginalised right-wing causes together. The 'Better Britain Society' worked to establish 'a code of morality and honesty in Britain'. The 'Anti-Strike Union' argued for wage cuts of 10%. 'Aims for Industry' which pre-dated NAFF by more than thirty years campaigned tirelessly against nationalisation. The 'Social Security Scroungers Campaign' started by Ian Sproat M.P. carried out its own review of cases in which they claimed people had duped the benefits system. The 'Silent Majority' campaigned for power to be given to the lower middle class who it felt had been the victims of collective labour for too long. 'Civil Assistance' was a collection of volunteers ready to intervene at any time if called upon during a disorder or industrial dispute. 'GB 75' was a similar enterprise.

The two most respected strategists behind the National Association for Freedom, both of whom had experience of working in secret government departments, were Robert Moss and Brian Crozier. Their politics are ideosyncratic, neither Conservative or straightforwardly Republican, they are both cold war warriors who would like to see the Soviet Union brought to its knees. They are both avid supporters of American foreign policy and they have both written about juntas. Crozier and Moss have both studied and written prolifically about Latin America. At different times both men have taken a keen interest in the state of democracy in Chile.

Moss and Crozier frequently expressed the view that the military would have to step in during a period of disorder in Britain. Writing in the *Daily Telegraph* in 1975, Brian Crozier lauded the military junta in Argentina; "The military saved the people from a fate worse than anything which is now happening''. What Crozier meant by 'what is now happening' is not clear. We know that right wing death squads killed thousands, that people went missing, that there was torture and malnutrition. ''We in Britain share the same problems as Argentina, excessive trade union power and an inflated state sector. I believe that Argentina has laid the pre-conditions for an economic miracle. Whether the miracle comes to pass will depend on whether the government has the will and the skill to *rid itself of trade unionism* and of a swollen state sector''. Again about Argentina, ''Now a newly drafted trade union reform bill calls for a limit of two years on executive office; prohibits political activity and rules out political levies''.

In his book 'The Collapse of Democracy', Robert Moss posits a situation where, through unchecked and permissive liberalism, the Communist Party begin to gain power in Britain. Moss's solution echoes Crozier's, he cites Brazil and Argentina as examples of societies where the military have been able to cleanse the nation of its left parties, trade unionists and thinkers.

At the same time as appearing to argue for regimes which came to power by slaughter and survive by torture, both Moss and Crozier in common with others in the NAFF were obsessed with the process and the rule of law. The law is, they said, an abstract system of ideas which men were subservient and answerable to. In their philosophy, the law has nothing to do with class but is an independent set of rules which treats everyone with a rational and independent fairness.

On picketing and Employment legislation the NAFF had this to say in the mid-seventies: ''All pickets should be part of the existing workforce of any place where picketing is taking place. Where threats of violence or obstruction are likely to occur the police should be given sufficient powers to prevent contact between pickets and those not engaged in picketing *by cordoning off a particular access route to a workplace*. It is for instance an offence... to shout insulting or derogatory words such as 'blackleg' or 'scab' and, within certain discretionary limits, this type of behaviour ought not to be tolerated''.

Many NAFF exponents were well aware that the rule of law can take you only so far down the road to power. Writing in *Free Nation*, Norris McWhirter in an article, 'Using the Law', had this to say; ''The law, particularly the civil law, works to a strict timetable. When the need arises however, law can move with remarkable speed. *Even the normally sacred procedural rules can be brushed aside*''.

By 1978, the new Conservative Party under Thatcher was in sight of power, through a series of campaigning groups and 'think tanks' their strategy had been worked out to the last dot and comma. In early 1978, a Report from the Conservative Party's policy group on nationalised industries was leaked to the Economist. It had been drafted by one of the party's leading right wing M.P.'s Nicholas Ridley. The report concluded that it would be far easier and more permanent to fragment some nationalised industries rather than sell them off whole to private interests. In relation to coal pits in particular it suggested that those which could not be sold off to private enterprise should be handed over to workers co-operatives. In an industry which by any analysis will become more capital intensive over the years, this would equal the closing of pits while concentrating investment on new technology in a few. But perhaps the most interesting thing which the Ridley Report had to say was in relation to the coming conflict between the unions and the state, which it considered would be the result of wage claims or redundancies.

The report anticipated that in the first or second year of the next Conservative government there would be a political threat from its enemies. It could come from a 'vulnerable' industry like the coal industry it suggested. The report outlined a five point plan to counter any such threat:

- Profit figures should be rigged so that high wage claims could be conceded.
- The eventual battle should be on ground chosen by the Conservatives, in a field which they think could be won. The report mentions the steel industry in particular.
- A Thatcher government should build up coal stocks, particularly in the power stations. Make contingency plans for the import of coal. Encourage the recruitment of non-union lorry drivers by haulage companies to help move coal where necessary. Introduce dual coal/oil firing in all power stations as quickly as possible.
- Be able to cut off the money supply to strikers and make the union finance them.
- There should be a large mobile squad of police equipped and prepared to uphold the law against violent picketing. "Good non-union drivers" should be recruited to cross picket lines with police protection.

From 1974 until 1979 the new right organised their government in exile and nothing that they have done since should have come as a shock. To any group which believes as vehemently as the Conservatives do in class struggle, civil war is the only possible solution to the 'problem' of the organised working class. The right have done nothing to disillusion us since coming to power, they have carried out their manifesto to the letter. It is a tragedy that many on the left did not bother to read it.

How could there be a settlement in the present dispute with a government and a political party which wants to cut the throat of the working class? Any worker who compromised would be aiding and abetting their own suicide and the death of the trade union movement.

As the strike goes on and the ideological intentions of the present government become evident the reality of the conflict will become obvious to more and more trade unionists. The government of course has its tactical solution well charted, it was documented by Robert Moss in the 'Collapse of Democracy' and in Brian Crozier's article 'Post Disaster Systems'; after a long and bitter struggle paralleled with destabalisation the government will fall back on military rule. Counter-insurgency policing will be endemic to this rule and cleansing of left elements will be ongoing. The way to victory for the miners is equally well documented and it can only be achieved by the concerted action of the whole working class. It is time that other trade unions rallied to the miners' side and to the call of their class.

The Background to the Strike

Four years ago in 1980 at the annual NUM conference a resolution was passed to take whatever action was necessary to oppose pit closures, other than those due to proven seam exhaustion. This decision was unanimous.

At that same conference, Arthur Scargill then President of the Yorkshire Area NUM, claimed that the National Coal Board (NCB) had a list of 50 proposed pit closures. This was denied by Sir Derek Ezra the Chairman of the NCB at that time.

In 1981 the Conservative Government backed down in the face of a threatened national miners' strike over pit closures and agreed instead to give more funding and support to the mining industry.

In 1982 Arthur Scargill, by then President of the NUM, was given leaked NCB documents classifying pits into short and long-life and outlining the 30 biggest loss making pits. Seventy five mines were listed as short life and Scargill claimed that these would be closed within five years. At that time the NUM National Executive's call for action was rebuffed on a ballot after a massive propaganda campaign by the NCB. Scargill, however, stuck to his 'hit-list' of proposed pit closures, still strenuously denied by the NCB.

In September 1983, Ian MacGregor, Chairman of British Steel, was appointed the new Chairman of the Coalboard. He has since presided over a massive 'rationalisation' of the industry, increasing redundancies (presently 450 a week) and accelerating pit closures. There has been progressively less consultation with the unions and the retraction by the NCB of previous agreements. Shortly after his appointment, McGregor stated that private foreign capital would be welcome in the British coal industry. It was evident that as in relation to all other nationalised industries, the present government had the long term objective of handing the coalfields over to private enterprise.

In the last week of February 1984 the South Yorkshire Panel, which comprises 15,000 men, went on strike over meal breaks at Manvers Colliery. On March 1st, the NCB announced the closure of Cortonwood pit near Rotherham and then on March 2nd, the closure of Bullcliffe Wood pit near Barnsley. The Yorkshire Area NUM Council met on March 5th, and called a Yorkshire Area strike from the end of the last shift on Friday March 9th.

Scotland also had two pits under threat, Bogside in Fife and Polmaise in Stirlingshire. Workers at these pits went on strike on March 7th, and Scotland also called an Area strike from the end of the last shift on March 9th.

On March 6th, following these decisions, McGregor announced that 20 pits would close and 20,000 jobs disappear in the next year. Even this was not the reality claimed Arthur Scargill; the ultimate loss would be in the region of 84,000 jobs. On the same day Scargill pressed McGregor for a guarantee that there would be no compulsory redundancies. McGregor refused to give it.

At the same time, to seduce younger workers into accepting voluntary redundancies the Government announced greatly increased severance payments. The new terms, to be introduced from the end of March, would guarantee £1,000 for every year of service for all miners between 21 and 50 who agreed to take voluntary redundancy. For some men this represented three times the amount they would have received under the old terms.

On March 8th, the National Executive Committee of the NUM agreed that the Areas of Scotland, Yorkshire, South Wales and Kent could have official Area disputes, with immediate official status for any other area which wished to join the dispute.

On the first day of the strike, all of the Yorkshire pits were out and more than a half of the coalfield was brought to a standstill by picketing. From the start Yorkshire miners concentrated their efforts on the moderate Nottinghamshire pits, where less than half of the workers were supporting the action. Nottinghamshire with some other areas was calling for a national ballot. There seems little doubt that many of the men in Nottinghamshire believed that in the short term their jobs were not threatened. There are also historical reasons for the moderation in Nottinghamshire. Notts miners had, for some time, received higher bonus payments and more overtime because of better geological conditions and advanced technology. Having no real tradition of militancy, they had been treated more favourably by the NCB, ensuring their continued moderation.

Within the next few days, with about 75% of the miners on strike, several areas held ballots rejecting strike action and there were calls, orchestrated by the government and the media, for a national ballot of all members.

On March 13th, only three days after apparently rejecting the use of the 1980 and 1982 Employment legislation, the NCB sought a high court injunction against 'flying pickets'. This was granted the following day and pickets were supposedly confined from then on to their own pits.

On the same day, the Nottinghamshire police were reinforced by officers drafted in from five other areas. There were battles with the police at Ollerton Colliery and the police began stopping pickets driving up the A1.

Pickets from Yorkshire continued to defy the High Court injunction and concentrated on the Nottinghamshire, Lancashire and Derbyshire pits. There was a high police presence at pits and in surrounding areas. At Ollerton pit in Nottinghamshire on March 15th, newspapers reported a clash between 300 pickets and 300 police officers following which a miner died. Leon Brittan, the Home Secretary, announced that 3,000 police reinforcements from seventeen forces were on standby. He stated that the police had clear power to prevent obstruction and intimidation of those who wanted to work and could 'take preventative action by stopping vehicles and people'.

By March 16, only eleven pits were working normally. The NCB and the Government stalled on court proceedings for contempt of the the injunctions against the miners and instead relied upon the criminal law and a heavy police presence. In the ensuing days picketing in the Nottinghamshire area drew a massive and unprecedented response from the police. Cars with pickets from Kent were refused entry to the Dartford Tunnel, and the Nottinghamshire border was virtually sealed off with police road blocks. Pickets were arrested either before they could arrive at the pits, or whilst standing peacefully picketing at pit entrances.

Throughout the next week, with 80% of the workforce on strike, pickets continued to put pressure on the Nottinghamshire pits while also beginning to shift the emphasis towards the picketing of power stations, wharves, road and rail traffic. Many of the unions involved had already expressed support, and on March 25th, the British Rail Board announced that support for the miners from ASLEF and the NUR had caused a 50% reduction in the movement of coal (80% of coal is moved by rail). By the beginning of April, the transport, rail and shipping unions had all given their official support and the National Union of Seamen had instructed members to block imports of coal. The Government began to bring coal in using workers from other countries or scab labour. The Central Electricity Generating Board increased its use of oil and imported fuel oil from Rotterdam despite claims to have up to six months' supply of coal at most power stations.

Amidst calls for a national ballot of all miners from the Government, the NCB and the media, picketing continued. Miners were by now making consistent allegations of police violence, phone tapping, the use of 'snatch squads' and special branch questioning on their political beliefs.

Gerald Kaufman, the Shadow Home Secretary, was given a file containing details of police misdemeanours (see Appendix 2) by the Yorkshire NUM. On April 6th, the backbench Labour MP for Barnsley West, Mr. Allen McKay gained an emergency debate on civil liberties and the police action in the Commons. This debate took place on April 10th. The opposition had gone into the debate badly equipped. So unsure were the Labour Party about their stand that Neil Kinnock, the leader, did not speak. The Government wiped the floor with Labour party politicians who could not divorce themselves from the historical bi-partisan approach to the police.

Replying to the debate Douglas Hurd, Minister of State at the Home Office, said: 'Those making allegations against the police could seek a remedy through the courts or the independent police complaints procedure'. Hurd accused Kaufman of 'generalised nonsense' and Tony Benn of 'living in a world of imagined conspiracies which has only to be exhibited to be seen to be absurd'.

By the end of the fifth week of the strike, 80% of the miners were still out and there had been in the region of 1,000 arrests. There were no signs that the miners were going to turn back now, and every sign that the Government and the NCB were striving to gain a military style advantage over the miners.

The National Reporting Centre and the Association of Chief of Police Officers

"The special 'built-in' riot-force concept provides the best means for the control of civil disturbances and violence in a democratic society"[1]

The policing of the miners' dispute has brought into sharp focus the wide discretionary powers available to the police. It has given the lie to the often repeated mythology that there are a number of autonomous and local constabulary forces in England and Wales. One of the most disturbing factors to emerge in the dispute is the national role of the Association of Chief of Police Officers (ACPO), a professional body representing Chief Constables, their Assistants and Deputies in England and Wales.

According to the text books, the police force in England and Wales is run on a constabulary basis and comprises 43 areas. The administration of the police service is carried out in a tri-partite agreement by the Home Secretary, the local police Authority or Committee and the Chief Constable. The Police Committee of a County Council consists of two thirds local councillors and one third magistrates. The six metropolitan County Councils, excluding London, constitute Police Authorities, as does the City of London. All the Police Committees report back to their County Councils although some of them are not a part of the County Council structure. Under the 1964 Police Act, the Chief Constable is responsible for the direction and control of the local force on operation and policy matters. The Police Committee deals with staffing, including the appointment of the Chief Constable, equipment, costs and accomodation and is responsible for 'the maintainance of an adequate and efficient police force'. It has no say on policy matters. While the Home Secretary does not have a general statutory responsibility for maintaining the efficiency of the police force, he does have a strong central role with powers of direction on various important matters. Recently there has been criticism from the Metropolitan Authorities that the Home Secretary himself is deciding upon the appointment of Chief Constables.

On the recommendation of the Home Secretary, Her Majesty's Inspector of Constabularies (HMI) are appointed to report to him on the efficiency of all constabulary areas. It was the HMI Sir Lawrence Byford that the Home Secretary instructed in the second week of the strike to go to Nottingham and report to him on the effectiveness of the Nottinghamshire constabulary in dealing with the strike. In this way the Home Secretary overode the Nottinghamshire Police Committee.

Given this structure, it comes as something of a surprise to find that the organising body in the policing of the miners' dispute is ACPO who have set themselves up in the National Reporting Centre (NRC) at Scotland Yard. The National Reporting Centre was set up in 1972, in the wake of the Saltley Gate, Shrewsbury pickets and Pentonville Five incidents. At that time Sir Robert Carr, the Home Secretary, announced that he had been discussing with Chief Constables how to combat 'violence and victimisation in industrial disputes'. The Special Patrol Group had in fact already been used in London against Bryant Colour workers and dockers picketing a paper warehouse during the dock strike. An anti-picket squad was set up in November 1973 so that 'Scotland Yard maintains a central picket branch under a Deputy Assistant Commissioner, where two sergeants collect and co-ordinate information on disputes, militant trade union points, flying pickets etc.'[2] This information was to be passed on to highly mobile para-military units (at that time the Special Patrol Group) to facilitate, national and prompt 'control'.[3]

By January 1974 the *Sunday Times* was reporting that there was a special squad of 800 trained police ready to go anywhere at any time during the miners strike, 'A special unit kept watch on known extremists in such areas as Stainforth near the Hatfield Main Colliery and Cadeby near Mexborough and the Chief Constable said he has identified possible trouble areas and a plan of action has been worked out.'

A *Times* report of March 19th, 1984 suggests that the Centre has been activated on at least three occasions since 1972, including the 1981 riots in Toxteth and Brixton. It's existance was virtually unknown in its advanced form until the current controller of the Centre made a public statement on March 18th 1984, about its' role in the miners' strike.

The Controller of the National Reporting Centre is always the current president of ACPO—presently the Chief Constable of Humberside, David Hall. It was his decision to put the centre into operation on March 13th. We now know however that on February 9th, there was a meeting at the Home Office between the Home Secretary, the Attorney General and all Chief Constables.[4] It appears that this meeting was to review the policing situation in the wake of the NGA dispute, but it is probable that the Attorney General briefed the Chief Constables on the legal strategy in the event of a miners' strike. A month before the strike began the police were already receiving political instructions by a method which by-passed the County Police Authorities.

Hall claimed that within three and a quarter hours of the picketing beginning in Nottinghamshire 1,000 officers had been mobilised from different forces. A few days later, after consultation with HMI and the Home Secretary, Hall organised the deployment of more than 8,000 officers involving *all but two* of the Constabularies in the country, to police the dispute. The officers deployed came from specialised Support Units; they are officers trained in riot control techniques and provided nationally with the same transport and similar equipment. These officers have been maintained at this level, on full alert, throughout the strike.

During the 1970's more than half of the 52 police forces in the United Kingdom created Special Patrol Groups or similar support units trained in riot control and the use of fire arms. The mutual aid agreement between constabularies is serviced by these support units (see Appendix 1). Each Police Support Unit consists of three sections of ten officers each, plus sergeants and an Inspector. Although we know that the building of these various support units began after Saltley Gate, the official reason for them possibly being drawn together was a pending nuclear attack. The force was then to be mobilised on 'receipt' by the Chief Constable of 'a message from the Home Office'. In reality the Police Support Units established across the country were to deal with public disorders, strikes and riots. It is estimated that even on the basis of one Police Support Unit per division there would be a standing force of 11,000 specially trained riot police available. It was intended from the beginning that this 'third force' would be controlled from a special operations room in Scotland Yard; we now know this is the National Reporting Centre.[5]

Hall and his assistant, the Chief Constable of Bedfordshire, Andrew Sloan, are personally responsible for the deployment of officers, after negotiations with the Chief Constable concerned. They do not however have any responsibility to the County Police Authorities. Hall and other officers at the National Reporting Centre have played down their role as a 'strategic command' for a National Riot Force, maintaining that they are simply monitoring the situation and helping local constabularies; 'If a problem moves from point A to point B we would move to assist local police forces as necessary', he stated on March 18th.

Even this short statement gives the lie to the notion of constabulary independence with which most Chief Constables claim to be acting. It also avoids the politically obvious fact that the National Reporting

Centre and the National Riot Force have developed with sole responsibility to the Home Secretary, a cabinet member. The fact that an organisation of senior police officers can make a major intervention in the controlling of an industrial dispute dispels any notion of the police being locally accountable.

ACPO is now the most powerful policing institution in the country, a management board of the country's police force, mapping out its policy and its direction. Over the last few years it has extended its influence into many areas of policing policy. John Alderson, the ex-Chief Constable of Devon and Cornwall, made it clear in an interview with *Marxism Today* that opposition to his liberal style of policing from APCO was one of the factors which led to his premature resignation from the force.

ACPO are not elected representatives, they are not accountable as an institution to anyone but the Home Secretary and the cabinet. The question must be asked: how have they been able to overide the statutory regulations for the organisation of local police forces in England and Wales? Publically ACPO have appeared to limit themselves to influencing policing policy through constitutional channels; covertly however, they have become the high command of a National Riot Force, what the Chair of the South Yorkshire Police Authority calls a 'junta' operating from the National Reporting Centre.

The uses of Employment Legislation

On March 14th, 1984, the National Coal Board were granted an injunction in the High Court under the 1980 Employment Act restraining the Yorkshire miners from picketing anywhere other than their place of work. The following day, the Yorkshire pickets were out again in force in the Nottinghamshire coalfield. The next week, the NCB drew back from an action for contempt in the High Court against the Yorkshire NUM for continued secondary picketing. Any action would have been against members of the union's executive and the NCB would have had to prove that the executive were expressly in control of the picketing and that individual officers were instructing men to picket. The reasons given by the NCB for their retreat at the time were: it was felt that the police were handling the pickets very successfully: and the situation might become more inflamed if the action was taken.

The 1980 Act, together with the 1982 Employment Act, represents the culmination of the Conservative Government's anti-union legislation. They attack the closed shop, restrict picketing and allow the seizure of union funds where the union fails to disown the ever-expanding variety of illegal industrial actions which are created under the Acts. Basically all forms of effective picketing are outlawed and any attempt by unions to escalate action or draw upon working class solidarity become illegal. It is lawful to picket at your own place of work in order to peacefully persuade someone to work or not to work or to communicate information. The Code of Practice, accompanying the Acts which is not legally binding, advises that picket lines should be generally restricted to six people or less, at the discretion of the police.

At the end of 1983 this legislation was used against the National Graphical Association (NGA). They were in dispute with the Stockport Messenger group of newspapers over a closed shop agreement and NGA members from other areas were picketing the Warrington premises where the dispute arose. An injunction was granted to the owner of the group of newspapers, Mr. Eddie Shah, against the NGA under the 1980 Act to stop the 'secondary picketing' by NGA members who did not work at the Warrington site. Since the members continued to picket, the NGA was fined, in the first instance £50,000, followed by further fines involving the seizure (sequestration) of union assets. This civil strategy in the case of a small union like the NGA aimed at the union's financial structure, together with a vicious policing operation on the ground, assured the government of a victory. A victory which was aided by the compliant role of the TUC which had failed to oppose the Government's anti-trade union legislation from the start.

The Government however, had another contingency plan for the miners, decided before the strike began. Political decisions had been made about the way in which the law would be used. The seizure of funds, the imprisonment of Executive officers would not crush the miners resolve, more likely it would strengthen it. Employment legislation would have been directed against officers and leaders, not the conscious rank and file. A previous Conservative Government had floundered in this respect by sending five dockers to prison and turning them into Labour martyrs. The use of the civil law would as well have handed the NUM the support of other unions in a struggle focussed upon anti-trade union legislation. The Government still had problems in this respect over Cheltenham GCHQ.

Perhaps the single most telling factor was that the use of civil employment legislation did not aid the Government's general policing policy developed specifically for use against the organised working class. This involved the highly mobile 'National Riot Force' and the new criminal law proposed in the Police and Criminal Evidence Bill. The miners were to be subjected to a confrontation with a para-military police force and mass criminalisation.

The Criminal Law and Civil Containment

The criminal law is the most powerful weapon in the state's armoury. There are many reasons for this, but perhaps one of the most obvious is that most people believe that the criminal law contains universal principles; it is brought to bear when someone has 'done something wrong'. What many people do not realise is that today it is often the police who decide what is 'wrong'. The criminal law appears to have a kind of infallibility which puts those who break it on the other side of reasonable society. Not only does it have the power to punish but to shame as well. To give someone a criminal record is to stigmatise them in the eyes of the community. At the end of the process there is prison, the punishment which makes an offender an untouchable.

The criminal law is very specific and so can be easily used in political situations; no matter of great legal concern is ever argued out in a Magistrates Court, nor is motive ever considered. Because the police officer is so well received in the Magistrates Court, it is an uphill struggle for the defendant to prove his or her innocence, while guilt is virtually taken for granted.

There are however problems for the state in using the criminal law for political repression. The general trend has been to take power away from the Magistrates and give it to the police. The police have constantly claimed that *they know* who commits crime and it is only the legal complexities of the court that enable offenders to escape punishment. The Government can only go so far in awarding a power of conviction to the police in the present climate. The next best thing which it can do, is to use the period of remand before trial as a punishment based upon a presumption of guilt. In exercising this extra-judicial function the police assume the power to contain dissent without recourse to a trial.

There are an increasing number of ways in which the police can act punitively prior to trial in a Magistrates Court. During our work in Yorkshire and Kent we found many such practices in operation.*

1. Men who were stopped on the way to pickets were told to present their driving documents to their local police station within five days. For men from Kent who were out of their area for periods of up to three weeks this presented problems.
2. Car drivers simply had their keys taken from them, this is effectively impounding the car.
3. Conditions of bail were demanded by Magistrates on the instructions of the police. These were such that men were unable to travel to counties outside their own while awaiting trial.
4. In one case in South Yorkshire and one in Kent, both involving large numbers of defendants, the prosecution withdrew its case knowing that the men had been wrongly charged, in exchange for the defence agreeing that the men be bound over (in Kent in the sum of £100 for a year). This tactic obviates the need for a trial and though the men had not infringed the law they were being contained and punished.
5. The most serious strategy which shows clearly the power of the police to control systems of punishment prior to trial, is that of 'remand in custody'. At the time of writing this report there were seven miners in prison; these men had not been found guilty of any offence, but simply broken conditions of bail.

Although these are all forms of restriction they appear legal subtleties when compared with the blocking off of the Dartford Tunnel or the massive erosion of rights brought about by road blocks and checks around Nottinghamshire. In these many and varied circumstances the police were determining who should travel where and what purpose was considered legitimate. They acted out their powers without recourse to the courts, statute or precedent, simply stopping people, searching their cars, breaking windscreens, and turning drivers back to where they had come from.

Many miners who were arrested in the first few weeks of the

---

* A number of the practices have been developed in relation to criminal charges, especially in London. Increasingly arrested persons are not charged after being held in the police station but told to report back there in a week or two's time. This is effectively a form of probation without an offence having been proved. Curfews have been instigated in London against suspects. The practice of 'signing on' every night or sometimes morning and night at a police station has a long history in serious criminal charges.

strike were surprised by the battery of criminal laws which the police used against them. They could not understand that the powers of arrest and the 'authority of force' which the police have, allows them to use criminal charges against them without having to present legal proof to Magistrates for many months. The most common charges which have been used during the strike: obstruction of a police officer, obstruction of the highway, breach of the peace, threatening behaviour and even assualt, are all charges which a police officer may give witness to without other witnesses or the need for independent or corroborative evidence. It is sufficient for the Magistrate that the constable says that he saw the offence take place.

Many of the arrested men believed that they would be able to make legal argument in court because, they said, they had not broken the law. The simple fact is, that before they began to picket the government had decided to criminalise them. It was irrelevant how or why they were arrested, the very fact that they were organised and in confrontation with the state criminalised them in the Government's eyes. To argue in legal terms anyway is foolish, at this level it is the police who make the law; they arrest, charge, question and prosecute, all on behalf of the state.

One other reason why the state uses the criminal law is that the police are the central collecting agency for information and intelligence. For the simplest misdemeanour, a massive amount of information can be gained on any individual who is taken into police custody. From the first instance of confronting the police, a person is accounted for and can in the future be more easily controlled. The use of employment legislation on the other hand deals impersonally with the union structure and so gains no information.

Intelligence gathering is not only important to the state with respect to further criminal charges which might be brought later, for example conspiracy, but is important in any post strike period. If the miners lose the strike the NCB will make a sweep of the union rooting out radicals, militants and political party members. The intelligence information for this sweep will have been gathered from the thousands of arrested men.

For all these reasons and others, the criminal law was the first weapon that the Government used to try and crush the physical structure and the will of the National Union of Mineworkers when it began its strike. The strategy had three objectives: firstly to criminallse the strikers both within their own organisations and in the eyes of broader society; secondly to physically thin out the numbers of men available for picketing and thirdly to gather masses of intelligence on activists for use in a post strike situation.

PART TWO
The Operation

The Dartford Tunnel Incident

In the first weeks of the strike all those areas which were unanimous in their strike action contributed pickets to those areas where men were still working. The focus for this picketing was in Nottinghamshire and the Midlands where a percentage of the men remained at work. The three Kent pits began sending men up to the Midlands or to Barnsley where they were re-located in Nottinghamshire.

There are a number of points at which the Thames can be crossed but the three most used crossings for travellers coming from Kent are the Dartford Tunnel, the Blackwall Tunnel and the Rotherhithe Tunnel. The Dartford Tunnel is exceptional in the sense that it has a multi-lane approach and car drivers have to pay a toll.

On Sunday March 18th, police officers from the Kent constabulary attempted to stop anyone who appeared to be a miner or who was going north to aid the miners' strike, from crossing the Thames through the Dartford Tunnel. It is not the first time that an operation of this kind has been mounted in this country (see Appendix 3). The Chief Constable of Kent was later to say that it was his decision to mount the blockade. However, it seems more probable that the operation was organised from the National Reporting Centre at Scotland Yard. Not only was the Dartford Tunnel blocked but both the Blackwall Tunnel and the Rotherhithe Tunnel were closed for 'building work'.

What police officers actually said to car drivers who they suspected of being pickets later became a matter of dispute. While miners contested that they had been told they would be arrested if they crossed the county border, police claimed they were warned that they could later be arrested for causing a breach of the peace.

The men were interviewed were quite clear about the determination of the police to turn them back and not allow them free passage to the north of England.

On March 18th, I set off to Barnsley in a van with five other men. We reached the Dartford Tunnel at about four in the afternoon. There were two or three cars already pulled over. There were about 25 police officers at the entrance. We were approached by an Inspector. He asked us if we were pickets, we said that we were miners on our way to Seafield Colliery in Scotland where we were to attend a conference. The Inspector said: 'No way are you going through this tunnel'. He didn't give any reason. He warned us that we would be arrested if we continued and he gave us a telephone number to call if we 'wanted to take the matter higher'. We turned round and left the area.

My first order for picketing was in the second week of the strike. On Sunday March 18th., four of us set off to Barnsley in South Yorkshire. We had no idea of where we were going to picket or even if we were going to picket. We set off between four and five in the afternoon and reached the Dartford Tunnel without any problems. There are a large number of lanes approaching the tunnel, there is a toll gate on each lane. The traffic was heavy. As we approached the tunnel we saw several white transit vans and there were groups of police officers gathered round the vans. Each toll booth had a police officer on it. There were also officers moving about in the traffic, they were looking inside the cars and scrutinising the passengers. We were about six car lengths away from the booths when we were flagged down by a police officer and as he came over two other officers converged on the car. The police officer asked the driver to wind down the window. When he did this, he was immediately asked questions, where the car was from, who owned it etc. The police officer then asked if we were miners. The driver answered the questions truthfully. The police officer then told us that they knew of our intentions and objectives and he lectured us on the laws regarding picketing. We were then told that if we left the County of Kent we would be arrested on the grounds that the police suspected our future actions would constitute a breach of the peace.

Some miners who put up a more spirited or devious defence of themselves and their company had their cars searched by police who tried to prove that they were miners.

Our driver was asked to get out of the car. We told the police that we were going to a wedding in Sheffield. The officer searched the boot of the car and found our sleeping bags. We were told that we were suspected of 'going picketing' which may cause a breach of the peace. We replied that picketing was not illegal, he said, 'I'm not going to argue, if you don't turn back, the driver of the car will be arrested, the car impounded and the rest of you will have to walk home.'

As is often the case when the police move suddenly into political and civil areas which do not concern them, many officers were themselves confused and tried to bluster through on their tacit authority.

There were four police officers, then an Inspector came over. They said, 'who are you?' we said, 'Kent pickets'. They said, 'Where are you going?' We said we were going to the Leicester-shire and Warwickshire coalfields. They said, 'You know that's secondary picketing?'. We said that this wasn't the case because Kent is part of the South Midlands Area. The police officer asked the driver for his licence and also asked to search the car for 'offensive weapons.'

In this particular case, the car was carrying two law lecturers (see Appendix 4) as well as two pickets and after a short cut and thrust of legal argument the car drove through the Dartford Tunnel. They were stopped later at a full road block, 'a barrier across the road consisting of a police car, traffic cones and flashing lights', when it approached Dawmill colliery in the Midlands.

The media attention after the closing of the Dartford tunnel was remarkably specific in light of the fact that this one incident was part of a much bigger police operation. It made little mention for example, of what happened to those miners who found other routes to the north of England. All the cars which were turned back were escorted by police officers out of the vicinity of the tunnel.

We drove right over to the West of London, crossed the M4 and then picked up the M1. At Epsom or thereabouts, we came to a roundabout and saw a white police Range Rover. We ducked down in the car but it followed us for about two miles, then it shot in front of us and signalled for us to pull over. One officer checked the car while the other spoke to the driver. The police said that our car was low at the back and they asked us where we were going. We said that we were going to South Wales. One officer said, 'What are you doing picketing in South Wales?' We told them that we were going to address meetings. The car driver was told to produce his documents within five days; he replied that he would be away for more than five days and asked if his wife could present them, but the officer was adamant and said that he had to do it.

The police operation at the Dartford tunnel carried on throughout the whole day of March 18th. The two reasons that different officers gave for their summary powers were: that secondary picketing is illegal and that men may in the future commit a breach of the peace. The first ground is not worthy of discussion; matters concerning picketing in the furtherance of a trade dispute come under the Employment legislation which is civil and not criminal. In fact none of these men were actually picketing at the time that they were stopped.

With respect to breach of the peace or disturbing the peace, the police have powers under two Acts: The Justice of the Peace Act 1361 and the Public Order Act 1936. The Justice of the Peace Act is little used now but it was created to stop gatherings and roaming bands, either peasants or the dispossessed aristocracy. It could be described as one of the first 'pre-emptive' policing measures; it assumes that if you are abroad in a large party then you must be about to challenge the state, or at least be up to no good.

The Public Order Act was brought into force before the second world war during the period of fascist meetings and marches through the East End of London. This Act does assume some kind of correlation between gatherings, marches, demonstrations and riots or disturbances. The relationship between an act and any disturbance has to be causal and it has to be immediate or fairly imminent.

The police had no proper legal grounds for refusing access to the Dartford Tunnel to miners or men who wanted to picket. It was essentially an exercise in which the police argued and effected legal powers which no one previously thought they had. The police carried out the exercise with the intention of criminalising a section of the working population in the knowledge that if anything had gone wrong they could have effected arrests for a great number of criminal misdemeanours.

The Government are well aware of this loophole in the criminal law which presently allows people to demonstrate peacefully. They are preparing a 'Trespass and Riotous Assembly Bill' which will no doubt resolve the problem. Also later this year the Police and Criminal Evidence Bill will give the police the legal power to set up road blocks and stop and search people if they wish to attend any political gathering, demonstration or picket. Under the Act the police will be able to argue that they suspect an offence might be committed within any area where there is to be a gathering.

In relation to road blocks generally, the police have assumed massive powers over the last year. Some of the Prime Minister's security advisers are experts on Latin America where the 'state of siege' strategy has been used to great effect, particularly in Uruguay in the late 60's and early 70's. The police now have the accepted authority to cut off whole areas and stop the free passage of citizens without giving a reason. In April this year when the Greenham camp was evicted from the front gates of the site, all the roads leading there were cut off while the eviction took place. At the same time, the police instructed the media that there had been a 'traffic incident'.

One twenty seven year old undergound fitter from a Kent colliery had his own very determined view of what it meant to him personally when he was turned back from the Dartford Tunnel:

> ...we were escorted back from the toll gate, the police holding up the traffic to allow us to reverse, turn back and leave for home. My own personal circumstances are that I have never been inside a police station in my life and have no criminal record. To be threatened with arrest on the basis of assumed future actions, by the police, I found disgusting and hard to believe. Now, on reflection, the meaning of the incident has struck home firmly. **The police state is here**.

Road Blocks in Nottinghamshire

At the same time that the Dartford tunnel was cut off by officers from the Kent Constabulary a massive exercise was being conducted in Nottinghamshire. Thousands of police were drafted in from other forces to police the pickets and towns near collieries. The County of Nottinghamshire was sealed off on its Northern border with South Yorkshire and its Western border with Derbyshire. All intersections on minor and main roads, motorway junctions and roundabouts were heavily policed.

The roads were narrowed with traffic cones allowing only a trickle of cars through at a time while police officers scrutinised occupants and then waived them to the side of the road. The operation was not only directed against miners or possible pickets, (Appendix 5), single male drivers and single female drivers were stopped and questioned. Taxi drivers were automatically stopped and taxi firms were approached by the police and told not to accept miners as fares.

Within Nottinghamshire itself, secondary blockades were set up as far as two miles outside pits and villages near pits. At Ollerton where the work force was divided roughly into two equal camps in the first weeks of the strike, villagers found it difficult to leave and more difficult to gain entry to the village on the way back. Because the road blocks acted as a series of filters, with registration numbers being radioed through to the next block, car drivers were sometimes stopped five or six times within a few miles on their outward and inward journeys. The fact that it is very hard to distinguish miners from other working class citizens meant that many cars were searched and occupants questioned; people who were not miners had their car keys taken from them.

These road blocks also existed in parts of the Midlands, Warwickshire and Leicestershire. Here is the experience of a Kent miner who picketed Warwickshire:

> At the beginning we had to leave our cars 150 yards away and walk because we found a back way in, but towards the end of our stay, the police took the road block out two miles from the pit. There were cones across half the road and a Range Rover parked up. Cars that approached were flagged down and the officers shone a torch in the car. On a number of occasions we had to leave our car and walk two miles. On the last occasion we turned our lights off and shot through.

Government politicians argued consistently throughout the first weeks of the strike that the massive police presence was there entirely to make sure that Nottinghamshire miners who wanted to work could do do. In order to validate this argument South Yorkshire miners were depicted as an 'alien horde' whose sole purpose was to intimidate through violence. The facts were often different. There is a lot of evidence to show that the police mounted a concerted attack upon Nottinghamshire miners who were on strike and who wanted to picket their own pits or play a part in the strike.

> Later that day at Cotgrave Pit (in Nottinghamshire) the Cotgrave branch officials approached us as we were picketing and we were joined by a police officer. The police officer asked who worked at the Colliery. The four branch officials identified themselves and the police officer told them: 'Either you get to fucking work or you fuck off home, but you're not standing here with these pickets.

This and other reports we received reinforced the view that the police were never impartial but acted simply as a strike breaking force from the beginning. It was in fact their role to uphold on the ground the political line that the government and senior police officers were pursuing.

*   *   *   *   *

The arrested miners we took statements from had been arrested in a variety of circumstances and charged with a number of different offences. One thing bound all the arrests together and that was the fact that we did not come across one case in which anyone had palpably broken the criminal law. Two other things stand out: firstly all those arrested were arrested because they came into confrontation with the police rather than other citizens. Secondly, it was quite evident that the arrests had always taken place on the terms of the police officers and in respect to a general policy which had been decided on by the police. Apart from the arrests at road blocks and the arrests during pickets there were a number of arrests which took place while miners were not actually involved in union work.

Arrests at roadblocks

This is the fifth week of our strike and we have picketed different places before our arrest; Haworth (Notts), Ollerton (Notts), Thornseby (Notts), Linby (Notts) and Dawmill (West Midlands). From the third week onwards we found it almost impossible to get to any of the pits mentioned.

The policy of the police appeared to be to stop cars with three or four men in them or follow them to the nearest road block. In the preliminary surveillance before road blocks, police helicopters often shadowed cars and no doubt reported them to the next road block. Men who were stopped were either arrested or told to turn back. On many occasions they were not told why they had been stopped, or why they were being arrested, until much later.

On April 9th, I was with three other people in a car going to Clipstone Colliery. We set off at one thirty in the morning. We went down the M1 and got off at junction 27 or 28. We went down the road about three miles and then saw a police car parked at the side of the road. It pulled out behind us and followed us for us for about eleven miles to a roundabout where there were about 60 to 70 police with mini-buses and other vehicles. They flagged us down and pulled in at the back of us. A policeman asked the driver his name and whether or not he had been to Nottingham before. He told him to turn the engine off and get out of the car. He looked into the car and said, 'I recognise one lad in the back and one in the front, have I see you on any previous occasion?' We said that we didn't know. He asked our names. He said to the driver and one of the other lads, 'Get back in the car and go back to Yorkshire; we don't want to see you in this County again while this dispute is on or you'll get arrested'. He told me and one other lad that we were under arrest, although he didn't say what for.

Not only were the police going beyond their powers in this case by refusing access to another County on that day, but they also intimidated the men by telling them that they could not come into the County again while the dispute lasted. Sometimes the intimidation included violence:

Two weeks ago, I went by car, with others to picket Clipstone Colliery. About three miles from Clipstone Colliery the police were pulling all the cars in. They asked our driver if we had been down the night before and then said to him, 'Turn the engine off, you're under arrest'. I asked if we were all under arrest, he said, 'No'. I phoned the miners' Welfare for transport to take us back. The driver had been arrested for obstructing the police, together with four others. As we were waiting for our transport in a bus shelter by the side of the road, four transits pulled up and the officers got out. I had a plastic bag with a thermos flask in it, which was on the floor. One of the policemen smashed it against the side of the bus shelter and said, 'Whose is this?'. I said that it was mine and he handed it back to me. Then he said to me, 'Are you all right?'. I said 'Yes', then six policemen encircled us all and one of them pushed me and I fell down. I got up and he said to me, 'Get back into the car and go back to Yorkshire'. He kicked me hard in the shin, but I didn't retaliate. We said that we couldn't all fit into the car (a Datsun Cherry) since there were six of us but they said that they'd arrest us if we didn't. They escorted us fifteen miles out of the County.

Most of the miners arrested at road blocks were arrested for obstruction of a police officer in the course of his duty. The police claimed that the men were likely to cause a breach of the peace.

However, as in the case of the Dartford Tunnel, the pickets were often miles away from pits when they were stopped and they were not charged with public order offences but with obstruction. None of the miners we interviewed believed that they had committed an offence and often tried to argue the point with police officers.

> On April 9th, I left at about ten in the morning to go to Hucknall pit. There were four of us in the car. At a roundabout near Clumber Park the police waived us down and pulled us in to the side. There was a police van in the side road, another further down the road and two or three where we had been stopped. One policeman came over to us and asked the driver where we were going, the driver told him that we were going to Hucknall pit to picket peacefully. The policeman advised us to turn round. The driver said, 'No, we are exercising our rights as citizens to travel to a peaceful picket'. The policeman said that if we didn't turn round then the driver would be arrested. The driver refused to turn round and the police officer asked him to get out and took him to one side. The other two officers asked all three of us to get out of the car, which we did. They said that if we carried on we'd be arrested. We said that we still wanted to go. I asked why we were being turned back and one of them said, 'We have reason to believe that you may cause a breach of the peace'. He then said that 'he was arresting us for obstructing a police officer in the course of his duty.

Some pickets were asked to produce their driving documents within a specified time at thier local police station.

> On March 17th, I set off in the company of three other men at about three thirty in the morning. Our car was stopped about two hundred yards away from the pit on the road approaching a round-about. There were about eight or nine police officers in uniform standing at the side of the road. An officer flagged us down and all the cars behind us had to stop. The driver wound down the window and a police officer asked, 'What are you doing?' I said that we were official pickets. He told us to turn round and go back otherwise we would be arrested. They looked at our documents and told me that I had to produce my licence to a police station within five days. The officer gave me a piece of paper to this effect. They then escorted us across the border out of Nottinghamshire into Derbyshire.

The police were also impounding cars and taking away the drivers keys.

On April 9th, we all set out from Brodsworth at eleven in the morning. We were going to Hucknall pit. We travelled down the M15 then the M1 and came off at junction 27. We travelled about one hundred yards down the B608. A police officer signalled us into the side of the road, they had one patrol car and one large dark green bus. We were waved in. The police officer asked us where we were going. I said that we were going to peacefully picket and he said, 'You're not going to the pit'. I found out later that this officer was from the Metropolitan police. The police officer went to get an Inspector and he came over and told us that we were going to Babbington. I assured him that we weren't but he said that if we continued we would be arrested. I said, 'You look like arresting me then because I'm continuing'. The Inspector told me to get out of the car. He asked for the keys and I gave them to him. One of the men who was with me asked a police officer if he was being arrested and was told no. He was asked how he would get home and he was told 'walk'. He asked for the keys to the car and was told that he couldn't have them back. He said that he would walk to the pit rather than walk home. The police officer said, 'O.K., you're arrested as well'.

We spoke to one man who had refused to hand over his keys or open the car door; the police had smashed his windscreen with truncheons. They claimed later that it had been necessary in order to 'gain entry'.

Arrests away from pickets

It is inevitable that during the strike miners would be arrested at times other than during pickets. The policing strategy dictates that the NUM as a working class organisation should be criminalised and the police on the ground have taken every opportunity to play out this strategy. While the police defined miners as criminals, the miners themselves found it a difficult role to slip into. Without the training and experience of criminals, the police were able to arrest them with no more difficulty than taking sweets from children. Four Kent miners were arrested in London after they had attended a meeting:

We got back to the digs in Hackney. Opposite the digs where we normally parked our car there was a white transit van belonging to an Instant Response Unit. We parked the car, got out and began to walk to our digs. The van came round by our side until it was just past us then the doors flew open and ten officers including an Inspector and a Sergeant got out. These officers surrounded us. The Sergeant said, 'Whose car is it?'. We all refused to speak, on the basis that we hadn't done anything wrong. When we refused to answer, they split us up and put two officers with each of us. I was asked who the driver of the car was and I still refused to speak. After five or ten minutes when they couldn't find out anything we were put in the white van. I want to make it clear that I was shepherded into the van but at no time was I formally arrested or cautioned. As far as I was concerned, I was going voluntarily, as far as that is possible, to the police station. At about 2.30 a.m. I was released from police custody and I was handed a piece of paper. I was not formally charged and I was not cautioned. Later when I looked at the paper I found that it said that I had 'wilfully obstructed a P.C.

Many of the arrests resemble kidnap more than the due process of law. Some men were not actually arrested but questioned on the basis that they were **suspected** of being pickets:

On one occasion I was at Blidworth in the town in the company of three other men. We had just bought fish and chips and we were stopped and questioned by about ten police officers from a white support vehicle. We were told that as we were pickets we had to leave the town and go back to South Yorkshire. We were asked our names and addresses. We were told that if we went anywhere near the pit we would be arrested. We returned to our car and were escorted out of the County.

On March 29th, at Newstead Colliery there were a number of arrests during a small and peaceful picket. Two witnesses saw a miner arrested as he walked down the road towards the picket.

There were twelve of us at the picket and we were later joined by eight other men. There were enough police officers there to screen us off from the road. About eleven thirty or so, I saw a man from my colliery get arrested as he walked towards the picket. I approached the police van that he was being held in and asked for details of the man and his arrest. I was told to 'Fuck Off' or I'd be joining him.

The media coverage of pickets has chosen to dwell almost solely on those physical clashes which have taken place at some of the larger pickets. Apart from these clashes, which we will look at later, there have been many small pickets. Often if men got through the road blocks they were physically stopped by police officers from joining such pickets. The closer men got to the colliery the more stringent became the police security.

The first time that I went picketing was on March 27th, I went to Silverhill Colliery in Nottinghamshire. We arrived at Silverhill at approximately ten in the morning. We parked the car in Derbyshire and then walked for about a mile partly along roads and partly across country. We were with seventeen other men who had also parked their vehicles. As we approached the road which passes the pit, by way of a public footpath, a group of six police officers approached us, one of them in plain clothes. There were a large number of other officers around the top of the footpath; the police obviously saw us coming. We were asked what we were doing and we replied that we were walking on a public footpath. We were told that if we went any further we would be charged with behaviour likely to cause a breach of the peace. We said that we were going to peacefully protest. We told the police that we simply wanted to stand at the other side of the pit entrance and communicate our views to anyone who wanted to approach us. We told the police that they could stand with us. We were told that if we crossed the fence (by a stile) we would be arrested. We had a strong discussion with the police and told them that we had a right to use the highway. One of our lads went over the fence and was arrested. By this time there was an Inspector with us on our side of the fence, he shouted to his men on the other side, 'Arrest that man'. An officer walked up to him and asked him his name and address. I then heard the officer say, 'I am arresting you for obstructing me in the course of my duty'. The officer went to put his hand on the man's shoulder and the man said, 'You don't have to do that, which van do you want me in?'. The officer said 'That one', pointing to a van. The rest of us all followed him into the van. I sat in a van but I was not arrested. I was not approached by a police officer, I was not cautioned. I did not at any time obstruct a police officer. I thought at this time that we would be escorted back to our cars. I was taken to Mansfield police station where we were all charged with obstruction.

A number of themes in police thinking emerge from the men we interviewed. One of these themes was that the police expected and considered that they had the authority to determine the number of pickets, where they stood, and even what they could shout or whether they could shout at all. The other theme which is consistent is a determination by the police to describe pickets as demonstrators. This had obviously been a pre-arranged policy decision linked to the desire to use the criminal law. 'An Inspector asked me about my official

NUM arm-band. I said that we were on picket duty and he said, 'No, you're demonstrators'.

Arrests at pickets

Arrests at pickets fall roughly into three different categories:

i)   *Arrests during disturbances*
ii) *Arrests of individuals legally picketing*
iii) *Police provoked 'snatch squad' arrests*

i) Arrest during disturbances

Only in the first of these three categories does the procedure used by the police resemble what one would expect under the 'rule of law'. Inevitably with large pickets, there is often a confrontation with police who are there en masse and individuals are bound to be arrested who have not specifically committed any offences. But it should be pointed out that there are ways of policing large pickets, especially by allowing numbers of representatives to stand in the road and speak to men going to work. The police in Nottinghamshire seemed to see a large picket as an incitement to confrontation. They almost always refused to allow delegates to communicate their views to workers.

> On April 9th, I went to Babbington to picket. Across the gate of the pit there was a dual carriageway.There were pickets on both sides of the gate and in the middle. Pickets on the other side of the dual carriageway started to move to get to the main gate and scuffles broke out. The police tried to shove pickets back and pushed them saying − you're not allowed here. I went to the left hand side of the main gate and a police sergeant came up and shoved me, I tried to stand my ground. By this time there were a large number of pickets and police around the main gate. The police officer pulled me out of the crowd and two or three policemen walked me out. My arm was held behind my back. The police kept saying to me, 'You're the first, you're going to pay for this'. I didn't struggle. I asked what I had been arrested for and they said Breach of the Peace. As I walked with them they were digging me in the ribs. They said to me, 'Are you going to go in the van peacefully', I said 'Yes'.

> On April 9th, I went to Babbington Colliery. There were roughly 100 to 150 men on the grass verge adjacent to the pit gate. We were completely hemmed in by police, unable to communicate with workers going on shift. About 50 men tried to get to the other side of the gate and a scuffle started with the police trying

to stop them. I saw a man I knew being apprehended by one officer, and I saw him being kicked in the legs. Other officers joined in and held his arms up his back; the man was small and had no chance to defend himself. While this was happening, the picket surged forward. I ended up on the floor and an officer who had been standing near me began kicking me. I was kicked on the legs and a couple of times in the stomach. I was kicked five or six times. I finally managed to get hold of an officer's foot and brought him down on top of me. Two other officers joined him. I was grabbed by the hair and taken into the pit area. I was taken to a police station where I was charged with threatening behaviour.

I went to Babbington Colliery on April 9th, when the first miner was arrested on the other side of the dual carriageway, everyone surged forward and into the road. In the surge, I tumbled to the floor. I wasn't hurt. I picked myself up off the floor and a police officer grabbed my arm. I said to him 'I've only fallen down, I've nothing to do with it'. He took me more firmly by the arm and took me down through the main entrance of the pit into the yard. I struggled and said, 'You're not taking me anywhere. I haven't done anything'. He made a swipe at me but missed. I hit out and caught him in the face. Two other officers came to help him. One got hold of my other arm and bent it behind my back and bent my fingers backwards. The other officer had his arm around my neck. I was charged with obstruction.

ii) Arrest of people legally picketing

These arrests show clearly the kind of powers that the police have assumed. They are determined to control legal picketing, hamper it and make it as ineffectual as possible. With the help of the criminal law they throw their weight behind the strike breakers.

On March 28th. I went to Newstead Colliery. There were about twenty of us and about eighty police officers. Around about twelve o'clock we were waiting to talk to the men coming on shift. We intended to go towards the men peacefully in two's. We were about fifty yards from the premises. As the first car came I stepped through the police line and stood in front of it; the driver wound down his window and I began to talk to him. I was given a short lecture by an Inspector who told me that if it happened again I would be arrested. We saw another car approach and two of us again went into the road, we didn't even get a sentence out. I was escorted away by two police officers. I was later charged with obstructing a police officer.

A car stopped and we began speaking to the driver. We introduced ourselves as Yorkshire miners and said that we would like to put our case. We were then approached by a police officer who told us to get back on the pavement. We told him that we were speaking to the occupant of the car and when we had finished we would go back on the pavement... another car arrived and we approached it; we were asked again to return to the pavement, which we began to go, but an Inspector told the police officer that we had to be arrested. I was charged with obstructing the highway.

We had agreed in the morning with the police to allow six men on the road to picket. I took up a position with five other men at the side of the road. As the second or third lorry came out, I raised my arm to stop it. A sergeant who had stood five or six yards from me grabbed my arm with one hand and my throat with the other. He pushed me against the gates. He said, 'I'll stop the fucking lorries, if they don't want to stop they won't.

iii) Snatch Squad arrests

Snatch Squad arrests have nothing to do with proper legal processes and the men who are arrested by this strategy are picked out not because they are suspected of any offence but because they are prominent union officers or activists or because they have had some personal confrontation with a police officer at some other time during the strike. Men are targeted and then 'lifted' from inside the picket by a wedge-shaped charge of police officers. The fact that the police manage to effect these arrests at all is a clear indication of the peaceful attitude of the great majority of pickets.

I am a safety team worker at a pit in South Yorkshire. I know something about 'snatch squads' or 'internal security training' because I was previously in the British Army. I served from 1964 to 1974 and saw service in Borneo and West Germany. I was part of a special unit which concentrated upon internal security. I got the G.S.M. after serving in Borneo. As I witnesed it when I was arrested at Babbington they work in the following way; there are seven to ten men in parallel rows, they begin marching forward, the police in the cordon break their linked arms and force the picket back. The fourteen or twenty men then run in and 'snatch' a person, retreat and the cordon closes behind them. The squads choose men either by them being pointed out by 'plants' in the picket or by previously obtained photographs and descriptions. In my case, I saw the squad line up, cross the road and then run 'at the double' through the cordon. Three officers grabbed me'.

Brian Walker, Branch Secretary at Newstead Colliery, was leaving a Nottinghamshire Area Council meeting at Berry Hill, Mansfield when he saw three men dressed like miners climbing into the back of a police van. The men were in the company of police officers but were obviously not under arrest and appeared familiar with the officers. Later that day while watching a news bulletin about a demonstration outside Berry Hill Miners' offices, Mr. Walker recognised the same three men and contacted a television company. He appeared on local and national television pointing out the activities of the officers over a re-run of the film. It could be seen clearly how they pushed a miner from within the picket to the front so that other officers could arrest him.

The use of agents provocateur in crowds and political demonstrations has been a common police tactic for many years; it was specifically used in the pickets at the Grunwick film processing laboratories in 1974. The police always make an effort to collect the paraphernalia of various struggles: newspapers, stickers, leaflets etc., for this very purpose; 'later that day an Inspector asked us for some NUM stickers and one of the lads gave him twenty or so'.

Two men we spoke to became victims of 'snatch squads' because they had had verbal disputes with individuals police officers some time before.

I was at Wyvenhoe on the 17th and 18th of April. On the 17th, the police were unable to contain us and on the 18th they brought in men from Chelmsford. I was arrested at about 7.30 a.m. on the 18th. The previous week I had been to another picket when I had been warned by a P.C. about using foul language (bastard). In fact, the officer came off worst in the argument because his sergeant told him not to bother. At Wyvenhoe, I noticed this P.C. who I had argued with; in fact, I changed my jacket and cap to confuse him in case he acted vengefully towards me. The picket surged forward at one point and a wedge of police officers ran in, they were in formation and they ran through the linked arms. I suddenly found myself grabbed from behind by the P.C. who I had argued with. He held my neck in the crook of his elbow. He tried to pull me out of the picket but we both fell to the ground on the edge of the road. Two other officers stood on my wrists and the P.C. extricated himself. I was taken to an Instant Response Unit van.

Processing After Arrest

The method of arrest, questioning in custody, the manner of being charged and such things as phone calls or the right to see a legal representative are not governed by law but by guidelines, most particularly The Judges' Rules. In order to see how far the police have departed from accepted convention and how far they have drifted towards the use of 'martial law' tactics in the miners' strike it is useful to look at how the system works in theory.

A person can be arrested on 'reasonable suspicion' or if they are seen by a constable actually committing an offence. This arrest allows the officer to take an 'offender' into custody and bring him or her before a Magistrate. On arrest a suspect is supposed to be cautioned and warned about answering questions. The period in custody inside a police station, which only began with the advent of a state police force, is meant to be short. Before the police force came into being the suspect would be brought before a Magistrate immediately and he would examine him or her. Since the nineteen-twenties the police have taken over the role of interrogators and this is now done without witnesses in the secrecy of a police station.

There is no law governing how long a person can be held by the police in custody after arrest. It is commonly accepted that the time in custody is to be used by the police to confirm their 'reasonable suspicion' and find proof of a crime. This can be done either with detective work, statements from witnesses or confessions from the suspect. There is no law governing the right of a suspect to see a legal representative. While in custody, a suspect has no rights except those which are deemed not to 'hamper the police in their enquiries'. If a suspect is to appear before a Magistrate they have to be formally charged with *an* offence, asked how they reply and presented to a Magistrate at the earliest opportunity.

There are no laws governing the taking of photographs or finger prints but the guidelines would suggest that the police are meant to take them if a suspect is charged with an imprisonable offence. If the police feel that they need fingerprints in order to prove their 'reasonable suspicion' and if a person refuses to give them, an order may be obtained from a Magistrate and they may be taken with 'reasonable force'.

As the police drift away from established custom and practice towards States of Emergency and martial law, a number of things usually follow. Arrests are made without an offence having taken place, cautions are not given. Brutality and intimidation can occur during the time in custody and while no attempt is made to find proof of an offence, low level intelligence is gathered and interrogation amounting to torture can be used in order to extract confessions. Long periods in custody can be expected with no communication with the outside world. Photographs and finger prints are taken as a matter of course.

Processing: 1. Polaroid Photographs

The practice of taking polaroid photographs of suspects seems to have started in London in the late seventies. It was introduced without any legislation or, to our knowledge 'guidelines', in response to police claims they they often found it difficult to keep track of arresting officers and appropriate suspects in 'riot' situations (see Appendix 6). A majority of men we spoke to who had been arrested in Nottinghamshire had been photographed in this way:

> I was held by the arms and from about four feet away a police officer photographed me with a polaroid camera. 'I had one polaroid picture taken on my own and another with the arresting officer'.

> There was a funnel of officers from the support vehicle to the cell van. I had a polaroid picture taken of me as I reached the cell van. I want to stress that this picture was taken of me alone.

Only one man we spoke to had found the strength of resist having his picture taken, he was an ex-soldier:

> When it came to my turn, I refused to have my photo taken, I kept my head down and as a consequence I cannot be sure exactly who was responsible for what happened. I know that an officer walked up from somewhere else and said to the two who were holding me: 'Get the bastard's head up' then, 'Pull his hair'. Someone did pull my hair but this did not make me raise my head. Next, after saying 'Grab his nose' the officer tried to force his fingers into my nostrils. I moved my head from side to side. Then I heard the same officer say, '*Right* bastard' and I was violently punched in the face. The punch landed on the top of my nose between my eyes. The officer then held my head in an arm lock and forced my head up. My glasses were broken and fell to the floor. They managed to take the photograph.

Processing: 2 Questioning

Arrested men were transferred from the scene of the picket either in white IRU vehicles or in large cell vans. On arrival at the police station they all had their personal effects taken from them, down to shoe laces, ear-rings and belts. Only one man we spoke to was assaulted inside a police station but another had to put up with physical intimidation:

> After an hour in the cell I wanted to go to the toilet. I was let out of the cell by an officer who was very aggressive. As he led me down the corridor he said, 'So you're the bastard who doesn't like coppers'. I simply said, 'Is this the way to the toilet'. He was walking alongside of me, he pushed up close to me and began pushing me into the wall and knocking my ankle with his foot. I felt that he was trying to make me respond physically but I didn't.

Two men who had both been charged with assaulting police officers actually made statements; these were the only men we spoke to who were asked anything at all about the incident which led to their arrest. One of the men who made a statement found that the officer taking it did not want to write down the fact that he, the suspect, had been assaulted by a police officer; the man only signed the statement under duress:

> A statement was taken from me but this did not deal with the assault committed against me. I was told that if I didn't sign the statement I would be held for up to two days.

All the men arrested in Nottinghamshire were questioned by plain clothes officers who did not formally introduce themselves. Men were taken individually into interview rooms and were usually questioned with two men present, one of whom stayed silent. There are signs that there was a strategy of trying to unnerve people before they were questioned: 'I was left in the room with the younger of the two men for some ten minutes but no word passed between us'. Most of the men found it hard not to answer the questions in some form and nearly all of them admitted to having been frightened or worried about what could happen to them if they didn't answer.

The interviews began with questions about how they had travelled and how they had received their instructions. There was every indication from the nature of the questions that often officers had a good deal of information already. They were asked about their families, their wives' or girlfriends' names, how many children they had and whether or not they had any debts. They were normally asked what they would vote in a ballot and what they had voted in the last ballot. Some were asked what they voted in the General Election. From this basic pattern the individual interviews diverge in different and mysterious ways.

I was asked if I was a member of a political party and what I thought of Arthur Scargill. I was asked if I was picketing for Arthur Scargill or myself. I was asked if I was being paid and whether it was a political strike.

I was asked about the 'envelope system' (of giving men their picketing instructions) which had only been started that day. I was asked how I voted in the last ballot and how I would vote in a future ballot.

The officers tried to appear familiar with my background. The first thing they said to me was, 'What's this London connection?' (The man's family had lived in London before and just after the war). They asked me what I thought of Arthur Scargill. I gave them a lot of rhetoric and they left.

They asked me what I thought of the strike and what I thought of Arthur Scargill. They asked me how much union subs I paid and whether I knew where it went. They wanted to know what I thought about Arthur Scargill being paid out of union money. They started to tell me that he had a chauffeur and did I know how he was paid. They asked about the Branch Secretary by name.

I was asked what newspaper I bought and who I had voted for in the pit union elections. I was asked about our Branch Secretary and where the strike headquarters were. What did I think about about Arthur Scargill trying to stop the Notts. miners from going to work.

A plain clothes officer came into the exercise yard and tried to draw us into a political discussion. I remember him specifically saying, 'Scargill and Benn are not Trade Unionists, they are political wreckers. At least under Joe Gormley you were in a position where you had a man who cared about your welfare.'

I was told that my 'picketing days' were over because the court would impose conditions of bail. I was told that they hoped for adjournments and postponements and said that the bail conditions would keep us away from the pickets. They said we would probably never come to court. I was asked if I was a communist or a member of any political party and who I voted for in the General Election. Then they asked, 'Have you got on the Council at X yet' (I was previously a parish Councillor in XX).

Q. Which way did you vote in the last General Election?

A. That's no business of your's.

Q. We both voted Conservative. We wondered which way you voted.

A. I didn't vote Conservative, that's for sure.

Q. Are you a left winger or an extreme left winger?

Although the suspects always assumed that the men who interviewed them were CID officers, in light of the questions it seems highly unlikely and one has to assume that they were Special Branch officers. All the questioning was political or an attempt to gain low level personal intelligence. It followed more or less the same pattern in every case. This method of gaining intelligence and personal details while people are in police custody is sinister in the extreme and is a real indication of the 'military' nature of the police operation.

Processing 3: Photographing and Fingerprinting

All the arrested men were photographed and finger printed before being charged. The photographs were standard record pictures, full front face and side view with a number at the bottom. Those men who put up discursive resistance (no one refused, or put up physical resistance) were told that if they actually refused a Magistrates' order would be sought and they would be held in custody for a much longer period. They were also told that force would be used if a Magistrates' order was granted.

Processing 4: Charges

No one we spoke to was formally charged in the proper manner or cautioned a second time, or asked to reply to the charge. A number of men were not charged but simply had charge sheets handed to them in court.

Processing 5: Conditions of Bail

Almost as soon as the arrests began conditions of bail were imposed upon those appearing before Magistrates' Court and a number of men are now in prison as a consequence of being in breach of these. This means effectively that defendants have received punitive prison sentences *even though* no charge has been proved against them. The bail condition itself, copied and given to defendants is a ludicrous illegality:

> (This man is) not to visit any premises or place for any purpose in connection with the current trade dispute between the NUM and the NCB. Other than peacefully to picket at his usual place of employment.

It is not in reality a condition of bail but an attempt to impose a curfew on persons who have been picketing. It is phrased in such a way to frighten and intimidate a person from going about their legal political business. It means in theory that if a man goes to another strikers house or a public meeting as part of the strike and if the police apprehend him, he may be sent to prison.

Phone Tapping

On April 29th, David Norman the General Treasurer of the Post Office Engineering Union (POEU) challenged the Home Secretary to let members of his union investigate claims of phone tapping during the miners strike. He said reassurances that phones were not being tapped were laughable and went on, 'If Mr. Brittan claims it is a 'smear' to suggest that members of the NUM are having their phones tapped during the current dispute, then I ask him if he would be prepared for the POEU to conduct its own public investigation into the allegation and give it immunity from prosecution under the Official Secrets Act if it publishes it's results. I think that we all know what the answer will be to my challenge.'

Early in the strike it became evident to many strikers that their phones were tapped. In South Wales the owner of a bus company was phoned by strikers who wanted to be taken to Derbyshire; the owner was rung minutes later by the Derbyshire police asking how many pickets he was bringing. In other areas pickets have laid traps for tappers directing them to wrong venues for pickets. Stories about phone tapping are inherantly unreliable and it is clear that the best people to conduct a public investigation of the matter are the POEU. We have recorded only three of the things we were told.

In order to tap phones the engineer first has to cut them off for a period (see Appendix 7). We have been told as well that though all the received information is recorded the computers which record the information work on a 'key word' system; this only delivers information for immediate use if it contains certain words. One strike centre organiser related to us the conversation which he had with a union member from British Telecom. This person had helped the miners in their two previous strikes.

> When we first came into the building the phones went dead and then were connected again. We had a visit from our friend at British Telecom, he told us that they had put a tap on our phone

and that though he could remove it there was no point because they would only put it on again. He told us to guess at the trigger words and use them in a random way as much as possible.

It would appear that this facility is so extended now that it can be used very quickly. When one area of the South Yorkshire 'Police Watch' organisation had its first open meeting to choose a co-ordinater, that person returned home to find that his phone had been cut off. Another striker gave us this statement.

I went to one of the pits in Nottinghamshire with my wife to give support to the pickets. I took a couple of flasks of coffee. When I arrived the forty or so pickets were completely encircled by a double row of police, there were about 120 police. I was allowed through to give them the coffee. Once inside the cordon the picket leader told me that he had been informed by the police that no one was allowed to leave the picket for another hour, until 11.30 p.m. After they had the coffee I was asked by the picket leader to make a phone call to the strike centre informing them that the police would not let them disperse. I invited the picket leader back to my home to make the call. An Inspector allowed us to leave but only after he had had a discussion with other police officers some distance away. When we got home about twenty minutes later I showed the picket leader where the phone was. He tried to use it but it had been cut off.

Because of the very nature of phone tapping and the State's interest in keeping it secret it would be impossible to *prove* that it was happening or even to surmise it's extent. However, we find no difficulty in saying that we believe there has been a blanket tapping operation involving strike centres and the personal phones of many union activists. An expansion in the activities of the Special Branch and other 'internal security' organisations is an integral part of this Government's policy to criminalising large numbers of working people. Intelligence is the key to control and containment.

Police and Military Co-operation

We would like to stress that to our mind it is irrelevant whether or not the army is being used to bolster the number of police at the pickets. The para-military police who are being used are trained with DII and other quasi-military police bodies. They are trained in the use of firearms and many of them are trained in the use of such weapons as the baton round repeater gun and gas guns. They are trained in internal security strategies like 'snatch squads.'

Some of the Constabularies have provided their officers with riot clothing which consists of reinforced leg guards and heavily fortified jerkins like bullet proof vests. It is clear that the police who are being used in the strike are what strategists would call a 'third force'; a force between the police and the army. It is no longer the case that we do not have a riot police like the CRS in France. This riot force is 'built in' as a unit within each constabulary. The British state, always subtle and covert has organised a riot force within each constabulary area and though they are called 'Instant Response Units' in London and 'Tactical Aid Groups' in Manchester, they are in fact one similarly trained and equipped national riot squad.

The majority of police officers in Nottinghamshire are para-military police officers. They travel to their destination in long convoys of white support unit vans, like an occupying army. During the day when there is no activity on the picket they inhabit the colliery which they are attending. Often they come on and off duty in drill formation. Inside the pit yards they do drill training:

> There were a large number of police there, inside the pit premises, it was my impression that they were billeted there. We could see them clearly marching in formation.

> At Cotgrave picket, we parked up in the village and walked into the pit yard. I saw about sixty police officers there drilling in a military fashion.

Since the strike began there have been many reports of Army or Air Force personnel being used to police the pickets. The two most authenticated reports can be found in the Appendix 8, they are from Brighton Voice and News Line. As we only spent a week and a half interviewing people we were unable to follow through the stories which were reported to us. There were eight different circumstances described to us at second or third hand. These stories were so often repeated and from such different sources that we feel it would be wrong not to draw attention to them.

On the basis of what we heard it seems possible that armed forces personnel are being used *as police officers*. Something we were told repeatedly by first hand witnesses was that they had seen police officers without numbers on their uniforms or coats.

When the Nottinghamshire County Council Police Committee was asked for premises in which to billet police officers who were pouring into the County, they refused, consequently the majority of the police were stationed in two army camps in Nottinghamshire and one in Derbyshire. Each day they mounted their campaigns from their command headquarters in Mansfield police station which was also becoming an interrogation centre.

It is perhaps of little matter that the constitutional niceties have not been observed and a state of emergency declared. The police are under political instructions to break the strike using para-military methods.

PART THREE
The Consequences

The Police Authorities

The miner's strike has brought about one of the most extensive and costly policing exercises ever organised during an industrial dispute. The organisation of the operation on a national basis by the Association of Police Officers, in consultation with HMI and the Home Secretary, has overridden the statutory arrangements for policing which presently exist. It has brought to the fore the increasing centralisation of state powers at the expense of local democracy, a strategy evident in many other policies of the present Conservative Government. The Police Committees and Police Authorities have come face to face with a situation which challenges any notion of police accountability on a local level.

In practice, this accountability has long been of a very limited kind. The main legislation currently covering police powers is the 1964 Police Act. This consolidated a series of changes which had been taking place in the organisation of police forces for many years. By the 1930's central government was paying half the costs of maintaining police forces and the power of the Home Office over local forces outside of London was increasing. The old 'watch committees' which were responsible for maintaining police forces outside of London and which had wide powers of local control over their areas when they were originally formed in 1835, began to lose out gradually to their Chief Constables. In turn, the Chief Constables looked increasingly to the HQ of the Metropolitan Police force, Scotland Yard, which had always had a closer relationship to the Home Office, for various national police functions, thereby developing the process of centralisation still further. Under the 1964 Act, the number of police forces was reduced, making each area larger with a consequent increase in power for the Chief Constable. This made it even more difficult for the local community or council to have any real say in the running of their police force. The new Police Authorities were created to replace the watch committees with little substantive powers over policing policies.

At the same time, the police force as a body began to make more public demands about the nature of policing, staffing levels, police powers and the criminal justice system as a whole. Previously, demands had come from other sources such as MP's and Magistrates but now senior police officers in particular were publicly demanding more money and more powers. Sir Robert Mark, who was appointed as Metropolitan Police Commissioner in 1972, played a large part in this development with his pronouncements on many different aspects of the criminal justice system, including comments on the stupidity and prejudice of juries. This undermined the supposed 'separation of powers' whereby the police merely enforced the law 'impartially' while our democratically elected representatives in Parliament made the law.

Under the 1964 Police Act, the functions of the local Police Committees are loosely defined. They are responsible for the appointment of the Chief Constable and can dismiss him on the basis that he is running an 'inefficient' force, or has committed a disciplinary offence, subject to the approval of the Home Secretary. They are responsible for paying half the costs (through the County Council) of maintaining the force, and for staffing, equipment, buildings, etc. This can give them *some* powers over policy—say in refusing to pay for riot equipment or for an increase in the number of panda cars when the Committee would like to see more foot patrols. The Chief Constable is solely responsible for 'operational matters' and the Authority for 'efficiency', neither of which terms are defined under the Act. The Chief Constable must present an Annual Report to the Committee on the policing of the area and the Committee can call for further reports and ask questions.

However, the Chief Constable can refuse to give details or provide reports, and is able to appeal to the Home Secretary on his own behalf, on the grounds that these are 'operational matters' and therefore his concern alone. He may also appeal to the Home Secretary on the grounds that information should not be released 'in the public interest'. The Police Committee cannot instruct their Chief Constable or control his actions. In effect, he is not accountable to them or to the local community despite the fact that large numbers of civilian police personnel are employed by the County Council. The Courts have upheld the view that the police are only accountable to the law. However, it is precisely because the police use a considerable amount of discretion in enforcing the law that more democratic mechanisms, based on the local authority structure for example, are needed to attain some real measure of police accountability.

This discretion and lack of accountability have led to wide differences in policing policies in different parts of the country, and considerable variation in the relationship between Chief Constables and their Committees. Some Committees have struggled with their Chief Constables for a measure of local democratic accountability. Chief Constables have, in turn, revealed the extent of their independence and in several cases, their contempt for both their Committees and the public they claim to serve. This contradiction between Chief Constables and Committees has been highlighted and made public at different times.

In 1983, for example, James Anderton, the Chief Constable of Greater Manchester made a decision, without consulting his Police Committee, to arm patrolling police officers in Manchester. When questioned by the Committee, he replied: 'The policies were mine, the responsibility mine and not yours'. He went on to blame members of the Police Committee for causing the public furore that had followed his decision. In constantly blaming his Committee for interference he has built for himself a virtually autonomous role in the policing of the area. He is not alone in this. Kenneth Oxford, the Chief Constable of Merseyside, has presided over an unprecedented decline in police-public relations, and an increase in the use of violence by his officers but he has successfully rebuffed all attempts by his Police Committee to call him to account for his force's activities. In 1979, having refused to let the members of the Committee see the result of a police inquiry into the death of Jimmy Kelly, he allegedly told them 'keep out of my force's business.'

The Police Committees in Manchester and Merseyside have made frequent attempts to make their Chief Constables more accountable. This constant public friction at least begins to define the reality of the relationship in the public mind. While observing these arguments other Police Committees have convinced themselves that they enjoy better relationships with their Chief Constables than do Manchester and Merseyside.

There can be little doubt however, that a measure of complacency has crept into their relations and consequently it has come as a considerable shock to discover that their relationships could be destroyed so easily. In the current situation, the Chairs of the South Yorkshire and Nottinghamshire Police Committees have expressed anger and frustration:

The Home Secretary sent in Sir Lawrence Byford, the Inspector of Constabularies to look at the position in Nottinghamshire. The Home Secretary pays fifty per cent of the bill so he has a right to come in and have a look. What I don't agree with is that the HMI has more power that I have, more power that the Police Authority has got and yet we pick up the same amount of the bill as the Home Secretary does. When I went to see the Home Secretary, he told me that neither I nor he could tell the Chief Constable what to do. I don't believe that. In fact the Act (1964) does give the Chief Constables some autonmomy but I think really their power comes from all the little bits that have followed, the little bits of law that get through. No one realises what has happened until you get something on this scale. Then you realise that it is totally out of your control.

(Cllr. Frank Taylor, Chair of Notts. Police Cttee.)

The National Recording Centre is destroying something that we have worked hard for in South Yorkshire—full consultation, policing by consent.

(Cllr. George Moores, Chair of S. Yorks. Police Cttee.)

In particular, both Chairs were angry about the costs of the police operation and the expenses incurred on their behalf, without consultation beforehand. Cllr. Taylor Felt that his Committee had to some extent been 'duped' over this.

I do think that to some extent we have been duped. We were not consulted at all about the billeting or the cost. I didn't know until the second day that they were drafting so many officers in.

'Mutual aid' agreements exist between the Counties for financing special police operations. There are three grades of payment—the policing of the strike has been agreed on the basis of 'large scale aid'. This means that the Authority which has asked for help pays any extra overtime and subsistence costs. If two Chief Constables, or two Councils cannot agree, then the Home Secretary can order an Authority to pay. In Nottinghamshire the first two weeks alone cost £6.4m; for the first two weeks of April the cost was estimated at £2.8m. In South Yorkshire the cost for the first 4 weeks was estimated at £1m. Both Committees have taken action on this: the South Yorkshire County Council's Labour Group passed a motion in the fifth week of the dispute that any further policing costs arising from the strike should be found from the existing budget. They have also cancelled the '84/'85 vehicle replacement orders and taken action on abandoning parts of the building programme. In Nottinghamshire a special sub-committee of the Police Committee has been formed to monitor the ongoing costs, and the Chief Constable cannot spend anything above day-to-day costs without the Chair's authority.

When we interviewed the Chairs of the Police Committees both condemned the police tactics in relation to phone tapping, the use of 'snatch squads' and roadblocks. Cllr. Moores felt that the police were responsible for much of the violence on the picket lines, placing the blame for this on police officers from outside of his area.

> What is happening is that police from other areas are coming in here knowing that they are going away again. They come here, they attend the pickets, the adrenalin starts flowing and then the thumping starts. We're not used to this kind of policing up here, and we never will be. We had experience here of a thirteen week strike in 1980 (the steel strike) and we had no problems at all, now we get this sudden swamping of police officers. It is absolutely opposed to everything that we have stood for. There is no doubt that the police can be blamed for a lot of the violence that occurred on the picket line.

He condemned the role of ACPO in the dispute and the extent of state intervention:

> If I had to sum up what was most worrying, I would say that it was the concept of national policies that are carried out by police officers, without any legal standing whatsoever. Here we have state repression against people who are on the whole most moderate in their attitudes.'

The South Yorkshire Police Committee have set up an inquiry into the police activities during the dispute, and are taking evidence from a wide number of organisations, including the NUM, NCB and the media. They have also asked their Chief Executive to investigate the legality of ACPO's role in the organisation of the police operation.

The power of Police Committees to take action against the police for their activities in such operations is limited. However, there can be little doubt that the chief Constables in both areas could have been called on publicly to account for their actions during this dispute. The Committees do have the power to sack their Chief Constables, even if this is subject to the agreement of the Home Secretary. Such an action would, at least, have drawn attention to the lack of public accountability with which Chief Constables operate generally and brought to the fore the way in which the police operation has been organised in order to break the strike. Cllr. Taylor commented that: 'although not a lot is being said now, the debate about his (the Chief

Constable's) powers will go on long into the night after this is all over.' This will be too late. The developing independence of Chief Constables from their local communities, and the increasing centralisation of various police functions have taken place over a number of years and Police Committees must accept some level of responsibility for allowing this development.

Despite their lack of substantive powers, Police Committees could bring their forces to some measure of public accountability by addressing themselves in Committee to the political questions raised by State power. Lack of political resolve and an inability to clearly support the working class, in this case the miners, by Labour Councils has allowed the police the space to organise a massive strike-breaking exercise from a national centre, using specially trained riot police and involving a complete erosion of rights.

> The implications can be summed up in the words 'state repression'. Frankly the only comparison that I can think of is that we are returning to the kind of scenes that we witnessed in 1933 and 1934 in Germany. The media have played a great part in this, in that they are voluntarily supporting a national propaganda campaign. They are showing the worst aspects of picketing, 98% of which is peaceful, they are creating a climate of mistrust. We seem to be going down the same path that Germany went down in 1934, state direction, state repression.
>
> *Cllr. Moores.*

Conclusions

This report was not undertaken as a scientific enquiry and is better described as a journalistic investigation. For this reason we have recommended a fuller and more independent Inquiry in the recommendations. However, on the basis of the men we took statements from and those we interviewed we feel able to draw the following conclusions:

1. That a National Riot Force has been developed and deployed in England. This force is trained in para-military strategies and is equipped with riot weapons. The lessons which this force is putting into practice are those learned in the north of Ireland since 1968. The National Riot Force appears to be answerable only to the Home Secretary. It has emerged and developed without any change in the 1964 Police Act to sanction it.

2. That the Association of Chief of Police Officers, ACPO, are now a command structure for this National Riot Force and the president of ACPO has operational control over it. That ACPO have acted without reference to the 1964 Police Act or to the County Police Authorities which individual Chief Constables are partly answerable to.

3. The Police officers who have been arresting men in Nottinghamshire have been briefed in what powers they should assume. Often they do not have these powers in law and they have been acting beyond the law to which they are apparently no longer answerable. Many of the things which they have been doing will be sanctioned in the Police and Criminal Evidence Bill when it becomes law. Witnessing what has been happening in the first weeks of the miners' strike confirms in our minds what many people have already said that the Police and Criminal Evidence Bill has little to do with crime and everything to do with criminalising the working class and those who dissent from the policies of the present Government.

4. That a campaign of mass criminalisation has been waged against the striking miners. The decision to wage this campaign rather than use the civil law was probably a political one which senior police officers were privy to.

5. That the police have been employed in a partisan and political way, not to keep order, or protect everyones' rights including pickets but simply to break the strike.

6. Very few of the men who we interviewed and who have been arrested since the strike began have committed any offence or infringed the criminal or common law.

7. Many of the arrests and charges made by the police have been of doubtfull legality or in contravention of Judges Rules.

8. Time and again in the cases of those people we interviewed the police have acted with utter contempt for the rights of citizens in that they have:

    i.   Arrested men with counter-insurgency methods, like snatch squads and agents provocateurs.

   ii.   Arrested men without reasonable suspicion of an offence having occurred

  iii.   Failed to caution arrested men.

  iv.   Arrested men on patently inadequate or legally dubious pretexts.

    v.   Taken polaroid photographs of men while using force.

    vi. Taken finger prints and palm prints of men being held in custody without informing them of their rights.

    vii. Taken photographs of men being held in custody without informing them of their rights.

    viii. That in the matter of both the issues above and in the taking of statements the police have used threats and pressures.

    ix. On every occasion not granted the person in custody access to a phone.

9. That Special Branch Officers have been employed in an intelligence gathering operation and have interrogated men in detention on political and personal matters without sanction in law. They have done this without making it clear to the subject who they were or for what purpose they wanted this information. They have done this without making the subject aware of his rights or giving him any opportunity to have sight of the notes or sign them as true.

10. That Magistrates have been compliant and weak in the face of the police and deprived the men brought before them of the protection which the law is supposed to offer to every innocent person. That Magistrates have awarded conditions of bail and bound men over, even in some cases, have refused bail and remanded people in custody without making the most cursory or preliminary enquiries into the circumstances of their arrest.

11. That a blanket phone tapping operation has taken place. That this in itself is such a massive erosion of the individual's rights that the Home Secretary should be called upon to resign.

12. That the police have generally used powers which they have not been granted in statute or precedent, such as, those powers used in the blocking off of the Dartford Tunnel and the arbitary turning back of working class people from the Nottinghamshire border.

13. That the County Police Authority in Nottinghamshire has not acted with sufficient decision or strength to challenge it's Chief Constable or the Home Secretary on the overriding of the Authority's power, or the collapse of 'normal' liberties in the County. We sympathise with and understand the predicament of the Police Authority but contest absolutely the idea that the financial implications of what has happened are most important. Without a doubt the state will pay and however much it costs it will be cheap for them if they have exercised a police state.

Recommendations

We recommend that the National Union of Mineworkers in conjunction with other trade unions which can contribute special knowledge set up a public Committee of Inquiry. The Inquiry would have terms of reference falling under three headings:

1. *A Committee of Inquiry* to look into the use of the criminal law during the miners' strike. It should make particular reference to the role of the Attorney General and the conduct of Magistrates during the strike.

2. *A Committee of Inquiry* to look into the role of the Association of Chief of Police Officers in the miners' strike. The Committee should make particular reference to the relationship between the Home Secretary and ACPO and the development of the National Recording Centre.

3. *A Committee of Inquiry* to look into the covert employment of para-military strategies during the miners' strike. The Committee should make particular reference to:

   i.   The growth, formation and training of a National Riot Force.
   ii. The use of polaroid photographs by the police.
   iii. The use of snatch squads.
   iv. The use of violence and intimidation within police stations.
   v.   The use of special branch officers to interrogate suspects.
   vi. Telephone tapping.
   vii. The use of propaganda based on lies in the media.
   viii. The use of various forms of surveillance and the keeping of records and information on trade unionists.

VOLUME II
The Iron Fist

PART ONE
Nottinghamshire—
Divided and Ruled

The Hearts and Minds of the Notts. Miners: A Background to the Last Six Weeks

By the sixth week of the dispute, 80% of the miners were still on strike and there had been 1,000 arrests at picket lines and roadblocks. Attitudes were becoming entrenched on all sides. Some Nottinghamshire miners were still scabbing and pickets from Yorkshire and Nottinghamshire were putting increased pressure on them to come out in solidarity. The next few weeks were also to see battles fought by the NUM with other trade unions for their support, particularly in the steel industry. The Labour and Trade Union movements seemed unable to throw their wholehearted support behind the miners, in spite of the NUM's history of standing firm behind other groups of workers during their struggles.

The violence by the police against the pickets was escalating and there was increasing evidence of direct intimidation by the police against striking miners and their families. The number of arrests more than trebled during this period: by the end of the twelfth week there had been 3,500 arrests. In the face of a huge propaganda campaign, the use of the police as strike-breakers and the government's absolute determination to destroy the NUM, the miners continued to fight for their futures with resolve.

The working miners in the Nottinghamshire coalfield were to come increasingly to the fore in a propaganda drive by the government and the NCB aimed at splitting the Nottinghamshire men away from other British miners. This propaganda campaign had begun even before the strike. On the same day that the NCB announced the closure of Corton Wood and Bulcliffe Wood, they also announced that no pits in Nottinghamshire would close.

The strike ballot in the Nottinghamshire Area was held on March 15th and 16th. From Monday March 12th pickets from Yorkshire entered the Nottinghamshire coalfield. The majority of them contented themselves with canvassing the Nottinghamshire miners to support them in the forthcoming ballot. They were joined by miners from Kent and South Wales. Large numbers of miners refused to cross the picket lines and it began to look as if the tactics would succeed. By the second day of picketing however the police were out in force to prevent pickets from approaching the Nottinghamshire miners and they waved those going in to work straight past the pickets. Angry scenes turned violent at some pits and the media had a field day.

On the day of the ballot in Nottinghamshire, the Nottinghamshire Evening Post published a blatant piece of misinformation propaganda. They published a letter from a woman claiming that Yorkshire miners had been paying £2 a week into a strike fund since 1972; now, she said, they were drawing £70 a week each in strike pay.

The Ballot result was heavily against the strike action; only 7,285 or 26.5% of those voting, voted in favour. Picketing was resumed on Monday March 18th, but the extra police were used to good effect. Pickets were prevented from entering the county by roadblocks. Those who managed to get through the cordon were kept well away from pit entrances and prevented from approaching those going into work. Many of the Nottinghamshire miners who had voted for a strike joined the pickets but they too were prevented from approaching their colleagues. By the end of the second week of the strike there were between eight and eleven thousand police officers in Nottinghamshire.

At the beginning of April the divisions within the Nottinghamshire NUM began to surface. Ray Chadburn and Henry Richardson, the President and General Secretary, both fully supported the action but felt that because they represented the Nottinghamshire Area they should suppress their own views and present the Area position. Most members of the left-dominated Area Executive were already on strike but they could do no more than make recommendations which the right-wing dominated Area Council promptly overturned. On Tuesday, April 3rd, the Area Executive Committee issued the following recommendation:

> In view of the fact that other Trade Unions throughout Britain are instructing their members not to cross picket lines in support of the miners' fight for jobs, this Area must search its Trade Union

principles regarding policy on picket lines. We therefore recommend that branches set up their own picket lines and the Area Executive Committee instructs our members not to cross those picket lines. We reiterate our support for a National Ballot Vote.

At a Council meeting two days later this recommendation was overturned and the splits grew wider. Chadburn and Richardson were both attacked verbally and Chadburn said afterwards that it was the worst meeting he had attended in his life. On April 12th when the National Executive Committee met in Sheffield, Chadburn and Richardson were abused and jostled by the waiting crowds as they left the meeting. Both men turned on the media who were expecting them to attack the strikers. Instead they condemned their own members for not having the guts to stand and fight for themselves and their fellow members.

Although there were now 10,000 Notts. miners on strike (April 12th) the Ballot result prevented any of the elected officials from taking an active role in organising those who were on strike into an effective force. To give the strikers a boost a rally was organised in Nottingham for Monday April 14th. An estimated 20,000 miners took part in the march and a packed meeting afterwards heard messages of support and solidarity for the Notts. miners who were on stike.

After the rally, late in the afternoon as marchers reached their coaches near Mansfield Leisure Centre, fighting broke out between police officers and miners. There were 88 arrests and 50 men were charged with riotous behaviour. These serious charges can carry unlimited fines or unlimited imprisonment.

In the second week of April, Arthur Scargill, the NUM President, announced that the NEC was seeking a change in the NUM's rules which would allow a national strike to be authorised by a simple majority in a ballot, rather than the 55% then required. This was to be discussed at a special Delegate Conference, the supreme body of the NUM, on 19th April. Ian McGregor, the National Coal Board (NCB) Chairman, responded to this with a call to miners to defy their union and return to work. As the day of the special delegate conference to discuss the ballot approached, McGregor's propaganda moves increased and on 15th April he hinted that troops might be used to move coal. He went on to claim that 25% of pits would be geologically unworkable in a long drawn out dispute, with the consequence that more jobs would be lost by compulsory redundancies. The NCB's position would not be changed in the short term, he added, by a national ballot calling for an official strike.

On 19th April, the day of the delegate conference, thousands of miners lobbied delegates outside the NUM Headquarters in Sheffield. The conference voted to make the strike official and voted in favour of the rule change. The following day the right wing dominated Nottinghamshire Area Council discussed the decision but avoided taking a vote on it. They agreed instead to send a circular to all Branches explaining that the decision to make the strike official was now national policy and anyone wishing to come out on strike would be on official strike. Now that the strike was 'official', the Nottinghamshire strikers were able to receive funds from the Area and display placards proclaiming 'Official NUM picket'. This gave them tremendous heart.

On May 22nd the Coal Board achieved what the NUM had been trying to do for seven weeks, it brought the Nottinghamshire coalfield to a standstill. May is the beginning of the annual holiday entitlement period and the NCB allowed all the working miners a rest day to participate in a 'Right to work' demonstration against the Union officers at the Miner's Offices in Mansfield. About 7,000 holidaying scabs were escorted by the police to the Miners' Offices. In stark contrast, striking miners who gathered in Pleasley to march to the Miners' Offices in support of the Area officials were met by a baton charge from the police and thousands of strikers were prevented from reaching their destination.

By Friday May 4th the right wing within the union had recovered enough ground to announce that they were going to the High Court to seek an injunction ordering the Area Council to withdraw its instruction not to cross picket lines.

During the first week of May, renewed efforts were made by the NUM leadership to bring out those still working in Nottinghamshire, South Derbyshire, Leicestershire, Lancashire and Warwickshire. The response from the Government, the NCB and the media was more propaganda, with claims that there was still 6 months' supply of coal available at power stations and that thousands of miners were responding to an advertisement in the NCB newspaper 'Coal News' about a telephone hot-line on redundancy payments.

On 10th May Arthur Scargill announced a new initiative with the transport unions (the National Union of Railwaymen, the Transport and General Workers Union, the National Union of Seamen and the train drivers' union, ASLEF) to stop the movement of coal. There had already been some local agreements and on 27th April a joint meeting of the triple alliance of rail, coal and steel unions agreed to halve the coal supply to the Ravenscraig steelworks in Scotland. This was to lead to a major battle between the NUM and the main steel union, the ISTC, led by Bill Sirs, in the coming weeks. It became clear that Sirs was intent on looking after his own workers' interests at the expense of the miners. This was flying in the face of the solidarity shown by the NUM during the 13-week steel strike; and overlooked the fact that a long-term decline in the coal industry would inevitably inflict great damages on the steel industry. The NUM stressed the steel production *must* stop, and that other groups of workers should be willing to make short-term sacrifices on behalf of the miners and of the Trade Union Movement as a whole.

Arrests in all areas continued to escalate. In Scotland on 10th May, 292 miners were arrested on their way to picket the Ravenscraig steel plant and the Hunterston Terminal. The compromise agreement made between the NUM and the steel unions was already faltering.

On 16th May Ann Scargill and three other women were arrested on the picket line outside Silverhill colliery in Nottinghamshire. Many women's support groups had been formed and a large number of women from many areas were joining the men in the organisation of the strike.

By 18th May, 2,164 people had been arrested in connection with the strike as part of the police's strike-breaking activities. Of these, 1,077 were in Nottinghamshire.

The only real foothold the Government had was the large number of miners still working in the Nottinghamshire area. The Chief Constable of Nottinghamshire stated that special units had been set up ostensibly to identify intimidators of working miners in pit villages. This was the beginning of a huge propaganda campaign aimed against striking miners which gathered momentum in the following weeks. The Home Secretary announced that these units were composed of special patrols, backed by CID investigators. Cabinet sources revealed that the Government hoped that the activities of these units would lead to a return to work by the strikers. As complaints against the police mounted, Leon Brittan, the Home Secretary, speaking at the Police Federation's Annual Conference, assured the police that their annual pay claim would be dealt with sympathetically.

On 15th May, two Nottinghamshire NUM branches issued writs against their executive members in an attempt to reverse the executive's official backing for the strike. On 10th May the National Executive of the NUM had made the decision, usual in strikes, to suspend all branch elections until the strike ended. The Nottinghamshire area executive were fearful that an injunction could have been granted to nullify this decision and hold elections. On 23rd May the Nottingham shire executive reversed this national decision to postpone the branch elections. In an area where more than half of the men were at work and showed no signs of joining the strike, the Nottinghamshire area executive had allowed the Government and the NCB the possibility of consolidating its position in what was becoming the most crucial coalfield in Britain. The elections are now due in August, and it seems likely that they will produce a right-wing victory on the executive, leaving the strikers stranded with no political or financial support.

On 25th May the High Court ordered that the NUM could not instruct any of its members in Nottinghamshire to join the strike. Arthur Scargill denounced this decision as 'consistent with over a century of anti-working class judgements'. Henry Richardson, Secretary of the Nottinghamshire area NUM, on the other hand, stated that the decision would make little difference, since miners already on strike would still receive the official support of the union.

The government meanwhile were stepping up pressure on miners and their families by attempting to starve them back to work. On 15th May it was announced that the value of groceries, firewood, and other 'gifts' would be deducted from social security payments to striking miners. Police at roadblocks began asking drivers not only if they were pickets, but also if they were taking food to striking miners. The local communities rallied round. Soup kitchens had already been set up in many mining areas, run on funds collected locally and some Labour Councils were providing free school meals for the children of striking miners.

Arguments about the level of coal stocks continued. By mid-April the Coal Board was buying in foreign coal. Arthur Scargill went to Paris urging the blocking of coal from Europe. He already had the agreement of miners' unions in Australia and Holland.

Towards the end of May a negotiations circus was promoted by the government and the media. The NUM had made it quite clear from the beginning that they would not discuss pit closures, yet pundits were suddenly forecasting an end to the dispute. Negotiations collapsed on 23rd May when McGregor showed himself incapable of the fine tuning the government required; he appeared bullying and aggressive. A day later it was announced that McGregor would be temporarily removed from negotiations because of his handling of the dispute.

On 21st May the Lancashire area executive suspended those still working from membership of the NUM of up to 5 years, a decision affecting up to 1,500 men.

The BSC's coke works at Orgreave suddenly became a focus for the confrontation when mass pickets were moved in to try to prevent movement of coke to their Scunthorpe works. On 27th May, Arthur Scargill called for increased picketing at the plant. The true nature of the state's preparations and their training of a national riot force was suddenly made clear. Thousands of officers on foot in full riot gear were supported by mounted police and dog handlers. There were 82 arrests and 28 pickets hurt.

Clashes continued throughout the following day after renewed provocation when Arthur Scargill was arrested in the early morning. In the middle of June the BSC suspended their convoys into Orgreave.

On 1st June Margaret Thatcher claimed there would be no early resolution of the dispute whilst continuing to deny that she was playing any role in it. However, on 6th June, Paul Foot published Cabinet documents in the Daily Mirror showing that the Cabinet had 'been involved up to its neck'. These leaked documents demonstrated the Cabinet's role in the railwaymen's pay talks. Thatcher had ordered that the talks be drawn out to keep the railwaymen working and moving coal. As industrial action became more likely, and with it, the possibility of the rail unions joining forces with the NUM, an increased pay offer was tabled and accepted. The government had succeeded in buying off the railwaymen while isolating the miners. During the Commons debate following this revelation on 7th June, Thatcher and other senior Cabinet ministers were absent, treating with contempt any efforts to bring them to account for their deceit. Outside the Commons 70 miners were arrested during a mass lobby of Parliament.

On June 13th the NCB, McGregor and the government finally brought an end to tentative private negotiations which had been taking place, by announcing a completely new 'Plan for Coal'. McGregor's next ploy was to threaten a rolling ballot of all miners, beginning in the Nottinghamshire area. The threat was idle and the plan poorly conceived. Cracks were becoming evident in what had appeared to be a united and co-ordinated opposition by the government, the NCB and McGregor; thieves were falling out.

The 'Jewel in the Crown': Union splitting in Nottinghamshire

The Area

The county of Nottinghamshire is bordered on its eastern side by the non-mining county of Lincoln and on its western side by the now relatively small mining areas of the North and South Derbyshire. The mines in the Nottinghamshire area have a long history having developed parallel to the heavy industry in the Black Country. Many of the present mines were dug in the second half of the nineteenth century. The coalfield consists of twenty-five working collieries scattered throughout the county, from Harworth, the most northerly on the Yorkshire border, to Cotgrave, the most southerly on the Leicestershire border.

For administrative purposed the National Coal Board (NCB) divided the county of Nottinghamshire into two areas, North Notts. and South Notts. The National Union of Mineworkers Nottinghamshire area however organises over the whole county. The NUM represents approximately 31,000 members in the county. Of the 31,000, twenty-eight are employed at the twenty-five collieries and the remaining three thousand or so are employed in various workshops, transport depots and training centres.

Historically the Nottinghamshire coalfield has always been profitable, first for the private owners then after 1947 for the NCB. This profitability has been due to relatively thick seams of good quality coal in generally good geological conditions. The proximity of the coalfield to the heavy industrialised Black Country provided ready markets while competition between coal and other industries for labour ensured that the Nottinghamshire miners were always amongst the highest paid in Britain. Even though they were highly paid as miners, other seasonal occupations and other industries attracted their labour and led to frequent shortages. There was always room for men from other coalfields to be re-located in Nottinghamshire.

As the demand for coal went into decline at the end of the postwar economic boom, the Nottinghamshire coalfield was spared the worst ravages of the late fifties and mid-sixties. In fact the Nottinghamshire area became the receiving area for those Welsh, Scottish and north east miners and their families displaced by the massive colliery closure programmes of that time.

A series of coal fired power stations were built along the Trent Valley and the majority output of the Notts. pits was earmarked for these power stations. As the economic crisis began to cut deeper, the Nottinghamshire NUM lost only 12,000 members between 1964 and the present day compared to 32,000 lost in the Yorkshire area over the same period. Now, though, the Nottinghamshire coalfield can no longer be regarded as secure. Many pits are old and in desperate need of investment. The evidence suggests that they will not receive this investment and in the long term face the same closure programme which is affecting other areas. The most immediate threat is posed by the 'break even' demand of the present government. The last Chairman of the NCB, Norman Siddall, claimed that if the 12% of uneconomic capacity could be removed the industry would be better able to achieve 'break even' point. Of the 25 pits in Nottinghamshire, twelve are operating at a loss.

The policy of the present Conservative government involves a commitment to a nuclear energy programme which demands that the NCB must 'break even' by 1986. Of the 28,000 colliery workers in Nottinghamshire, 23,630 depend in varying degrees on the Trent Valley power stations to buy their output. It is clear that the government intends to phase out these power stations. The Central Electricity Generating Board has admitted that it has no plans to order any coal-fired power stations in the foreseeable future. On the other hand it is their stated intention to build fifteen new nuclear power stations over the next twenty years. Given that there is already sufficient generating capacity available to cope with any upsurge in demand, and that demand for electricity has been steadily declining, it is reasonable to assume that nuclear power stations will replace existing coal-fired stations.

The Union

In order to understand why such a large number of workers in the Nottinghamshire area have consistently failed to fight for the interest of their class it is necessary to look at both the structure of the Union and its history. The National Union of Mineworkers is a federated union made up of twenty areas, each one with its own structure and rule book. Although the areas are very similar, no two are exactly the same either in their structure or their rule book. The Union developed from pit to company level and then to county level; each county area has jealously guarded its rule book.

There are four full time officials of the Nottinghamshire area; they are elected by individual ballot. They are, the President: Ray Chadburn; the Area General Secretary: Henry Richardson; the Financial Secretary: Roy Link and the Pension/Benevolent Officer: David Prendergast. These four men also act as the Area Agents, that is, they are each responsible, especially in relation to grievance procedures, for a given number of pits within the area. In most areas the Agents and Officials are separate.

The Area Council is the general management body of the Union and as such is responsible for the affairs of the Union. Every branch at a pit or other specific place of work elects a delegate by individual ballot each year. These delegates and the four Area Officials consititute the *Area Council*.

The *Area Executive Committee* comprises ten lay members, plus the four full-time Area Officials and the Vice President who is also a lay official elected by the Area Council from amongst its own members. The ten lay members to the Executive are also elected by the Area Council.

The Executive meets at least twice a month or sooner as necessary and conducts the Union's business between Council meetings which are held every two months. The Executive is responsible for: dealing with matters which may be delegated from time to time by the Council; dealing with matters of urgency; preparing recommendations to the Council and preparing the Agenda for Council Meetings.

The Executive does not have the power to vary a decision already on record by the Council and it is written into its constitution that it shall not deal with political questions unrelated to the Industry. The Area Council is under no obligation to accept the recommendations of the Executive Committee.

A History of Division

Given the power of the Council described above, influencing the direction of the Union depends upon influencing the consciousness of the working miners at Branch Committee level. This consciousness is changed and directed by many factors within the everyday life of the working miner both at work and outside work. Not only does the political complexion of the rest of the county affect miners, but whether they own their own property and how incentive schemes at work are organised.

Now, just as in the coal strike of 1926, the tactics of the Conservative government have been aimed at isolating the miners in different areas from each other and splitting and dividing within the miners' own ranks inside areas wherever possible. These tactics can only succeed where there are those within the Labour movement and the miners' organisation prepared to collaborate with the Conservatives and the employer.

Many parallels inevitably do come to mind between the present strike and that of 1926. Both were long drawn out strikes during the summer months, with a Tory government with a massive parliamentary majority, an ineffective opposition in the House of Commons, the harassment of miners and their families by the police and debtors and the frequent police baton charges which ease the way for scabs to get to work.

In Nottinghamshire in particular there are other similarities which relate to divisions within the union. A possibility is reappearing which few miners imagined could happen again in the Nottinghamshire coalfield: Spencerism. Spencerism means 'non-political' unionism, a Union working for the government rather than its members. It means anti-communism and anti-socialism. Spencerism is the kind of trade unionism which the Conservative government has been trying to bring about through employment legislation. The right approves of it now just as much if not more than it did in 1926.

In 1926, George Spencer, a right wing Labour M.P. and elected officer of the Nottinghamshire Miners Association, negotiated a District Agreement with the coal owners and led a return to work mid-way through the six weeks' strike. He was expelled from the Nottinghamshire Miners Association (NMA) and the national organisation, the Miners Federation of Great Britain. With the full co-operation and the financial assistance of the coal owners, Spencer formed his own 'non-political' union, the Nottinghamshire Miners Industrial Union (NMIU).

Dr A.R. Griffin, the official historian for the Notts. miners and recently retired Head of Industrial Relations for the NCB North Nottinghamshire Area, said of Spencers Union:

The anti-political section were entirely right wing... they were not opposed to political action as such; they were opposed rather to politics of the wrong shade.

Spencer and his Union were upheld by the establishment as the model Trade Union. The extreme right wing organisation 'The Economic League' used to send in flying squads of organisers to have propaganda drives and get people to join the Union. Any suggestion that they should use their trade union power either in political or industrial action was decried as communistic.

Once they were isolated from the rest of the miners, the men in Nottinghamshire suffered more than most. A policy of 'co-operation not confrontation' which included no-strike agreements ensured that by 1937 when the Nottinghamshire miners were finally able to rid themselves of the NMIU their wages and working conditions had deteriorated to such an extent that they were among the worst in the British coalfield.

In the present dispute, we have seen the emergence of the Nottinghamshire Working Miners Committee (NWMC) and Henry Richardson has spoken of 'a union within a union'. The NWMC meets in secret and the police 'vet' anyone entering the villages where its meetings are held. At present, only two members of this Committee (they claim twenty-five members, one from each pit) are prepared to identify themselves. In an interview in the *Financial Times* on May 26th, they claimed that they had no intention of taking over the function of the Union. Later in the same article they admitted that at those collieries where the elected branch officials were on strike members of their organisation had taken over their role, 'with the blessing of the NCB'. The Secretary of the group told the *Financial Times* that: "Up to twelve weeks ago, I had not been to a union meeting in my life."

He and other key figures in the organisation stood for office in the recent Branch elections ordered by the High Court. The declared function of the NWMC is to raise funds for those working miners who are *enduring hardship as a result of the strike*. Letters of appeal are sent to various organisations; these letters contain the following statement: "The Notts. Area NUM leaders, typical of the National Executive, are now no longer reflecting the views of the majority". Local Liberals and Conservatives have promised donations. Dr Griffin, writing in the *Coventry Evening Telegraph* in May, said: "There is a distinct possibility of the NUM breaking up. Already some officials have approached me for advice for setting up breakaway unions".

Clearly, the government and the NCB will do all in their power to support and encourage these factions within the union for the present. It remains to be seen however whether the Coal Board would be prepared to allow negotiating rights to any group other than the NUM once the strike is over. A victorious NUM will undoubtedly demand the removal of anyone who actively campaigned against them. Those elected officers who are presently collaborating with the NCB and the Conservatives must know that they are playing for much higher stakes than just their weekly wage.

Mention of Spencerism, The Economic League, non-political unionism and anti-communism in 1926, brings us back full circle, not only to the activities of union splitters in 1984 but to the Radical Right and the group which brought Thatcher to the leadership of the Conservative Party. The nature of class struggle does not change; the Economic League was one of the many organisations which aided the National Association For Freedom. It provides an information service on 'subversives' and union activists for industry.

The Economic League has always been particularly involved in the mining industry because as a bosses' organisation it was financed and run by coal owners when the mines were privately owned. Although the working class has made considerable gains in many areas since 1926 the aims of the League, as they were stated then, can be seen to be central to Thatcher's Liberalism today:

> To uphold the principles of private ownership upon which the greatness of Britain has been built. To discourage any undue political interference with industry that may result eventually in some form of bureaucratic control or State Socialism. To oppose all subversive elements which may attempt, by stirring up strikes and disaffection, to interrupt the smooth working of the industrial machine.

Since the National Association for Freedom realised its aim in achieving a government of the Radical Right there can be less use for such organisations. Those on the fringe have been taken within the state and such organisations as the Economic League probably provide only a small proportion of the intelligence on trade unionists that state security organisations like MI5 collect and record.

The police can pursue the objectives of such organisations on the ground and there is little point now in the right organising vigilante groups or private armies. Nevertheless the Nottinghamshire NUM suffered disastrously from the activities of organisations with similar aims to the National Association for Freedom before the Conservative government came to power and one can see the same hand at work during the present dispute in respect of the private High Court actions taken against the Union.

During the office of the Callaghan government from 1974 to 1979, Bill Richardson of the Blidworth Branch of the Nottinghamshire NUM instigated a number of High Court actions against the Area Union. Richardson was often accused of creating situations whereby the Branch Chairman made a ruling based upon an interpretation of the rule book only to find himself challenged in the High Court. Invariably Richardson won in the High Court not only because the courts were in league with the right but also because over the years the rule book had developed many contradictions.

The most disastrous aspect of this kind of litigation was, however, the space it allowed for the judiciary to make interventions in the NUM Area rule book. Through the court cases the High Court was allowed access to the book and was responsible for its modification. In a protracted and subtle way this is rather like allowing management to play a part in the Union or to put it more simply: Spencerism.

Richardson's challenges in the High Court required specialised legal knowledge and a lot more finance than an ordinary working miner could reasonably be expected to have. The question arises: where did the expertise and finance come from?

Although Richardson has now retired and NAFF no longer appears to exist in its original form it is significant that the right has made a number of applications to the High Court recently. Before the strike began, the Barnsley Winders, whose leader Bob Copping is one of only two men who have scabbed in Yorkshire since the strike began, took the Yorkshire Area of the NUM to the High Court. The Yorkshire Area had tried to suspend the officials of Barnsley Winders from holding office for contravening area policy. The High Court ruled against the Union.

Similarly, Lancashire miners won a High Court ruling preventing their area from suspending them from Union membership for scabbing. The case which has had most publicity is that of the Notting-hamshire miners who took the area officials, Chadburn and Richardson, and the National Officials Scargill and Heathfield, to the High Court to get the Court to declare the strike illegal. Although they did not achieve their purpose they were granted an order making the area rescind it's instructions to members not to cross picket lines. They also won an order forcing the Union to hold local branch elections at a time when a third of the workforce is on strike.

Where is the work and the finance coming from for those legal actions? We can only speculate, but the tactics are familiar, splitting and dividing. They have been the central tactics of the anti-socialist right within the Union for over fifty years. Now the State itself is completely behind them and endorsing them.

PART TWO
The Dirty War in Nottinghamshire

Intimidation and Misinformation: The Northern Ireland Card

The attitude of striking miners of all areas, earlier in the dispute, to the call for a National ballot was eminently sensible and truly democratic. How, they asked, could it be right for men in safe pits, who earned good money, to vote away the jobs of others? This was a class view of democracy and the state did its best to distort and break it, preferring instead to illustrate the anomalies in small areas and hold these up as undemocratic. Even after the call for a National ballot had run its course, striking miners felt the same way. Those who were still working in Nottinghamshire were being divisive, they were prejudicing the chances of victory for the vast majority. Quite naturally the strikers wished to impose the needs and the views of the majority on that recalcitrant and selfish minority.

Left to the union to resolve this question, a democratic view would have prevailed and those still working would either have been picketed out or cut asunder from the union which had gained for them the very benefits which they now enjoyed. The matter was not left to the union. The state is well practised in the exploitation of right-wing minorities, it has used and manipulated them not just by splitting unions as the British and Americans did across Europe after the second world war, but also by dividing countries as it has done in India, Cyprus and Ireland; wherever there has been democratic resistance to British rule.

By May it had become obvious that the position of the Nottinghamshire miners was crucial to the strike. Not so crucial to the NUM because working miners in that area constituted only a very small percentage of the total mining workforce. Those who did work though were extremely important to the government: by stressing the condition of working miners in one coalfield it was possible to distort and misrepresent the position nationally. In Nottinghamshire alone a majority of men still worked so this was where the government poured in resources and propaganda. The Conservative government took up the slogan, 'The Right to Work'.

This ploy has echoes of Northern Ireland. In 1918 in the General election, Irish voters returned Sinn Fein members in 24 of the 32 counties of Ireland. The first Irish government was set up independently of Westminster. The English doggedly insisted upon its military presence even though they had been voted out of the country. After a bitter war the Irish Republican Army signed a treaty with the British, agreeing a division of Ireland into two separate states, one comprised of 26 counties in the South and the other comprised of 9 counties in the North. Of the 9 counties in Ulster, Unionists had polled a majority in only four. As soon as Ulster became an English statelet, Westminister gerrymandered the county boundaries making it six counties, most of which had a Unionist majority. In voting terms the Catholics in the north were in a minority and this fact has been used by the British state as an argument for their continued oppression. Within the context of a united Ireland this false democracy would be seen as absurd.

The analogy with Ireland went further as the government poured thousands of police officers into Nottinghamshire, briefed to take the side of the working miners. To give this massive presence validity and to make its role of 'protecting' the majority plausible the move was accompanied by a propaganda campaign. The central theme of this campaign was that the minority of strikers were intimidating the majority of men going to work.

The government faced another problem which it would have to find a covert solution to: as the illegal road blocks, searches and arrests began to bite, Yorkshire Area NUM began letting pickets across the border to stay in Nottinghamshire. These men went in groups to various rallies and events and then stayed on as 'static pickets'. The campaign of propaganda and misinformation was orchestrated to obscure the violence being used by the police against these Yorkshire miners who chose to stay in Nottinghamshire.

Rarely was there any evidence of intimidation of working miners by strikers; if there were cases they were poorly documented by the media and amounted to innuendo. One or two stories were repeated in most newspapers and they bore such a similarity of intent and content that they were clearly concocted within some government department.

On May 11th the *Daily Telegraph* reported that, 'striking miners picketed the homes of miners in Nottinghamshire yesterday in an attempt to stop them going to work'. According to the *Telegraph*, working miners had to get dressed in the dark because strikers were out in the early morning identifying scabs by their bedroom lights. Many of the stories came from interviews or letters sent in apparently by working Nottinghamshire miners:

> The police action is necessary and the intimidation must be stopped. I have to put up with abusive telephone calls and abuse when I go to work. It is the only way of keeping law and order which would otherwise break down. I have only been stopped once by the police and asked where I was going. Left wingers have been trying to make out that the police were intimidating people.

> A Nottinghamshire miner: *Daily Telegraph* May 19th.

The Chief Constable of Nottinghamshire, Mr. McLoughlin, had some contradictory things to say about the role of the police and their impartiality, in the dispute. Speaking at a press conference on May 14th he had this to say:

> Intimidation of working miners and their families by strikers from other coalfields has led to the police establishing special squads which have been patrolling pit villages.

He added that, "the police have no axe to grind in this dispute; we must steer an absolutely middle course'. The middle course which he described was "intended to stop people getting into the county". The discrete middle course also involved lauding working miners who he said were having, "a bloody awful time". He admitted that there were people in the county who had managed to avoid 'police interceptor squads'. If these remarks were not enough to confirm his complete impartiality, Mr. McLoughlin hinted at there being people in Nottinghamshire who came from even more distant parts than Yorkshire: "The police are aware that others apart from miners have been on the picket lines. Some have been students and others were foreigners".

McLoughlin claimed that the Home Office was not involved in any of the decisions taken in Nottinghamshire concerning police tactics. Unfortunately, three days later Leon Brittan made a statement in the Commons following a Cabinet meeting, that extra police patrols and a special squad of detectives had been moved into pit villages to counter the intimidation of miners and their families. The *Daily Telegraph* of May 18th made it clear that special squads of detectives had been in Nottinghamshire for the past two weeks. Brittan's announcement in the Commons was followed by 'angry exchanges' on the Labour benches when Don Concannon, Labour M.P. for Mansfield, endorsed Brittan's claims of "intimidation, damage and threats to families". Concannon's helping hand to the right-wing Home Secretary was greeted by shouts of 'coppers nark' from other Labour M.P.'s.

While the *Daily Telegraph* had its rather detached and serious way of presenting this new propaganda strategy, the gutter press gave it more popular appeal. The *Express* and the *Daily Star* even came up with the same expression to describe those who carried out the intimidation: 'Britain cracks down on the pit bully boys' (*Daily Express* 18th May 1984). 'Police step up war on pit bullies' (*Daily Star* 18th May 1984). The *Daily Star* carried a picture of Leon Brittan looking decidely like a pit bully. The *Express* drew attention to a catalogue of incidents: 'The crackdown follows a spate of violence in which a kitten died after paint was poured over it, cars have been damaged, windows smashed and homes daubed with paint'.

Throughout May and early June it was difficult to pick up a paper which did not carry an intimidation story. It was a very useful propaganda campaign by the state, which must have convinced many working people outside Nottinghamshire that Yorkshire miners who travelled into the county of Nottinghamshire were just as Brian James described them in the *Daily Mail*, "militant hordes from over the border exporting the miners' dispute from Yorkshire into Nottinghamshire".

Beneath this blanket of propaganda and misinformation the police organised a campaign of terror against striking miners and their families. They bullied and terrorised any Yorkshire strikers who had gone to stay in Nottinghamshire and drove them out of the county while continuing a ceaseless war against strikers and their families; asking wives to produce identity documents; threatenting to arrest people for, 'harbouring Yorkshire pickets'; and questioning small children about the number of people living in their houses. The propaganda campaign died a death in June when, as all propaganda campaigns do, it began to lose ground to the facts which slowly and painfully emerged.

Torture in Rainworth

Whenever special squads are trained and given a degree of autonomy they develop an *'espirit de corps'*. This fraternity is something which the police force develops and builds upon. Each special squad develops an ethos of its own, it imagines it is beyond the rules, above the institution. Men make up their own language, they have pass words and nicknames. Prison officers slash the peaks of their caps to make them come straight down over the eyes. Police Support Unit officers stick up posters and paper plates in the windows of their vans with group names which give them and their team a new potency. When units develop like this, they are inhabiting a sinister and dangerous world; their discipline disappears; any accountability is thrown out of the window and they become vigilantes, goon squads with their own codes.

On Monday, 14th May 1984, there was a miners' rally in Mansfield. After the rally, as miners gathered in the car park of the leisure complex, fighting broke out between the police and marchers. Word of this confrontation spread quickly amongst police officers in surrounding areas. Mansfield or its environs was a dangerous place to be if you were a Yorkshire miner on that evening. Squads of officers were out looking for blood to avenge any injuries which their comrades might have received in the fight.

Twenty men from Frickley colliery in Yorkshire volunteered to stay in Nottinghamshire after the rally. Having got into the county they were to stay with the families of striking Nottinghamshire miners, as a static picket. At the end of the rally these men made their way by bus to Rainworth, a small pit village just east of Mansfield. Rainworth is a collection of red brick houses owned by the National Coal Board, which litter themselves around a major road junction. In the centre is Rufford Pit and nothing much else besides the Robin Hood public house, a chemist and a fish and chip shop.

It was around five o'clock when the party arrived at the Drill Hall in Rainworth. The Drill Hall is an NCB property; like many of the premises being used by strikers it is also being used by working miners. At the Drill Hall the Yorkshire miners found that the strikers, frightened of repercussions from working miners and the police, did not want to give them accommodation.

The position soon became clear; while a few men had been found accommodation in caravans the majority had nowhere to stay. This group made their way to the Robin Hood public house in the centre of Rainworth, where they waited until Notts. miners tried to sort out their accommodation. At seven thirty they were taken by car to Berry Hill, the Notts. Area Miners' Offices, and they were told they could sleep there. Having time on their hands they decided to go back into Rainworth and have a drink.

At around 9 o'clock the group had gathered together in the Miners' Institute. At 10.30 the men from Frickley decided to leave. Just as they were about to go a local person came over and told them that there were a number of police officers waiting outside. So concerned were the men at being 'illegals' in a foreign county, they considered running from the back of the club. They decided to leave by the front and hoped that the police were not in an ugly mood. Now, almost two months later, one of the men wishes that they had either stayed in the club or left by another entrance. What happened that night has left an irreparable mark on his mind and he has become obsessed with what he saw and had done to him:

> On reaching the bottom of the steps outside the Rainworth Miners' Institute Club a group of policemen were waiting. The one who appeared to be in charge of them, and who I learned later was an Inspector, approached my companions and me, about fifteen of us, and said, "Where are you going lads?" He spoke in a friendly manner. Some of us replied Berry Hill and others replied 'home'. The officer, who had a strong Geordie accent, said: "Well, off you go then".

As they set off to the bus stop, near the Robin Hood, some two hundred yards down the road, it was evident that they were being followed by a group of eight police officers:

> It was obvious from the start that the policemen were following us. After a while they started harassing some of my companions by pushing them; eventually one of them was struck in the back of the neck.

> When we came out of the Institute there were policemen outside. The group of us were strung out along the pavement and I was near the back, I was next to Clive. We had walked along the main road as far as the Robin Hood public house. During the walk from the Institute to the Robin Hood, Clive who was the last person in the group, was being pushed, slapped about the head and insulted; he was protesting about this.

When the men reached the corner of the road near the Robin Hood, three police support unit vans arrived. As the vans drew to a halt across the road, uniformed officers ran from them: "The officers ran across the road, a number of them holding truncheons. They ran up in two's and three's and set about us individually".

Suddenly there was running and shouting and I thought some police officers were coming for me but they went for the man who was in front of me. They started pushing him one to the other and then threw him to the floor and then began jumping on him. I stood there shocked and stunned. I could only watch because this was the worst manifestation of evil I have ever witnessed; four or five police officers bullying a man and enjoying it. I have seen violence before but this was sheer sadism.

The miner stood there rooted to the spot. Now perhaps in retrospect he felt guilty; being a peaceful man he didn't move to help his friend. Nor did he run which was probably the best thing he could have done.

The next thing I knew was that the Inspector who I had spoken to outside the club came up to me and said to his rank of uniformed thugs, "We'll have this bastard next!" and also perhaps "Give him the special treatment". I remember two or three police officers coming up to me casually, grinning. They seized me and frog marched me to the rear of the transit van. They put me on the ground in a prone position, with my arms out in front of me, my hands handcuffed tightly. From then on began the most traumatic experience of my life. A truncheon was brought horizontally from the back over my head, in front of my eyebrows and across the bridge of my nose. My head and torso were then levered up from the ground with the truncheon. Some kind of foreign body was inserted into each nostril and stuffed up my nose with what I assumed to be a ball point pen. I think that the foreign body was paper of some kind; throughout my stay in the police station I was constantly picking largish crumbs of what I thought was dried blood or matter out of my nose. The truncheon was then placed under my nose and this was used as a levering point instead of the bridge of my nose. I was lowered back to the ground and my back was jumped on several times, rhythmically so that the air in my lungs evacuated explosively every time that my back was jumped on. This created the effect that my body was being used as a bellows. I remember thinking at the time, in a detached manner, how organised it was; not a bit spontaneous and that they must do this quite often, and must be confident of getting away with it. Finally my head was turned sideways to the ground and something soft like a cloth was put under it, then someone jumped on my head. I was then thrown bodily into the back of the transit and I believe that two other men were thrown in on top of me. I couldn't breathe and I struggled to get out from under them.

Torture is the same the world over; there are only a limited number of things which can be done to a person to cause pain. Such organisation and method though, needs training and these processes must have been practised. While this man was going through his ordeal his younger companions were coping no better:

I was standing on my own on the pavement. One police officer ran at me, he came from the back of me and put his truncheon across my throat, holding it at both ends and pulled on it. I was pushed from behind across the road to a van. I was gasping for breath. I was thrown into a van on the floor with the truncheon still around my neck. I was face down on the floor and he had one knee in the small of my back. He said something like, ''put your hands behind your back bastard''. I did that and I was hand-cuffed. After I had been handcuffed and the officer had taken the truncheon from my neck he hit me hard with it twice, once on the right hip, once on the right shoulder.

The officers ran across the road, a number of them were holding truncheons. Two officers ran towards me; they held me by my arms and hair, one of them grabbed one of my legs. I struggled because I had done nothing wrong and I was being assaulted. As I was carried to one of the vans, halfway across the road, a third officer came up and hit me violently on the back of the head with a truncheon. My scalp was split by that blow and I began to bleed. I did not struggle after that.

The worst treatment was reserved for a twenty four year old face worker who has worked for the NCB since leaving school at sixteen. He had been found a place to stay by a Nottinghamshire miner who he had met in the Drill Hall. He hadn't been to Berry Hill but had had a drink in the Robin Hood. At about 10.15 he left the pub with three others and walked across the road to the fish and chip shop:

We were standing outside the chip shop eating our chips when we saw the rest of our lads being attacked by three van loads of police officers. We walked up the road towards this which was happening outside the Robin Hood. I shouted to the police to leave the lads alone and that we were all witnesses to what was happening. A senior police officer, I think an Inspector, came across and told me to "Shut up and fuck off". I protested and told him that I was a witness.

He recrossed the road and pointed me out to four policemen who started to run across the road towards me. I was frightened that I was going to be attacked too, so I ran. A man who was sitting in a car jumped out and grabbed me. This man (I presume a plain clothes officer) handed me over to the uniformed P.C's. I was not assaulted and I did not resist; I had my hands hand-cuffed behind me. As I was being marched up the street to the police vans I began to protest about the police treatment of myself and my colleagues. One P.C. grabbed me by the throat and bent me backwards over a fence and told me to, "Fucking shut up".

This lad was thrown into a van on top of the man who had paper stuffed up his nostrils.

I was eventually pushed on to a seat still handcuffed; the two P.C's sat behind me and began swearing at me then nudging me. I stood up to try and move to the front of the van away from these two. One grabbed me by the hair and pulled me forward over the seat. I was then dragged out of the van and thrown to the floor. I was circled by officers who began kicking me on the body and one kicked me in the face. My lip was cut on my teeth when this happened and my left eye began swelling. I was very frightened and I began shouting at them to leave me alone. I was then picked up and dropped onto a metal fence round the edge of the pavement; one officer was pushing down on my neck and forcing me to lift my feet off the ground. This meant that all my weight was on my stomach across the fence and I couldn't breathe. One P.C. then pulled a sticker from my cardigan (Support the miners NUM Stop Pit Closures) and said, "What's this fucking rubbish"; he then folded the sticker up and pushed it up my left nostril and pushed his finger up my nose to push it further up. The two officers stood talking almost conversationally to each other and began kneeing me in the face in turn. After a while an Inspector came over and said, "Has he quietened down yet?"

The men were charged with a variety of offences from Breach of the Peace to Assaulting a Police Officer. There is something in the intelligent mind which revolts as if with sickness at what happened to these men. But the anger is not just blind, against the world in general, it is keen and specific. It has to be directed against the politi-cians who know clearly what is happening, who stand up in the

Commons, clean and safe from the rigours of poverty and the smell of torture, to mouth homilies about the police force which sanctions thuggery. Such politicians are guilty of the very acts themselves because they know that this terrorism is a necessary part of their political programme.

Kidnap in Blidworth

Blidworth village surrounds Blidworth pit; it is just down the road from Rufford pit and Rainworth. The feeling in the North Nottinghamshire pit villages and strike centres is completely different from that in Yorkshire or in Kent. In the 'Glass House', the pre-fabricated building where food is dispensed in Blidworth, there is a large notice which says: 'We cannot feed pickets from other areas in here'. The building belongs to the NCB; the strikers were given it at the last minute, after the local Labour Council had refused to help them. The 'Glass House' is a couple of hundred yards away from the pit entrance. There is an atmosphere of frustration. While in other areas strikers have offices and facilities, here in North Nottinghamshire they are in a minority, hemmed in by an overbearing red brick village which is owned almost completely by the National Coal Board.

Nevertheless, Blidworth strikers are thriving and the women in the 'Glass House' are optimistic and full of energy. Here, unlike in Rainworth, the women have come to the fore and they have prepared themselves for speaking and organising as well as working in the soup kitchen. They have also had to bear the brunt of massive police intimidation, and organising against that, with all the strains and decisions which it brings suddenly to people who only two months ago lived a normal social and working life.

What happened in Blidworth on the evening of Wednesday, May 16th, is unparalleled even during the present dispute. This incident and those which followed it graphically map out the direction in which the police are travelling. For those involved, these matters seem to pass as a nightmare, like disturbing memories recalled by other generations and other communities. It takes time before the mind grasps that the centre of this reality is England in 1984.

On Monday, May 14th, just as others had gone to the rally in Mansfield with the intention of staying at Rainworth, eighty Yorkshire miners set off with the intention of staying in Blidworth. These men came from Yorkshire Main Colliery. On Monday night some of them were billeted at numbers 50, 52 and 54, Thorney Abbey Road in Blidworth. The houses in Thorney Abbey Road are small squat houses and the Notts. families let the Yorkshire men stay in their gardens. There were four in a tent behind number 50, twelve in a dormobile, a tent and a caravan behind number 52 and four more in a tent behind number 54. Other men in the static picket stayed in houses in the surrounding area.

On the first picket of Tuesday morning the Yorkshire lads had six of their number arrested on a picket at Blidworth pit. Apart from the arrests on the Tuesday the picketing passed off peacefully until the night of Wednesday, May 16th. The men wanted to return to Yorkshire on Friday morning and in order to make arrangements and be together with their hosts they all went out to the 'Jolly Friar' public house for a drink and a 'meeting'. Nothing out of the ordinary happened in the pub except for the fact that a group of uniformed officers came in towards the end of the evening and spoke to the publican.

At around 10.45 the twenty men from Thorney Abbey Road left the pub with the families who were putting them up. There was a police transit van parked outside the pub when they left but again this was not an unfamiliar sight. The pickets and the families sat in number 54 talking for about five or ten minutes before one of them decided to go to the caravan and get some bread. It was now about twelve o'clock. The miner quickly returned to the house and told everyone that he had seen police officers in the garden going through the tents. Immediately, people left the house to see what was going on; a branch committee member was one of the first out of the back door. He is a wiry, slightly built man in his late twenties:

> There were police officers in the drive and I saw at least two officers coming out of the back gardens of number 52. There was a sergeant immediately next to me in the drive. I asked him what he was doing. He asked me who I was and I told him that I stayed in the houses. He asked me to go to the top of the drive and I told him that I wouldn't. While we were talking four or five officers were in the immediate vicinity. The police officer was still demanding that I go to the top of the drive and finally I decided that I had better do this. By this time, the owners of the house had also drifted out onto the drive. I walked to the end of the drive but did not step on the pavement, I leaned on the gate post. By this time, there were at least eight officers surrounding me and the sergeant began leaning on me, chest forward, his face right up to mine. He said to me in an aggressive and

intimidating way, "Get back to work tomorrow". I told him that he seemed to be overstepping his powers and that he was there to police the dispute not act as an industrial relations officer. The next thing which the officer said to me led me to believe that he thought I lived in one of the houses and that I was a striking Notts miner; he said: "If you don't get the Yorkshire pickets away from here and out of these houses by tomorrow I will arrest you, your wife and your neighbours". I said, "I think you've got the wrong bloke then". All this time he was literally leaning on me and it was all I could do to keep pushing him away. Then I realised that I was being pushed from the left; I was tired of being pushed and also I realised that it was their intention to push me onto the pavement. I said, "How much room do you want?" and then I was forced to step onto the pavement. As soon as I stepped back onto the pavement I heard a shout. It was either, "That's him Sarge" or, "Get him Sarge". I knew then that they were going to arrest me and I thought that my best chance was to run round onto the road and try to jump back into the garden. I ran round a police van and almost got to the wall but seven or eight officers threw themselves at me. They forced my arms behind me and my head down, I felt a number of blows to my face and chest. One blow in particular hit me violently on the bridge of the nose and my nose was bleeding badly. One other blow which I felt was to my left breast; this hurt very much. My wrists were handcuffed. The handcuffs were so tight that they cut into my wrists and my left wrist bled. They then bundled me into a police van and drove off at speed. I lay on one of the long seats on the side of the van trying to work out what injuries I had. After about six seconds or so I sat up. There were about ten officers in the van. When I sat up I was met with a wall of hatred and abuse, to miners and Yorkshire miners in particular. I didn't rise to this but at one point I was hit in the chest again by an officer. After a minute or so, the van stopped and I was bundled out and thrown in another van. In the second van the attitude of the two officers was utterly different. They loosened the handcuffs and talked in a reasonable, almost friendly manner to me.

The twenty five year old woman who lives at number 52 Thorney Abbey Road had seen everything that happened from the drive; she then went back to her own house to see how her babysitter was. "She was crying and shaking because the police had been to the house earlier and questioned her. She had been asked where we were". The woman on the other side also found that her young son had been woken by noises in the kitchen. Within a short time of the committee man being kidnapped a massive contingent of police turned up in the narrow road. Different estimates put the number of police between two or three hundred, the support unit vehicles parked in the road, and the officers standing in ranks on the opposite pavement facing the houses.

They lined up against the wall across the road. Three police officers came across and told us all to get back in the house. One of the Yorkshire lads told them that we weren't going back into the house until they had gone. A police officer told him that we were in for a long night. One of the officers told my husband that they would arrest all the house occupants for 'harbouring' Yorkshire pickets. We then all went back in the house and locked the door. We decided to try and get in touch with the media but the phone kept going dead. Not long after we began using the phone, the police left; it must have been about three in the morning.

They had managed to get in touch with a Yorkshire solicitor and he had set off for the house but had been stopped and turned back by the police. No doubt everyone thought that was the end of the matter; surely, having committed their numerous crimes, the police would not come back again.

At midday on Thursday while I was calling on number 54, a police van arrived and two officers came down the drive. I asked them to leave. They pushed me to one side and then demanded the names and addresses of everyone stopping at all three houses. They asked my husband his name, address, date of birth and place of birth. He told the Yorkshire lads that they had to produce all their driving documents, stand by their cars and prove legal ownership of them. Mrs. H. asked the police to leave her property; they told her to produce evidence that it was her property. We went back indoors and tried to get help on the phone. The police left saying that they would get a warrant for the houses.

After what happened, the Yorkshire miners decided to leave Blidworth so that the families would not suffer any more harassment. They drove off that afternoon escorted by a solicitor in a convoy. Even with the pickets gone, this was not the end of the bullying and harassment. One of the most startling incidents that occurred concerned a torch and a button from a police uniform, both of which had been dropped in one of the tents. The householder in whose garden the torch had been found was visited by CID officers who told him that if he did not return it to the police station by the end of the week he would be arrested. In fact, the torch was by then in the possession of a solicitor. A week later, in the early hours of the morning, the householder was arrested and taken from his home to Mansfield police station where he was held for two days on suspicion of an assault. He was released without any charges being brought against him. The following week he was visited again by the CID, who told him that he would be charged with 'stealing by finding' unless he produced the torch. At this time the police were told that the torch was with a solicitor.

Since that night in May the families concerned have been subjected to frequent harassment and the 'Glass House' has been under constant surveillance. Two of the sons of families concerned have been arrested and at the remand hearing for one, in court, a senior officer again stated that the family concerned had been, 'harbouring Yorkshire pickets'.

The disturbing memory that comes most quickly to mind on hearing what these miners' families have gone through is that of British soldiers breaking down doors with rifle butts in the Nationalist communities of Belfast.

Police Riot at Tuxford Junction

The riot at Tuxford junction is unlikely to go down in the annals of class or crime as a great landmark—mainly because Tuxford does not roll easily off the tongue and secondly because it was a police riot and historians have a way of writing out such matters. On the 24th of May, men from Grimethorpe set off to picket Bevercotes Colliery in Nottinghamshire; they had picketed this colliery the week previously and there had been no incident.

They travelled down the A1 into Nottinghamshire and pulled off at Tuxford junction. Here, a slip road leads off to the left, sweeps round and bridges the A1 before continuing to Bevercotes colliery which is about a mile away. The pickets decided to park their vehicles on the grass verge at the side of the slip road and walk to the colliery. As they arrived and began walking up the slip road other vehicles arrived from other pits and parked up.

As they walked on the pavement over the bridge, there was no problem; it was a pleasant day and they were hoping for a peaceful picket:

It was apparent from our view on the bridge that the police presence here was such that we would not be allowed through. We continued to walk across the bridge and up to the first slip road off on the left. There were a number of officers standing at this point. They appeared to be manning a road block on the slip road. As soon as we got over the bridge other officers ran from vans towards us and reinforced the police presence on the bridge. I heard a police officer say, "No way are you going to demonstrate at Bevercotes". A local branch official objected to this, saying, "Are you saying we have no right as mineworkers to picket? Are you the judge and jury?" By this time an Inspector had arrived and the Branch Official addressed his remarks to him. The Inspector said, "Yes". There were now some fifty or sixty officers on the bridge and they began bullying and shoving us back across the bridge.

About two hundred pickets had arrived at the bridge and they turned and allowed themselves to be shepherded back to the slip road. As they went they were pushed and jostled and sworn at. On reaching the slip road they turned to face the police in an attempt to put a stop to the harassment.

It was quite evident that none of the officers were willing to explain or be reasonable. The pickets turned to face the police. By this time the police formed a solid line across the road and pavement. At the head of them and in front of their line was officer. As the pickets turned and faced the police a number of us asked questions of the police about the nature of their powers. No questions were answered. Instead the officer drew his truncheon very quickly, held it aloft above his head and said words to the effect of, "You have been warned". It was at this time that I heard a whistle being blown.

The pickets had no time to defend themselves. All the officers had their truncheons drawn and some of them went berserk. They arrested and beat people indiscriminately.

I am twenty one, I am an underground worker at Grimethorpe Colliery. I have worked for the NCB for four years. When the police charged I panicked and tried to run away. I was struck on the head. Everything stopped and all the noise was echoing. The next thing I remember I was being taken out of an ambulance and one of the ambulance men was asking me my name. I was then examined by a doctor. X-rays were taken of my head, chest and the right hand side of my body. A urine sample was taken and it was found to have blood in it. I had a bruise about four inches long above my kidneys.

I am a forty three year old miner. I have been employed by the NCB for twenty years. The police charge was brutal, callous, unnecessary and violent. Police were lashing out indiscriminately. Out of the corner of my eye I saw a picket fall to the ground. Neither myself nor anyone else offered any resistance. As I ran back down the road I could see a number of people being attacked indiscriminately with truncheons. A number of us returned to carry the injured lad to the side of the road where we placed him on the grass verge. He appeared to be deeply unconcious. We spoke to an Inspector nearby and asked him to get an ambulance. The Inspector went away. An ambulance did not arrive and after fifteen minutes I approached another officer who had just arrived.

One other person, a twenty two year old lad from Barnsley, was seriously hurt in the riot:

A police sergeant pulled out his truncheon and started laying into us. He hit me first as I was one of those in the front. He hit me on the head. I tried to get out of the way but he hit me again, either three or four times, I cannot quite remember. I was dragged away and one of the lads put a dressing on my head. An ambulance was called for and I was taken to Mansfield General Hospital, where I had six stitches put in my head. I am now experiencing dizzy spells.

When the first lad was knocked unconscious, one miner who had been a Special Constable had the foresight to attempt an identification of the officer who had committed the assualt.

I took charge of the situation and borrowed a note book and pencil. I approached the rest of the pickets and asked what had happened. I ran back to where the rest of the pickets were penned in by the police and asked if anyone had seen any P.C. hit the unconscious man. A number of men shouted that they had seen him being hit but none of them had got a number. At this point, Kevin came up and told me, "I didn't see him being knocked down, but I saw the bastard who hit him twice while he lay on the ground. I didn't get his number but I will recognise him. I'll never forget that face. He was evil. I approached a police Inspector and asked for and was eventually given permission to take Kevin to try and identify the officer who had hit the lad. By this time, the police were herding everyone off the road and into thier cars and threatening them with arrest if they did not leave. We had to run after the police to catch up. As we ran Kevin shouted, "That's him, that's him". He then ran in front of this P.C. and began running backwards in front of him and said, "Yes that's him, that's the bastard who hit the lad twice when he was on the floor". The P.C. said, "Fuck off". I then said to the P.C., "I have your number, would you mind giving me your name." He replied, "Fuck off".

Kevin and myself began to go back to see the lad who had been injured when we were stopped by five officers who questioned us. They told Kevin he could go but I had to go back with them. As soon as Kevin left, these five officers tried to snatch my notebook from me. They then encircled me and began pushing me down the road. All the time they were kicking my ankles and jostling me. I did not retaliate because I knew that if I did, they would arrest me and the notebook would be gone.

None of the men from Grimethorpe were arrested but they returned from the picket angry and incensed that one of their younger members had been taken away unconscious from Tuxford Junction. This incident, like many others, had taken place far away from the television cameras and the officers who committed the violence were unlikely to suffer any official sanctions.

Orgreave: One Day's 'Riot', Provocation and Violence

Orgreave is in South Yorkshire and not Nottinghamshire. However, Orgreave was important because it showed clearly the massive intervention of the state in the dispute. George Moores, the Chair of South Yorkshire Police Committee, is fond of saying that the South Yorkshire police managed the national steel strike and the picketing without any more trouble than can usually be expected at a Sheffield Wednesday football match. There can be little doubt that if South Yorkshire Police Committee had handled Orgreave, what did happen would not have happened. But policing now in South Yorkshire and Nottinghamshire is controlled by the Cabinet.

Orgreave and all that it entailed was organised as a military operation by the Cabinet. There was no chance of mineworkers communicating their views to the wagon drivers who drove in and then drove coke out of the plant; they were not union men, they were hand picked drivers who might have come from the dole queue or even from the army. They did not go about their business as if doing a day's work for British Steel, they were mercenaries hired by the state. From the time that they set out they were guarded by police motorcycle outriders who stopped all other traffic. They were accompanied by transit vans containing serials of riot police. The police were so heavily implicated on the side of the government that they might just as well have driven the wagons themselves.

Around the coking plant thousands of riot police ensured that the strike-breaking operation was carried out without the interference of picketing miners. These police officers were equipped with all the technology of a modern police state. They were trained to smash any opposition to the state's run-down of the mining industry and its continuing programme of economic rationalisation and concomitant unemployment. Throughout the dispute, one's attention has been drawn to the similarity of tactics used by the private coal owners earlier in the century and those now used by the state. There is one difference however: the coal owners never claimed that they did not have a vested interest. The present Conservative government wants us to believe that they are outside the dispute and apparently aloof from it. Above all else, Orgreave showed clearly the hand of the government and illustrated just how well equipped they believe they are to break the Trade Union movement and handle a prolonged or spreading strike.

Violence is central to the cases in Nottinghamshire which we have so far described. And for the Conservative government aspects of the violence at Orgreave were central to their propaganda war. Violence by servants of the state has been endemic to the whole dispute; it is a violence woven deeply into the fabric of policing as it is now being practised. It is not a violence which is seen on television (except in fictional form), nor is it a violence which is often reported by photo-journalists because it is violence which takes place outside the public arena.

It was ultimately very convenient for the government that the was able to show edited highlights during the last two weeks of what must have looked to most viewers like concerted rioting. The media, however, were never on the battlefield, nor did they show the massive build up of police at the depot. Any serious journalist or photogrpaher who tried to get a picture of the police organisation at Orgreave was approached and risked being arrested. In the main, the media allowed themselves, supple and pliant creatures of received opinion that they are, to be corralled by the police from the first day.

Violence by the police in the dispute began long before

Orgreave—and the miners coped with it stoically for some twelve weeks before they began to act offensively. They had been assaulted individually on picket lines and before they reached picket lines. They had been subjected to baton charges in Sheffield and Mansfield. They had been handcuffed and beaten until they were tired of meeting such provocation.

The first day of picketing at Orgreave was Friday, May 25th. There were only a few pickets and only two arrests. These two arrests are significant:

> I am a thirty four year old underground belt man. Up until Orgreave I had no problems with the police. I attended the morning picket, and as far as I saw, there were no problems; we were with Rotherham police officers and it was obvious that they wanted a quiet picket. At lunch time I had one drink with my friends and then returned to the picket. I was standing up the road next to Pete when the police ran at us. They grabbed Pete, they pulled and pushed and thumped him until he fell to the floor; however, they didn't arrest him. As soon as they grabbed Pete, everyone shouted at them to leave him alone. Officers were standing in front of us hemming us in and staring at us. I stared back at one. The next thing, three of them grabbed me and pulled me to the floor, they got my arm up my back and began dragging me along on my backside. Inside the station I was polaroid photographed and then taken before an Inspector who asked who was charging me; none of them seemed to know. An officer picked one out to charge me. This officer then asked what the charge was, again they didn't know, so the Inspector got up, came towards me and smelt my breath and said, 'Drunk and disorderly'. I began laughing.

That was the first arrest at Orgreave and together with the second it stinks of provocation. The second arrest was of a young one-armed lamp room attendant:

> As soon as the lorries went in, without any warning and without any provocation, the police broke ranks and ran at the pickets. They ran past me and my companions and when they got to the main body of pickets they picked on the smallest lad, Peter, and they knocked him to the floor. When I saw this assault I decided to complain to the most senior officer. As I began to move towards him, an officer close to me grabbed my arm and began pushing me. The officer pushed my back and said, 'Right, you're under arrest'. I was marched down to the offices, they took me to the

desk and an Inspector said, 'What are you going to charge him with?' The officer just shrugged his shoulders so the Inspector said, 'Use Section 5'. After I had been locked in the cell van the arresting officer came to the grill and threatened me, waving his fist at me saying, 'Don't you ever try anything like that with me again'. Later I was told that I had been charged with assaulting a police officer. Their story was that I had swung on the officer's arm and head butted another officer.

There was no picket over the following weekend and Monday was a Bank Holiday. Picketing began in earnest on Tuesday, May 29th, and by the end of the day there had been some sixty arrests.

A grey tarmacadam road runs the full length of Orgreave Coking Depot. It is a large depot put down oddly in the middle of a small piece of dirty countryside which is sandwiched between the M1 and Handsworth, a suburb of Sheffield. Across the road opposite the coking plant there are numerous office buildings. At the southern end of the depot the road runs through a small, red brick pit village. At the northern end, beyond two or three fields, the road goes uphill, over a railway bridge and then runs straight into a large post-war housing estate.

Standing in the first field, on the left past the depot, one has a good view of Orgreave works. It sits squat, black and very ugly by the side of the road. Its chimneys and metal storage tanks reach into the sky. It was in this field and on the road that runs along it that the pickets gathered on the twenty ninth. Even before the trouble started they were some two hundred yards from the entrance of the plant. Looking down the road they could see the lorry convoys speeding into the plant and later leaving. Between the pickets and the coking plant were line upon line of police across the road and the field. These officers were supported by mounted police, transit vans and dogs.

On May 29th, the first day of serious picketing at Orgreave, the police came out fighting. In the early morning a number of pickets had managed to take up position immediately opposite the entrance on the pavement. These men were forced by mounted police over the wall and onto a small square of grass where they were surrounded by riot officers in a cordon two or three deep.

Well away from the entrance, further up the road towards the bridge, the pickets pushed against the police lines as the lorry convoy came in:

The pushing and shoving was good humoured until someone shouted over a loud hailer, 'Take some prisoners'. As soon as that was shouted police reinforcements ran up and the mood changed. I had a thumb pushed in my right eye from amidst the police ranks. Another officer grabbed my hair and began to drag me forward. The police ranks broke and I was dragged through. I was punched and kicked on the throat, legs, arms and body as I was taken through the police lines. I was taken to the charging offices. The officer who had 'arrested' me kicked my legs all the way for about two hundred yards.

I was in the picket and an officer in front of me got his hand round my throat. As soon as I managed to get it away another officer grabbed my hair. Two other officers then grabbed me. One came from behind and caught me round the throat with his forearm.

I was walking towards the plant as the lorry convoy came in. A group of three officers came up to us and asked what we were doing. I heard a voice behind me said, 'You're obstructing the footway'. I didn't look round but I said: 'That's ridiculous there is plenty of room for anyone who wants to pass'. I then felt a sharp push or blow in the small of my back. I was propelled forward by it and fell to the floor. I was immediately surrounded by police officers who began punching and kicking me. I was then dragged into a transit van by a PC who had me in a headlock. I was punched in the face by the PC who was holding me. In the van I was thrown on the floor and about four officers began punching, kicking and throwing me about.

On the afternoon of Tuesday, May 29th, the police brought out their riot equipment for the first time. For the rest of the afternoon, from about two o'clock until four, they gave a varied demonstration of riot control tactics which were evidently well rehearsed and which had next to nothing to do with what the pickets were doing.

The police lines (2 or 3 deep) stretched across the road and across the adjoining field. The lorry convoy had passed into the plant. The pickets stood in the road and in the field facing the police lines. Pickets at the back, up the road, began to throw stones. Suddenly, in the corner of the field the police lines opened and columns of shield-bearing officers ran through and fanned out. Within seconds there was a solid line of perspex shields across the field and the road. The incongruity of this line was spectacular; police officers with blue riot helmets and perspex visors holding shields in the middle of a field, while in the background the heavily industrial coking plant, squat, black and belching white smoke.

Mounted police were brought up behind the lines on the road and after more stone throwing a warning was given about the use of horses. The lines opened again and the horses' hooves could be heard as they reared up and broke into a gallop. Riders in full riot gear swung long batons as they charged up the road. Pickets ran, or jumped the dry stone walls on either side of the road. At the top of the road the riders wheeled round and charged down into the field. The pickets ran into the wheat field.

In three charges throughout the afternoon, horse riders were followed by shield-carrying officers who used truncheons against anyone who hadn't run further up the road. These officers were followed by Instant Response Unit vans which edged their way up the road accompanied by walking officers. The charges stopped late in the afternoon when the police had moved their lines forward to the bridge at the top of the road. There was no hand to hand fighting from the pickets because they ran whenever the police charged.

All the arrests which were gained by the police in these cir- cumstances were carried out with brutality. The police, by virtue of their training and preparation, had obviously passed that point where they ceased to be police officers and became a para-military third force:

> I was asked to move, as the police ran past. I refused; I was punched in the face by one officer and another hit me on the back of my head with a truncheon. I was held against the wall and punched. As I was dragged back through the police lines I was punched and kicked.

> I was sat on the wall, the horses charged close to me and I jumped in the field. Officers on foot ran at me. I was knocked to the floor and two or three officers punched and kicked me on the floor. I was handcuffed and dragged away.

> I was sat behind a tree at the top of the field. Foot officers follow- ing the horses jumped on me; I argued with the police as they arrested me and I was hit over the ear with a truncheon.

> As the foot officers following the horse charge came up the road, I ran up to a portacabin which was at the side of the road. I was hit on the back of the head with a truncheon. I fell to the floor and was kicked and punched in the face by five or six officers.

> I was walking towards the bridge and about five or six officers grabbed me. I was kicked while I fell to the floor.

> I was standing on the wall as the horses charged. I was pushed

off the wall by an officer on foot who said, 'Get over there bastard'. I landed in the field in the path of other foot officers. I was hit with truncheons. I didn't resist; as I was held an officer came up and hit me in the head with his fist.

I ran towards the railway embankment to escape the riot police. I tried to help an older injured man but then two officers caught up with me. One struck me with his truncheon on the elbow. I was struck on the knees and ribs repeatedly. One officer hit me last on the elbow and said, 'Fuck off back to where you come from'.

I was in the field; I had been arrested. A senior police officer grabbed me by the hair and dragged me over a wall. He said, 'You and all those other bastards are going to lose this one and so is that bald headed bastard Scargill'.

Much of the police plausibility collapsed in the last week of picketing at Orgreave when the television cameras clearly caught an officer going berserk. He repeatedly truncheoned a miner who was on the floor. It seems possible that this piece of film heralded a change in the attitude of the media to the pickets. It did not herald any change in attitude of the state to the police or the violence which they have used since the strike began. To anyone who understands the role of the Director of Public Prosecutions in supporting the morale of the police on behalf of the state, it came as no surprise when he announced that the officer who had gone berserk would not face criminal charges.

Cabinet members and functionaries within the state are well aware that violence is an inherent part of their strategy. In fact, this is the role of the police in the dispute—to use both the criminal law and a high level of violence to defeat the strike with military tactics. Unfortunately, the media is not always there to record the violence; they are well managed by the police to this end. Even if they do witness it, they refrain from publishing it because of their ideological position, or sub judice rules are invoked to foreclose on publicity, or drag out an investigation after which the actual act will have been long forgotten.

The Union and its members are left to explain and carry their own history. Unfortunately, in the present climate it all too often becomes a kind of sub-history and is easily ridiculed by official sources as extreme or unfounded. Many of the men who picketed Orgreave have stories similar to the one below; after the strike few of them will forget Orgreave or the police violence.

We sat on the grass and from where we sat we had a good view of the coking depot. As we watched we saw the police at the junction charge the pickets. I ran to the boundary wall across the other side of the field. As I did so, I saw police on horses charging up the road. I ran over the bridge, and I think I ran over another bridge and then there were houses on my right. I was on my own and had been separated from the group I was with. I met some Yorkshire miners sitting on a wall and I had a drink of water with them. As I was drinking the water pickets ran up from the direction of the coke works. I looked to my left down the road towards the coke works and saw police in riot gear with shields and truncheons. They were hitting the running pickets. I saw a policeman lash out at a running man and hit him three times. I saw policemen were lashing out at everyone and the man I was with stood up and shouted, 'Stop running, don't throw'. The pickets had started throwing stones at the police who were laying about them. I could see that the police were hitting anyone, so I ran. I ran down a dead end alley. Then more pickets began to run in there, until it was full of pickets. The police came to the end of the alley, there were three of them and they were waving their truncheons. Two of them were shouting, 'Come on, out, out'. The pickets started to run out and the police clubbed every picket. As they ran out they struck the pickets violently on their heads and back. The police just assaulted them, they made no attempt to arrest any of them. I was the last one out. As I came out I was grabbed by one officer and hit by another who brought his truncheon down on my back near my left shoulder.

The Developing Use of the Criminal Law

We would have liked to have dealt at greater length with the way in which the government is continuing to use the criminal law; unfortunately we have had to restrict ourselves to the short update in this section.

In Appendix 12 we have included the full statement of Mr. S. who was arrested at Thoresby pit in Nottinghamshire early in the dispute. It is an important statement and an important case; we wanted to include it in the section in the first volume on arrests at pickets but were unable to.

In Volume I of *A State of Seige* we explained how the law was being used against miners on strike in an attempt to criminalise them. Since then the Lord Chancellor, Lord Hailsham, has appeared on television telling the public at large that Arthur Scargill should be arrested and tried; Thatcher has made references to the 'rule of law' and Leon Brittan, the Home Secretary, has appeared on television saying specifically that pickets at Orgreave were 'criminals'. While the law might well be a very exacting instrument as it is written in the criminal code, all the procedures which bring people to trial and govern their imprisonment are carried out by people with a political view of what constitutes crime and punishment.

The processes which govern the conduct of police officers and magistrates are not specific, they are so general and in need of repair, so completely without accountability that the state can drive a coach and horses through any semblance of human rights. For Thatcher and Brittan to say that the police are not partisan but are servants of the law is laughable in the context of the massive and well tuned apparatus of repression which is presently operating in South Yorkshire and Nottinghamshire.

During the miners' strike we have observed various illegal trends and procedures in the police activity and the prosecution process being brought into the open. Many of these practices have been observed before, being used by the most corrupt elements in the Metropolitan police. Few of these practices are governed or restricted by law and as in other serious confrontations between the state and working people, any rules or guidelines which might previously have been adhered to have now been thrown out of the window.

Handcuffs

Handcuffs are used indiscriminately on youth and adults alike. Putting handcuffs on suspects often involves systematic brutality. One arrested man who complained that the handcuffs were too tight was told by an officer; "They aren't tight enough until they draw blood". We have spoken to many men who have scars on their wrists and lower arms where the handcuffs have bitten into them. Two cases were reported to us where the handcuffs were on so tight that someone had to be called to get them off; in one case this was a village blacksmith; in another two officers in the police station.

Charging

The proper procedure for charging a person has also been abandoned. Charges are often made up inside the police station depending on which officers are available to say later that they witnessed the crime. Cases have been reported to us where officers without arrests went looking in the cells to find people they could charge. Cases have been reported to us where officers have stood round in groups joking, while trying to think of charges that might stick.

Judges' Rules

We have not come across one case in which a suspect was allowed a telephone call. We have recorded one case in which the police made a call for a suspect and so harangued his young daughter that she broke down crying. We have not come across one case in which a suspect was allowed to see a solicitor during the period in police custody. Solicitors have been given minutes with defendants after they have been charged, either in cells or in the magistrates' courts.

Special Courts

In order to speed up processing, magistrates' courts have been sitting at night or out of usual hours. On a number of occasions, friends and relatives have been turned away from these courts being told by the police that they are 'Special Courts' or 'Private hearings'. Denying access to the public in a court of law is perhaps one of the most sinister developments in the dispute.

Bail

Magistrates are ignoring the conditions of the Bail Act and processing large groups of defendants without regard to their circumstances or the evidence against them. The court has been turned into a factory system.

Conditions of Bail

Conditions of bail have escalated to ridiculous proportions and are given without regard to the circumstances of the defendant, leading to bizarre situations where some defendants cannot even go to their own house or their own pit. Conditions of bail now include: curfews from 8 pm to 8 am in which the defendant is not allowed out of their house; enforced reporting to police stations three times a day, or reporting to a senior police officer for permission to attend a person's own pit; being bound over *as well as* being on bail, without being convicted.

Release from custody

On release from police custody a person is supposed to be given over to the court. If they are then released by the court they are free to go. In a number of cases reported to us the police have been retaining peoples belongings and so making them return to the police station after being released by the court. On a number of occasions the police have then taken these released people back into custody and taken their photographs and finger prints; this is an unlawful practice.

Agents provocateur

We have had two particular cases reported to us which illustrate clearly how police officers in plain clothes have moved from their original task of 'spotting' people for snatch squads or general observation to acting as agents provocateur:

> I was running away from the picket near where some people had been stoning a police vehicle. Suddenly one of the men who was running with me grabbed my arm and said, "I'm arresting you." I realised then that he was a police officer even though he was dressed like the pickets. He had been with us all day from when we sat in the soup kitchen that morning.

Confrontational Indentification

The formal rules for identification are clearly laid down by the Home Office in a series of guidelines to all Constabularies. If a person refuses to stand on an identification parade, a police officer may find some other way of having him identified. A last resort is the confrontation; it is strictly against any guidelines to use confrontation without first trying to arrange a parade:

> I was sitting in the interview room with a CID officer; he was trying to get me to admit having injured a police constable. The door opened and an Inspector came in accompanied by a constable. The Inspector looked at the constable and said, "That's him isn't it?" The constable looked at me and said, "Yes that's him". I realised then that this was the constable that I had supposedly injured.

Common Informers

Common Informers were first used in the eighteenth century. They were employed by a variety of voluntary and religious societies to spy on people in the community. Sometimes these men were constables, sometimes they made their living from informing. Up until 1952 there were many statutes under which a person could gain a reward for informing. When the Metropolitan police came into being in 1829, the use of common informers began to slacken off. Informers or 'informants' as the police like to call them are now recruited by the CID and are paid money from the police informants fund. We have been told that informers in the pit villages are earning a regular wage of thirty or forty pounds a week for reporting gossip and incidents to the police.

Informers in police cells

When the police are having difficulty gaining information from suspects in custody, they will sometimes put an informer in the cell with them. The informer strikes up a conversation and is then taken from the cell. This information is used as the basis for questioning later. We have had one report of this technique being used in Mansfield police station.

The Caution for adults

Up until recently, cautions have only been used in the case of juveniles. The police request the appearance of the suspect and their parents at the police station and rather than appearing before a court they are 'cautioned' by a senior officer. In 1981 the Attorney General issued guidelines for the cautioning of adults. The implications of this development amounts to trial by the police within the police station. The practice has been experimented with in London over the last year. Many suspects are confused when they are not charged but told to report back to the police station in two or three weeks time. Having been let out on police bail they can see clearly that the duration of their custody has been extended even though they have not appeared before a Magistrates Court. In effect they have been put on probation to the police. The condition can be extended on two or three occasions unless the suspect takes a solicitor who demands that the client is either charged or released. With this process the police gain absolute power within the prosecution process and no independent or outside agency is involved. At least one of the miners arrested in London during the lobby of Parliament has been subjected to this new process. And five men caught 'stealing' coal in Yorkshire were also subject to it. As well as this giving the police greater control of the prosecution process, when it is used in the community the police may try to use it as a means of recruiting common informers.

PART THREE
The Police and Democracy

According to Sir Robert Mark, an ex-Commissioner of the Metropolitan Police, the basis of police accountability in this country is:

> 'The fact that the British police are answerable to the law, that we act on behalf of the community and not under the mantle of government, makes us the least powerful, the most accountable and therefore the most acceptable force in the world'.
>
> (1977, quoted in 'Policing London, GLC, 1982')

The notion that the police are only accountable to the law and are responsible for impartial law enforcement has always been a myth. There is inevitably a choice facing the police about *which* laws and which policies to enforce at any particular time. At the most basic level, decisions have to be made about whether or not, for example, to charge an elderly person with shoplifting or who to stop and search in the street. These decisions are made constantly and are informed by overall policies as to who the police believe deserves to be criminalised (See for example, Deputy Assistant Commissioner (Crime) David Powis' book : 'The Signs of Crime').

At a policy level, both senior officers and the Home Office enforce certain laws in particular ways in accordance with their ideological position. Furthermore, this is constantly changing as new legislation is created to deal with whatever a particular government feels are the biggest threats to the state. The 'Rule of Law' is never a static, impartial instrument. For example, the introduction in the mid-1970's of the Criminal Trespass Law, which prevented factory sit-ins, was aimed against the Trade Union movement and the organised working class who were increasingly turning to direct action. Far worse is to come, with the Police and Criminal Evidence Bill, which will come into effect early in 1985. This Bill will attack the most fundamental civil liberties and represents a major onslaught by the present government against the working class, the black community and an ever-widening series of politically marginalised groups defined as 'subversives' by the state. It is no accident that it comes at a time of economic recession and mass unemployment when political and industrial confrontations must be contained by the state.

The working class as a whole has always been criminalised by the state, and there is no sense in which we can ever say there has been 'policing by consent' in this country. In the post-war period, the re-building of a social-democratic consensus also required, of necessity, the creation of a largely mythical consensus around policing. This was, for the most part, achieved with a great deal of propaganda and without real opposition from the Parliamentary Labour Party.

In recent years, the idea of consensus has been constantly eroded with increasingly widespread knowledge of police racism, violence and corruption. The increased use by the police of 'fire-brigade' tactics; rushing into 'problem areas' with the Special Patrol Group (SPG) or other Instant Response Units (IRU's) has made a mockery of so-called police/community relations and has made visible a deep-seated contempt by the police for the communities they claim to serve. Despite intensive media management, police illegalities have forced themselves to the surface. A co-ordinated attempt to cover up firstly the brief, and secondly the findings, of the Operation Countryman investigation into police corruption in the Metropolitan Police did not slip by in the public imagination as easily as it had done ten years before in the *Times* inquiry. The cover-up of Countryman, and the propaganda campaign following the *Times* inquiry, went as far as character assassination of senior officers who were 'unfortunate' enough to become involved in these investigations.

It is evident that the last ten years have seen the resolving of major contradictions within the police establishment. Democratic or humanitarian officers, like John Alderson, ex-Chief Constable of Devon and Cornwall, have been weeded out, with the ascendancy of the hard right. The kind of policing espoused by the 'new' right in the police force is fully in line with the policies of the present government. These policies are based around preparations for confrontations between the state and the working class.

The continuing realisation that the consensus never existed, that in fact we live in a class society, has been illustrated in many ways; notably the riots of 1981 and the Southall disturbances before them. Since Kenneth Newman took office in 1983 as Commissioner of the

Metropolitan Police, radical and energetic attempts have been made to re-arrange the consensual image of the police. Neighbourhood Watch Schemes, Consultation Committees, police questionnaires and multi-agency policing have all been used in a 'Satchi and Satchi' type operation to re-conquer 'consensus'. The police role in the miners' strike has brought the illusion crashing down again.

There is no way at present in which the police are *collectively* accountable for their activities. The realisation of this has led to campaigns for police accountability which have gained momentum in the past few years. Calls have come from both outside of London, where the Police Authorities in the Metropolitan areas are calling for increased powers, and within London where there is currently no statutory mechanism at all for the local Boroughs or the Great London Council (GLC) to have a say in the policing of London.

The Police Complaints Procedure

While the police establishment works hard to manipulate ideas of consensus within the community, they attempt to calm public fears about increased powers by reference to formal means of redress against police misconduct. At present, there are two means of redress that citizens have against police illegalities: a Police Complaints procedure or a civil action in law both of which must be taken against a named police officer. A few individuals have been successful in suing the police for misconduct; for example, an elderly black couple in Stoke Newington were brutally assaulted by 17 police officers who raided their house one night in 1976. *Six* years later in 1982, they were awarded damages of £50,000 by a High Court Judge. To use the civil law is, though, a long, arduous, and often unpleasant procedure which can also turn out to be very expensive for the individual if they lose. Legal Aid is sometimes difficult to obtain for civil actions against police officers and the vast majority of those affected by police illegalities cannot afford to take private actions against the police.

As far as the police complaints system is concerned, we describe the text book version below. The present system for dealing with complaints against the police was established under S.49 of the 1964 Police Act and the 1976 Police Act; although it has remained basically unchanged since 1908. When a member of the public makes a complaint against an officer, the Chief Police Officer of the Force concerned is responsible for recording the complaint and ensuring that it is investigated. The Chief Officer (in practice, the deputy) then requests an officer from the same force to conduct the investigation, although he can request an officer from another force to carry out investigations into serious complaints. When the report of the investigating officer is presented to the Chief Police Officer, if he considers that there is evidence of a criminal offence committed by a police officer, he must send the report to the Director of Public Prosecutions (DPP). The DPP then advises whether or not the officer should be charged with an offence. After a reference to the DPP and in the event of no criminal charges, the Chief Officer decides whether or not to bring a disciplinary action against the officer.

At this stage, the Chief Officer must send a copy of the investigating officer's report to the Police Complaints Board, together with a memorandum stating whether or not disciplinary charges are to be brought and if not, his reasons for this decision. It is only at this late stage that the Board can intervene and disagree with the Chief Officer's decision, recommending that charges be brought. Where an officer denies disciplinary charges the Board can recommend that the charge is heard by a tribunal of 2 Board members and the Chief Constable, instead of the Chief Constable alone, although this is exceptional.

From the point of view of reform, one problem with the present system is that the police investigate themselves; this enables them, in secret, to make decisions about the moral and legal legitimacy of the complainant. Lord Scarman, in his Report on the Brixton Riots, stated that:

'There is a widespread and dangerous lack of public confidence in the existing system for handling complaints against the police. By and large, people do not trust the police to investigate the police'.

(‘The Brixton Disorders’ by Lord Scarman, Nov. 1981)

There *can* be no public confidence in a procedure which, like the prosecution process itself, is completely structured and determined by people in the police service. Hardly any disciplinary charges, let alone criminal prosecutions, result. Out of 17,514 complaints brought in 1982, only 263 disciplinary actions were taken by Chief Constables. The police take, on average, *8 months* to investigate a complaint, and in the meantime complainants are not kept informed of the progress of the investigation, on the grounds that it is sub judice.

As far as criminal proceedings are concerned, the DPP is reluctant to take action on the peculiar basis that a jury is less likely to convict a police officer than a member of the public. In the Operation

Countryman investigation, the DPP demanded 52% proof of conviction before charging an officer. Neither does he appear very willing to extend investigations into conduct which would seem to require thorough examination. As far as the Police Complaints Board is concerned, they very rarely use the powers they have, insufficient though they are. The Board was introduced in order to provide an 'independent' element into the proceedings, but in practice they very rarely challenge the Chief Constable: in the four years between the beginning of 1978 and the end of 1981, the Board only challenged the Chief Constable on 77 occasions, when there were in the region of 60,000 complaints.

Complaints under the present system also suffer from the 'before and after trial' syndrome. Where an individual has been charged with a criminal offence, and has at the same time put in a complaint about an officer's behaviour, they will be interviewed by a police officer before their case comes to court. In this way, a full and detailed statement taken from the complainant will inevitably reveal elements of their defence case, which could then be passed to the prosecution. The police prosecution could then have, in advance of any criminal proceedings, a head start against the complainant in their case. If the individual is found guilty of a criminal offence, then their complaint will inevitably be dealt with less seriously since they will appear to have been discredited.

One of the supposed cornerstones of the present system is that complaints are investigated, if not independently of the police themselves, then by a separate constabulary. With respect to democracy and the police, a great emphasis has always been placed, by the police establishment itself, upon the idea of constabulary independence. We now know that the Association of Chief Police Officers (ACPO) are in control of the policing operation in the miners' strike and that information is being passed from force to force. The biggest of the present 'big lies', and the one which the police establishment have to defend to the hilt, is that there is still constabulary autonomy and a separation between the executive and the police.

Fear of future harassment and intimidation, and actual harassment, cause about half of the complaints to be withdrawn; and many are not reported at all. The police are quick to claim that such complaints had no basis in the first instance. The police also claim that they have no defence against malicious complaints, although with the Police and Criminal Evidence Bill it seems likely that officers will be given the opportunity for legal representation. This is a far cry from the situation in and before the nineteenth century, when complaints against individual officers were taken far more seriously: the officer could be brought before a Magistrates Court and disciplinary charges, including possible dismissal from the force, imposed immediately.

The evident inability of the citizenry to master or control the police has become more apparent as the police force itself has grown politically closer to the state. When the police in London came into being in the last century, even the middle class were concerned about the new powers which they assumed. From 1829 to 1930 the police were subject to rigorous discipline, low standards of pay and small compensation for injury or bereavement. Now, in 1984, with the police on the threshold of the state itself, their loyalty has been paid for and proved, at the expense of any possible criticism from those outside the state.

Reforming elements have, in fact, been partially successful in their lobbying for change in the police complaints system. A new procedure is proposed with the Police Bill which makes minor adjustments; these go nowhere near providing a fully independent system. Under the proposals, a new Police Complaints Authority, or Independent Assessor, would be established to replace the Police Complaints Board. Any 'trivial' complaints (and it would be the police who decided whether or not a complaint was 'trivial'), would be dealt with informally by conciliation between the officer and the complainant. Serious complaints would be investigated by a Police Officer from another force under the supervision of the Independent Assessor. However, the bulk of complaints would be dealt with as at present i.e. by the police, with the provision that the Assessor would supervise the investigation if he or she wished. The role of the Assessor is still unclear because it depends on regulations not included in the Bill. It is however known that she or he will not have any staff attached and this will severely limit the extent of his or her interventions. Quite clearly this is not a properly independent system and will not alleviate public fears about the lack of thorough and impartial investigations of police complaints.

Any reforms which are considered to the police complaints system can be of no relevance to situations in which the state turns against the people. Policing in these circumstances has nothing to do with the protection of the population from crime, or the fear of crime, but is, by it's very nature, an open attack upon those without power. In confrontations with the state, as Brian Crozier says:

> 'What of human rights? The quick answer is that in a war, human rights are unfortunately likely to suffer.'

The Police and Criminal Evidence Bill

Throughout this volume and the last we have made a number of references to the Police and Criminal Evidence Bill. The miners' strike has shown that this Bill is not simply as the police have claimed, one which rationalises the prosecution process or makes statutory the Judges' Rules, it is like many other pieces of legislation, a major weapon to be used by the police against the people. It gives the police the powers to criminalise a larger section of the population than were encompassed by previous criminal legislation. The Bill is likely to be passed by the end of the year with most of its provisions in force early in 1985.

The Bill was based on the findings of the Royal Commission on Criminal Procedure, set up in 1978 by a Labour government. The Royal Commission was set up following the Confait case, in which 3 young men had been found guilty of murder on the basis of admissions made to the police while in custody. It was later established that the confessions had been given under duress and the convictions were quashed. The case gave rise to a good deal of concern about the rights of suspects in custody. At the same time, allegations of the police abusing their powers in other directions were increasing. The biggest problems arose at times when the police had people in custody, a period when the police themselves are completely and secretly in control. There were frequent accusations about the mismanagement of identification parades and claims that officers fabricated verbal admissions.

The brief of the Royal Commission was to rationalise the police role in the prosecution process, in particular with respect to the Judges' Rules. It reported in 1981 and its findings even at that time showed a ready accommodation of the views of the police establishment. Two members, Jack Jones, the trade unionist and Archdeacon Wilfred Woods, dissented from its uncritical acceptance of the police's demand for increased powers. The Commission acceded in part to the police demand for the erosion of the right to silence while in police custody. It argued for longer periods of detention and gave the police greater opportunity to extract confessions. Generally it relaxed the rules which governed the onus of proof on the prosecution and by doing that allowed the suspect a greater possibility of being criminalised. Senior police officers had for some years argued that suspects had too many rights which interfered with their investigations.

David Macnee, then Metropolitan Police Commissioner, argued in his evidence to the Commission that 'Many police officers have, early in their careers, learned to use methods bordering on trickery and stealth in their investigations because they were deprived of proper powers by the legislature.'

Despite tipping the balance in favour of the police, the Royal Commission did suggest three reforms which it believed would give adequate safeguards to the suspect while in police custody. These were: an independent system of investigating complaints against the police, a regional system of public prosecutors and the tape recording of police interviews with suspects. However, by the time Conservative Government drafted the Bill, and after further behind the scenes lobbying by the police, these safeguards had either been watered down or had disappeared.

We have already seen what happened with the police complaints system. The Bill makes no reference to any procedure of accountability in relation to the local authorities, although there is a section which formalises arrangements for liaison with the community.

The Police Bill will give the police sweeping new powers to move against large sections of the working class and those involved in political activity. It is more than coincidence that both Southern Ireland and Portugal are both introducing similar Bills at the present time. This points to a concerted move on the European periphery to extend police powers in 'vulnerable' countries.

Under the Bill the police will be able to stop and search people in the street, and for the first time will be able to use 'reasonable force' if necessary. This power already exists in London and has led to a great deal of conflict between the police and young people, particularly in the black community. Those refusing to give their name and address when stopped, or those disbelieved by the police will be arrested. The police will be given the power to set up roadblocks according to the 'pattern of crime' in an area. The police have preempted this last power during the miners' strike. A person's home can be searched and articles seized, even if they are not suspected of an offence. In some cases this may be done without a warrant. This power will allow the police to go on 'fishing expeditions' into the homes and workplaces of trade unionists, political activists and those they consider subversive, in order to gain information.

Once in police custody, a suspect can be detained for up to *4 days* for questioning, and access to a lawyer may be refused for up to 36 hours. It will make situations like the Confait case, where statements were given under duress, far more likely. There is no legal obligation on the police to tape-record interviews. The police will also be given new powers to carry out intimate body searches of the mouth, vagina and anus or take fingerprints without consent and using 'reasonable force' if necessary. The power to take fingerprints by force can be used against anyone from the age of *10* upwards. If doctors refuse to take part in intimate body searches, they will be carried out by an *untrained* police officer who is of the same sex as the suspect. This could not only involve physical damage, but for many women could constitute a serious sexual assault if carried out with force.

The police claim that many of these powers only relate to 'serious arrestable offences'. However, this term is only vaguely defined in the Bill. It does include rape and manslaughter but also any other arrestable offence, however minor, if the committing of that offence might lead to serious injury, harm to the security of the state, or serious financial loss or gain to anybody, *as defined by the police*. This will give massive discretionary powers to individual police officers, allowing them to use the Bill for trivial offences.

The police establishment claims that the police need the new powers in order to fight increased street offences, auto crime and burglary. The Bill, however, is not centrally concerned with reducing or preventing crime. It is far more concerned with controlling the working class population particularly that part which is unemployed. It legitimises current abuses of power by the police and fails in any way to increase their accountability to the public. Lord Salmon, a former Law Lord, described the Bill as bringing Britain closer to a 'Police State'.

The policing strategy used during the miners' strike has pre-empted many of the powers the police will be given under the Bill, such as the power to set up roadblocks; a general power which they do not presently have. The Bill will bring home to more individuals and communities the kind of policing that working class youth in general and black communities in particular have faced for many years. It will also extend criminalisation to ever-widening sections of the working class, trade unionists and anyone who challenges the policies of the present Conservative Government.

The Police and Criminal Evidence Bill is basically giving the police the powers to act with greater confidence as overt agents of social control. It will do this particularly by giving the police the power to gather information on people both in the home and on the streets, where they will be increasingly forced to justify their presence.

Changing the nature of the criminal law is a covert way of intro-ducing greater repression into a society. Many people have not campaigned against the Police and Criminal Evidence Bill simply because it appears to be concerned with the policing of the criminal world. They do not appreciate that a strong and authoritarian state inevitably sees the great mass of the working class as potentially criminal. This is particularly true in a period of high unemployment; crimes against persons and property which in the past were personalised and individual may become acts which are carried out collectively by workers or tenants and so threaten the very property and person of the state. Under such a Bill the police are given powers to combat the mass rather than the individual law breaker.

In the confrontation between the police and a class or whole groups of 'criminals', the police need not only the powers to detain and question possible law breakers before crimes have been committed, they also need equipment and training to do the job which the army has previously done in wars between nation states. The police need to be trained and equipped to deal with the 'enemy within' when it acts collectively.

Training For Confrontation

We showed in Volume I that one of the major changes in the police force in this country over the past 15 years has been the creation of a National Riot Force. This has taken place without recourse to parliament and inevitably without any public consultation. The police are now trained in a wide range of riot control techniques, including the use of water cannon, firearms, CS gas and plastic bullets. This reflects the increasing concern of the police with 'public order' which includes the containment of industrial disputes, political demonstrations and a wide range of other situations which are designated as 'problematic' by the police. This is not to say that the police have not in the past been used to contain political conflicts but the scale and the national co-ordination are new facets of this.

The use of firearms by the police on the streets of our towns and cities is justified with the argument that the police are faced with an increasingly violent and disordered society. However, in most situations where the police are armed, they are not facing violent and armed bank robbers, as they would have us believe. After the shooting down of an innocent man by the police in London in January 1983 (Stephen Waldorf), the Home Secretary, William Whitelaw, issued guidelines on the use of firearms by the police which stated that they should only be issued 'where there is reason to suppose that a police officer may have to face a person who is armed or otherwise so dangerous that he could not be safely restrained without the use of firearms'. Three months later the Chief Constable of Greater Manchester, James Anderton, put armed police officers on the streets of Manchester on 24 hour patrols. Whitelaw responded by stating that the guidelines were not binding. In June 1984, 2 unarmed men were shot and wounded by the police when they were ambushed in a post office in London. It is estimated that at any time there is an average of 215 armed police officers on the streets of London. It is the *police* who decide when officers should be armed.

Developments in the field of riot control are just as disturbing. The Home Secretary in 1983 allowed the Chief Constable of Merseyside, Kenneth Oxford, to conduct an internal investigation into the use of the potentially deadly ferret CS gas cartridges against the public. In 1983 the Home Secretary announced in response to a parliamentary question that 20,000 baton rounds (plastic bullets) and 1,000 CS projectiles 'of a type suitable for public disturbances' are held by police forces around the country, although he declined to state how they were distributed.

The riot control equipment and techniques now an everyday part of policing in England have all been tried and tested in the North of Ireland. When the British Army entered the 6 counties in the 1960's during civil disturbances their equipment consisted of 'a few mesh shields and batons inherited from Cyprus' (Bunyan, 1976). Since then well over 300 different items of riot equipment have been developed for use by the army and the police. Furthermore, joint police and army manoeuvres and training have been taking place in Britain in preparation for civil disturbances and political upheavals. At a seminar held in 1973, the Chairman of the Royal United Services Institute for Defence Studies stated:

> What happens in Londonderry is very relevant to what happens in London and if we lose in Belfast then we may have to fight in Brixton or Birmingham. Just as Spain in the '30s was a rehearsal for a wider European conflict, so perhaps what is happening in Northern Ireland is a rehearsal for urban guerilla war more widely in Europe, and particularly in Great Britain. (quoted in BSSRS, 1974).

This preparation goes back many decades and has intensified since the mid-1960s. The economic recession and the states of emergency declared during the early '70s led to the development of full-scale plans to suppress internal conflicts. In 1973 a Working Party was set up to investigate technical equipment available for intelligence purposes; crowd-control equipment produced for Northern Ireland and to look at the re-equipment of the British police. (Bunyan, 1976) It included representatives from the Ministry of Defence, Home Office and Sir Robert Mark, then Deputy Commissioner of the Metropolitan Police, who had been a member of the advisory body concerned with the re-organisation of the Royal Ulster Constabulary (RUC). The expected major confrontation was, at that time, forestalled, but the preparations were there for a future battle and are now being put into action during the miners' strike.

What the police establishment obscures and what the media always fail to point out is the fact that the police have their own ideological position; they are a political body. Although this might not be obvious when they are dealing individually with 'crime', or patrolling the streets, as soon as they weld themselves into an elite or a corporate body for public order they inhabit an ideological position. This position is anti-socialist and anti-working class; it is deeply conservative.

The police were at Orgreave in such numbers and so equipped for two reasons: firstly to inflict a serious defeat on the mineworkers, secondly to experiment with riot control techniques. We interviewed one miner who told us that before one police charge an officer fired something which landed in front of him and his 2 friends. As he went to pick it up the police ran up and an officer put his foot on it saying 'That's ours'. The miner described the object which he thought was a CS gas cannister as about six inches long, round about an inch and a half in diameter, dark grey or black with a white stripe round it. This is a very exact description of a certain make of plastic bullet, or CS gas cannister still in its cartridge.

The violence that the police were able to use at Orgreave has given them the confidence to move into the pit villages and use that same violence against the community. This is the strategy of the state, to slowly push forward the boundaries of violence and military repression to the point at which large numbers of uninvolved people will believe that it is necessary to see the army brought in. It is classic provocation.

The police are not simply involved in a confrontation with the National Union of Mineworkers, they are working out a counter-insurgency strategy. A massive internal security operation is being carried out against working class resistance to the present government. The strategy involves much more than simply defeating pickets or making sure that scabs get into work. It involves pursuing working people off the streets and into the confinement of their homes.

It is aimed at stopping organisation and curtailing working class culture. These things are seen as seed beds of dissent. The strike is an experimental ground within which techniques of counter-insurgency can be practiced and honed. Part of this operation involves confusing and debilitating the working class community by violence and spreading doubt within their ranks about the morality of the strike and the use of violence by their own members

Behind the very public violence of the one berserk police office at Orgreave something much more sinister is being prepared. It involves provocation away from the picket line as well out of view of the press. It is the dirty undercover warfare of counter-insurgency brought directly from Ireland to the North of England via Brixton and Toxteth. It began in Nottinghamshire under the cover of 'intimidation' propaganda but it is creeping from there to other counties away from the picket lines and into the working class community:

> I am a thirty-four year old mineworker from Scotland. I am presently staying in Ollerton, Nottinghamshire. I set off in the early morning for the picket. I was walking up Whinney Lane and a car stopped. I cannot recall the make or the registration number. The window was rolled down and I was asked if I was going to the picket line. I replied yes. There were two men in the car and I was offered a lift. I got in the back seat. We appeared to be going away from the picket line and I was told, 'You're all right Jock'. I was getting worried. They stopped at a junction and I tried the back door which was locked. The car stopped in a wooded area. I was told to get out and they opened the door. I was told to put my hands on the roof of the car. I asked what was going on. The man on the right spoke to me and the man on the left hit me in the ribs. Then the same man hit me with an instrument which was black and was like a cosh. On the ground, I was hit twice on my right leg. They said to me, 'It's a waste of time lifting you fucking Jocks, this is the only way to deal with you. You found your way down here, so you can find your way back'. They then drove off and left me. When I later saw a doctor he diagnosed a ruptured vein in my right leg and bruised ribs which were possibly cracked. I presume that the men who attacked me were police officers because of the language they used.

It is important to understand that these outbreaks of violence are not idiosyncratic, or confined to a few officers; they are part of a strategy. Over the last two months the incident of 'riot' and affray within the pit villages has escalated. Quite abruptly villages which have the occasional problems on a Friday or a Saturday night and which are usually patrolled by one or two familiar police officers have exploded into battle grounds.

There are lessons which were obscured for the working class as a whole during the 'riots' in 1981. In many small places, far from the scene of major disturbances, rumours of riots were spread, marches were said to be coming. Shopkeepers boarded up their windows, school children were sent home. In some areas hospitals were put on alert and army medics could be seen. Massive police reinforcements were drafted in but never used. Plain clothes police officers were seen carrying pick-axe handles and iron bars. Unidentified people with balaclavas were said to be leading looting and rioting.

This is the other side of Orgreave. Orgreave was a practise ground for offensive action in urban disorders but was portrayed publicly on television as an attack upon the police by the miners. While this set piece practice goes on other counter-insurgency tactics are being developed; in these the police are only the foot soldiers.

VOLUME III

Agitate!
Educate!
Organise!

A Background to June and July

By early August, the miners had been on strike for five months. During that time, the Government has employed many different strategies in its attempt to break the NUM, including the use of massive amounts of propaganda. Part of this propaganda battle has relied on the creation of a host of issues intended to divert attention away from the central facets of the dispute: the number of miners taking redundancy payments; the supposed lack of support from other Unions and so on.

On the face of it, this might appear to be a very one-sided battle. The Government has the backing of big business, including the newspaper proprietors, and its own financial resources to call upon, as well as the implicit control of much television news coverage to throw behind a propaganda campaign against the miners. On the ground it has the police to carry out its policies by force and the judiciary to sanction police action in the Courts.

Despite all of this, there was never any sign from the miners that they would relent in their struggle. As a result, new strategies had to be created constantly by the state; more devices sought and employed; more propaganda pushed out in order to sustain an immense amount of pressure on miners and their families.

From the beginning, the Government's major strategy was to criminalise the miners with the use of the criminal law and the National Riot Police Force. By August there had been six and a half thousand arrests at picket lines, at illegal roadblocks and in the miners' own villages and homes.

Within a couple of months, the Government responded to the miners' continued determination to win by stepping up this strategy into its second phase. This constituted the organisation of a campaign of terror in pit villages carried out by the police, together with a new turn in the propaganda war: as the media spewed forth lies about 'pit bullies' (*Daily Star*) intimidating working miners, the police were laying communities to siege with violence, threats and intimidation. The third, and most recent, major strategy created by the state has been the organisation and funding of a 'Back to Work' campaign.

From the very beginning the Nottinghamshire coalfield lay at the centre of the strike; and this was no exception during it's fourth and fifth months. Nottinghamshire miners who had refused to strike from the start had hung their refusal on different excuses—initially that they wanted a national ballot. However, the history of moderation in the Nottinghamshire coalfield gives the lie to such excuses. The number of Nottinghamshire miners at work has fluctuated throughout the long months of the dispute. As striking miners were torn between conscience and financial considerations, the position was highlighted by the sight of scabs with full shopping baskets, while striking men and their families were relying on food parcels.

Several Court actions were taken by working miners in Nottinghamshire including an attempt to declare the strike illegal, which failed. However, they succeeded in forcing the Nottinghamshire Area NUM to hold Branch elections, which had been suspended throughout the coalfields as is usual during industrial action. The elections took place amid a storm of protest from striking miners, since the police refused them access to the ballots which were held in pit yards. By the end of June the elections had taken place and showed a massive swing to the right, as had been expected, thus consolidating the position of the working miners. Rumours of a breakaway union in Nottinghamshire were further fuelled by the announcement that the Nottinghamshire Working Miners Group had been formed, and had in fact run a slate of candidates for the recent elections—against Union rules. Some pits had to have new elections organised as a result of large numbers of miners being denied access to pit yards to vote.

The new Area Council immediately began to make things difficult for the striking miners. They froze Nottinghamshire NUM funds, some of which included donations to prevent hardship amongst striking miners and their families. They threatened to close down the main strike centre for North Nottinghamshire and the Legal Centre at Ollerton.

According to a report in the *Observer* on July 1st, a group of six working miners had set up a central committee and taken legal advice about forming a new union, provisionally called 'Notts. '84'. The *Observer* report went on to point out that the names of the candidates of the working miners group were on posters displayed at collieries which were 'apparently produced on NCB printing facilities'.

The working miners in Nottinghamshire were well and truly set on a throat-cutting exercise. Unable to see that fighting for jobs means fighting for *all* jobs and that Thatcher is on course to destroy one of the last strongly organised sections of the working class, they are continuing in their attempts to divide the NUM in support of their own 'principles'. In fact, they are acting against all basic trade union principles, and are willing to hand Thatcher the miners on a plate; to abandon fellow workers and their jobs; and allow a victory for the police and the Courts to take over the running of industrial disputes.

The working miners' divisive threats to form a breakaway union were at least partly as a result of fears for their expulsion from the

NUM. The possibility of disciplinary action heightened as the NUM special delegate conference on 12th/13th July endorsed a new rule, agreed at last year's annual conference. This rule change allows the setting up of a 7-man Committee, headed by Mick McGahey, President of the Scottish NUM, and Vice-President of the NUM nationally, which has the power to expel or suspend individual members or to dissolve or suspend a branch or area. NUM officials can be removed from office or an individual can be disqualified from holding office. The day before the special delegate conference a case attempting to prevent the conference from changing the union rules was heard by Sir Robert Megarry, the Vice-Chancellor. The case was brought by the 17 working miners on the Nottinghamshire NUM Area Council and Megarry ruled in their favour. The conference ignored and defied this attempt to interfere in democratic union procedures and voted overwhelmingly in favour of the rule change.

As the weeks of July and August went by the NCB attempted to gain momentum for the 'Back to Work' campaign. Unsubstantiated figures were released daily about the numbers returning to work. What was never made clear was that even if a miner only returned for one shift, and then went back on strike, he was still counted among the numbers of working miners; or that as men returned to pits, larger numbers of safety men were removed by the NUM. We never saw these working miners' pictures or names in the press, and were never provided with any proof of the NCB's figures of those at work. In one case in Scotland the NCB announced that two people had returned to work at Castle Hill Mine. Union investigations revealed the 'scabs' were in fact two nursing sisters employed at the pit who had worked throughout the strike with the NUM's blessing.

The working miners were clearly getting worried at their lack of support. They would have to increase their numbers and consolidate their position further, because they knew that the NUM would not allow scabs in the union when the strike was over, and that striking miners would not work with scabs. By mid-July the Press grabbed eagerly at the enigmatic figure of the unnamed 'Silver Birch', supposedly leading the 'Back to Work' campaign. An intrepid team of investigators at the *Observer* announced on July 29th that 'Silver Birch' was in fact a group of men meeting for 'a talk and a drink' in different coalfields. However, in early August, Chris Butcher, obviously not an *Observer* reader, emerged as the 'Silver Birch' himself. He worked at Bevercotes Colliery in Nottinghamshire and had revealed his identity, he claimed, because striking miners' attempts to find him led him to fear that someone else may be wrongly accused of being him. He was given round-the-clock police protection.

Butcher claimed that he had donations and pledges of thousands of pounds from businesses and branches of the Liberal and Conservative Parties. After travelling the coalfields with a *Daily Mail* reporter for two weeks, he also claimed that 80% of miners wanted to return to work and meetings were being held to encourage them. Coincidental with the appearance of 'Silver Birch' came the news that Gerald Hartup of the Freedom Association had embarked on a 'fact-finding' mission in the coalfields.

Meanwhile the NCB were running their own campaign to encourage miners back to work. They took a series of initiatives, including the laying on of special buses in the North East and Scotland. In Derbyshire, letters were sent early in July to men at nine pits guaranteeing them employment even if expelled from the Union, offering wages of £200 per week and promising police protection. The police, acting in their traditionally impartial role, provided escorts for men from their homes to the NCB buses. The bus windows were reinforced with steel mesh and the drivers wore crash helmets, while the scabs wore balaclavas to conceal their identities.

Despite these moves: the backing of working miners with anti-union money, the police protection and the NCB guarantees, the campaign to get miners back to the pits has been a dismal failure. It could be partially due to the fact that the initiatives were taken while most pits were closed for the annual holiday. But the single most important reason for its failure is that the vast majority of the NUM will not settle for anything less than the continued future of their industry and a solid, undivided Union.

Throughout June and July the support of other Unions whose members were moving coal became crucial. Coal stocks were getting dangerously low and Arthur Scargill predicted power cuts by August or September, based on leaked documents from the Central Electricity Generating Board (CEGB). Although Peter Walker, the Energy Secretary, issued the routine denial, Mr Scargill's prediction was supported by two separate studies issued in July, based on figures from the Department of Energy and the CEGB.

The overshadowing display of support for the miners came during this period with a national docks strike. The British Steel Corporation (BSC) had brought in 'contract' i.e. non-registered labour at Immingham to handle iron ore for its Scunthorpe works. This was a flagrant breach of the national Docks Labour Scheme, dating from a joint agreement between the dockers union, the TGWU, the Government and the National Association of Port Employers (NAPE) in 1947. The scheme guarantees that no non-registered labour is used and the union controls the number of registered dockers. NAPE had been pressing the Government for some time to bring an end to this agreement. Just before the strike began, Nicholas Ridley, Transport Secretary and a leading right-winger in the Conservative Party, had made an attack on the Docks Labour Scheme on the basis that it hampered free trade.

The country's 35,000 harbourmen were called out on strike from midnight on July 9th. Ports were brought to a standstill immediately and more than three quarters of the country's imports and exports were stranded at quaysides. The City panicked: a financial crisis looked imminent.

Within a few days freight services at Dover were blocked and passenger services threatened. This cross-channel blockade was helped by the NUS ban on freight in Sealink ferries as a protest against the privatisation of Sealink.

Thatcher was worried as the Press in mid-July hailed this as her 'worst week', and she quickly organised a rally in her Finchley constituency to boost her flagging ego. She also seemed to be walking around with her eyes and ears closed as she stated that 'the country would not be held to ransom by a tiny minority of strikers'. Ministers rushed to the press denouncing the dockers as subjects of political manipulation on behalf of the miners. The NUM were jubilant and it provided them with a much needed boost of confidence.

The docks strike was over, however, almost as quickly as it began. An agreement was being negotiated and was virtually concluded when the dockers at Dover removed their cross-channel freight ban. Self-employed lorry drivers, selfishly frustrated at not being able to cross the channel, threatened violence and arson if the ban was not called off. This represented a victory for the force of violence alone, and was not in itself the cause of the strike coming to an end, although it was hailed as such in the press.

By July 23rd it was all over. At mass meetings throughout the country the dockers voted to accept the recommendations of their special delegate conference to return to work. NAPE had made a renewed pledge concerning the use of non-registered labour at the docks. The Government was left in no doubt about the strength of feeling amongst sections of the trade union movement in support of their own futures and the future of the coal industry.

The other major battle the miners were fighting during the summer months was to stop the movement of coal, coke and iron ore for steel production. Support amongst the rail unions, ASLEF and the NUR, was biting into coal stocks but had always been patchy. Additionally, lorry drivers were being encouraged by the BSC to drive through picket lines at coal and coking depots, with reported payments of £300 per week. Bill Sirs, leader of the main steel union, the ISTC, was backing management in his determination that steel production was not going to be affected by the strike.

The ISTC's complete contempt for the NUM was displayed at their annual conference in mid-June. They did not even discuss the strike until the end of the week, as though the trade union movement were not in the midst of its biggest struggle for years. They offered talks the following week, which, in the event, led no further than the possibility of a 'modest' cutback in steel production at some future, unspecified point.

Picketing was focused at the Ravenscraig, Llanwern and Port Talbot Steel Works, and again at the Orgreave coking plant. The rail unions were stopping supplies of coal and iron ore to and from the plants and depots, but these blockades were being broken by supplies brought in by road. In June there was serious police violence again at Orgreave. The Government openly encouraged BSC to use the employment legislation against the NUM.

The rail unions' supportive action was, however, biting by July and the ISTC planned with BSC management to break the railway blockade at Ravenscraig. The steel union's leadership stated that they were willing to use coal from anywhere to save their plants. The cost of breaking the miners' blockade of Llanwern was now £50,000 a day.

Towards the end of July the Employment legislation was finally used against the NUM. A firm of road hauliers took the South Wales NUM to the High Court for breaking the terms of an injunction granted in April to prevent picketing of their lorries. The South Wales NUM were fined £50,000. They refused to pay the fine and the area offices were occupied by miners expecting the bailiffs to come and claim the building and its contents. The money was, however, removed by gaining access to the South Wales NUM's bank account through their accountants. Although the area officials had for some time been putting the Union's funds into different accounts to prevent seizure, the Court was able to locate and sequester well in excess of £50,000, including money donated for striking miners and their families.

Throughout the summer months, several attempts had been made to 'negotiate' a settlement to the dispute, but despite occasional bouts of press hysteria presaging an end, it was obvious that the Government had no intention of allowing a negotiated settlement at that stage. At the beginning of July, the NCB announced that new talks would begin soon. The NCB launched another massive publicity campaign involving full page advertisements in all the national daily papers for 8 days, costing at least £500,000. These advertisements were aimed at telling rank and file NUM members how they had been 'misled' by their leadership about pit closures. Stan Orme, the Labour Party's Energy Secretary, was involved in 'behind the scenes' negotiations. However, the only thing to emerge from the latest set of talks was a change in the wording: pits would be closed which could 'not be beneficially developed', rather then being 'uneconomic'. The NUM turned this ludicrous offer down. In any case, McGregor's statement on June 27th that he wanted to see the NUM leadership roundly defeated rather than negotiate a quick settlement to the strike was clear proof of the real state of play.

A day later, Sir Robert Megarry, the Vice-Chancellor, gave 3 Derbyshire miners the right to challenge the legality of the strike in the High Court in September. This attack came amidst numerous press stories about the return to work in areas other than Nottinghamshire. A similar action was taken soon afterwards by 2 working Yorkshire miners.

The support of other unions was made clear with a series of one-day stoppages throughout the country in June. Transport was badly disrupted on the South-East's day of action on June 27th, and several daily newspapers did not appear as a result of their refusal to publish a statement by the print unions in support of the miners. Fifty thousand people in London marched on a rally to show the strength of feeling and counter the propaganda about the miners being completely isolated from other unions.

The Government's propaganda efforts had remained fairly consistently high throughout the months of the dispute: condemnation of 'mob rule'; flagrant attacks on the rule of law, and so on. As the Parliamentary recess approached, however, their outburst built up to a positive cresendo, with Thatcher's infamous 'Enemy Within' speech on July 19th. This was the end of term address to her hard working team, and its poetry was not wasted on the Conservative backbench 1922 Committee. The Government, she said, had fought the enemy without in the Falklands, and now was faced with the enemy within. She did not add that America and Britain had put into power the right wing politicians in Argentina and had been giving them support for many years. In a rather unflattering comparison, she likened Arthur Scargill to General Galtieri and accused Neil Kinnock of leading official opposition support to mob rule, the destruction of democracy etc.

Coincidentally, up and down the country on the same day, other senior Cabinet Ministers were also firing a major attack on the NUM. If there had even been any doubt, it now became crystal clear how important it was to Thatcher to win this battle, and the lengths to which she would go to do so. It was certainly important enough to spend a minimum of *£70—80 million* every week to defeat the NUM, in losses to industry, extra policing costs and tax losses. (J. Harrison and B. Morgan in *City Limits*, 10th August). Nigel Lawson, the Chancellor, had considered that this was a worthwhile investment to the nation, in a recent speech in the House of Commons.

There was no doubt that by the end of July some men succumbed and went back to work in Nottinghamshire and other areas, although the figures were greatly exaggerated. What was important to remember, though, was that huge numbers of men were still on strike, despite the resources being used to break them: the full force of the state, police, courts, Government, the NCB, the press, and the big business, anti-union backing of 'Silver Birch'. The 'Back to Work' campaign had been seriously defeated by the miners' ever vigilant watch at all pits and their determination to win. The miners were settling in for a cold Christmas.

PART ONE
Riots and Resistance

A history of police action against organised labour clearly contradicts the assertion that Britain has always had a moderate, benign police tradition. From the 1840's onwards, if not before, police worker confrontations were bloody and brutal affairs. The police moved against the Chartists in the 1840's and firmly put down riots in the Black Country between 1835 and 1860. Where Labour disputes were concerned the police everywhere protected the interest of the industrialist against the workers—many of the former actually determining, as local government officers, where and by what means the police should act. In Scotland in 1880 and 1881 in the Lanark and Ayrshire coalfields the police acted on behalf of the owners and were responsible to the law of the owners. In Wales in 1910, the police also acted brutally to quash the strike then affecting several Glamorgan collieries. To put down the strikes the whole of the 500 strong Glamorgan Constabulary was brought to support the local police, along with 50 Bristol police officers, 40 Swansea police, 40 Cardiff police, plus 100 mounted and 700 foot police of the London Metropolitan force. As an additional precaution troops were mobilised. Following the disturbances in Wales, literally thousands of police were used to break strikes in 1911 in Hull and Salford. In Liverpool, in the same year, pitched battles occurred between police and workers. However, the most serious crop of incidents occurred in December 1931 and on into the New Year of 1932. Then, violent police-worker confrontations occurred simultaneously in Liverpool, Wallsend, London, Leeds, Glasgow, Kirkcaldy, Wigan and Stoke. The violence eventually peaked in Birkenhead in the autumn of 1932 when the police in Birkenhead broke and conducted what can only be termed a 'reign of terror'.

Tom Bowden
Beyond the Limits of the Law, Pelican 1978.

Introduction

If, for the ruling class, war is 'the continuation of politics by other means', then riot is just that for the working class. When the mechanisms of diplomacy break down between nation states, war breaks out. When the illusion of consensus breaks down in the community, when conflicting values are un-negotiable, the people take to the streets. Under feudalism and capitalism it has been that way for hundreds of years.

In this present time of crisis, the people and the state are standing toe to toe and as the state will not give a hand in its own demise, the people are forced to fight. There are now no formal mechanisms left to resolve the injustice of the rule of capital; reform is only possible when there is slack in the rope round the neck of the working class; when the rope is tight it is a fight for life and death. When no formal procedures exist, riot, disorder, resistance and organisation are the only alternatives.

Nowhere is this conflict sharper than in the relationship between the people and the police. As an organisation of the state the police force has a monopoly of both legal authority and the use of violence. On the other hand there exists no viable or independent formal or informal procedure for the resolution of the injustices which they perpetrate. For the first time since the second world war, the police have now come under serious critical attack. Those who should have done, did not speak out against them at Grunwicks or against their attacks on the Greenham Peace women, nor after the NGA picket at Warrington.

Now under attack, the Chief Constables have coined a new language. They are, they say, only 'the jam in the sandwich ', the 'piggy in the middle'. They now whine that they have been caught in a conflict which is none of their making. These views, expressed in peculiarly inarticulate language, are simply a more extreme version of the propaganda which they have always expressed. They are, they say, an independent force, left with the duty of resolving conflicts between different parties. The problem is of course that increasingly since the beginning of the nineteenth century the party most involved in major conflicts has been the state—the employers of the police force. Rather than being the jam in the sandwich they are one of the slabs on either side of the filling which, in this case, is the people.

Public Order Policing

The organisation of a state police force which began in London in 1829 did not simply change or broaden the role of the constable which had existed since the thirteenth century, it increased their numbers massively. The nineteenth century, marked by the coming to power of a new capital-owning middle class was governed by a completely different philosophy from that which had shaped the chaos of the eighteenth. While the watchword of the eighteenth century was individual liberty, extending even so far as the common acceptance of riot, the nineteenth century was dedicated to the discipline and control of the mass.

The two major nineteenth century developments in policing: a state financed uniformed police and in the eighteen sixties a plain clothed police establishment, were determined by the need of the new middle class to impose order and discipline on the working class outside the factory. Inside the factory, the machine itself imposed a new order on the worker. The uniformity of production by machine meant that workers themselves had to act as part of the larger machinery of production. The police force, itself organised in a military and machine-like way, regulated and controlled the population during the time when it was not working within the factory. In order to do this the police had to be buried within the working class community and legitimised as part of it. This determination by the state to impose order by physical punishment was resisted at every turn by the working class. Previously, resistance to the constabulary had been easier because there were fewer constables and they were not always granted the authority of the court; now they were backed by the power of the new state.

One of the most notable attempts by the people to collectively resist the new uniformly equipped and trained police force took place in Clerkenwell in 1833. In May of that year the National Union of the Working Classes, campaigning for the vote, announced a meeting at Cold Bath Fields. Two days before the meeting was due to take place, Lord Melbourne, the Home Secretary, following a discussion with the Commissioner of the Metropolitan Police, publicly warned the population "not to attend such a meeting" which he claimed would result in a breach of the peace.

On the day of the meeting the police set plain clothed officers and army officers in the vicinity of the field and paid police spies were sent to mingle with workers. One and a half thousand mounted and foot police hid themselves at various strategic points near the meeting. By two thirty when the meeting began there were between five hundred and a thousand people in Cold Bath Fields. Shortly after the first speaker had begun and while the assembly was listening, a column of marching police came into view from a road adjoining the field. The meeting came under attack as they turned to face the police and a pitched battle ensued. In the course of this fight a police constable was stabbed to death. Within ten minutes the meeting had been broken up, some thirty or forty of the audience badly injured by truncheon blows and a number of arrests made. Magistrates held a special hearing that evening and into the night, defendants and witnesses spoke of police violence and arrests effected for no reason.

The police had no immediate suspect for the death of the constable and the Home Secretary offered a pardon and £100 reward to anyone who came forward to convict him. Two days after the attack by the police an inquest was held into the death of the constable. The inquest lasted four days and during the hearing it became apparent that there was an unbridgeable class gulf between the Coroner and the working people who formed the jury. The jury was incensed by witness descriptions of the police presence and the evidence of unprovoked brutality; they returned the following verdict:

> We find a verdict of *justifiable homicide* on these grounds—that no Riot Act was read, nor any proclamation advising the people to disperse; that the Government did not take the proper precautions to prevent the meeting from assembling; and that the conduct of the police was ferocious, brutal and unprovoked by the people; and we moreover, express our anxious hope that the Government will, in future take better precautions to prevent the recurrence of such disgraceful transactions in the Metropolis.

When the verdict was announced the sound of cheering from the public inside and outside the courtroom was deafening; rejoicing overflowed into the streets. For two hours the Coroner sulkily ordered the jury to retire again and reconsider the verdict but they refused and in the end he was forced to accept it. For weeks, the jury was honoured and feted by middle class radicals and working people throughout London and medals were struck in their name.

Since the organisation of a state police force, by careful manipulation and propaganda, the state has prised the working class apart from its history. It has separated the working class from its historical consciousness and enticed it into a world of bourgeois history and morality. Such is the balance of consciousness in the latter part of the twentieth century that many people believe that there has existed a consensus within the working class on policing. The tide has completely turned to such a point that the police now assume a legitimate power to kill people or seriously injure them; if resistance does occur 'more of the same' is considered a viable resolution, and the police receive accolades for defending democracy and civilised values.

The police took over the role of the military with respect to combating the collective resistance of the working class. In effect, this role, of putting down large groups which threaten the state, changed little except in as much as the constabulary were not initially armed with the same weaponry as the military. There was a reason for this: if the new constables were to infiltrate civil society they had to break down the separation which existed between the people and the military. They had to appear as much like ordinary citizens as other members of the community. This role within the community was as important to the state as their role in combating collective resistance.

The constabulary, with the Magistrate, is also that power which has regulated the morality and the culture of the working class population. This role has been evident since the thirteenth century. Constables and common informers were sent out into the community to regulate the leisure of the working class, whether by constraints on licences for dancing and drinking or by the regulation of the people on the streets after daylight hours. The constabulary and the common informers prosecuted rural and industrial workers for blasphemy, sacrilege and breaking the observance of the Lord's Day. It still is the case that a person may be taken before a Magistrate for swearing with only the witness of a single constable.

The police discipline and punish the working class and those of the middle class who stray too far beyond its morality. They are enforcers of morality and behaviour; the bouncers and the minders for the values of the state. In the tradition of all authoritarian teachers, they teach neither by example nor by wisdom but by the intimidation of punishment. It comes as no surprise then to find that during the course of the miners' strike, a period in which the working class and particularly the youth have broken the boundaries of imposed morality and discipline, the police are more zealous in their enactment of punishment and revenge.

This process of moral 're-education' goes on not only formally and 'legally' on the picket line, but within the community as well. Exemplary lessons have to be taught to a working class which is becoming conscious. As with 'breaches of the peace', lessons have to be taught *before* the results of consciousness are seen because than it will be too late; unruly behaviour will have turned to riot and riot to revolution.

The way in which the police seek to teach lessons is no different in the present age from that which it was in the nineteen twenties and thirties. If we find it hard to understand the reasons for certain police actions within the community, we need look no further than the tacit instruction which their service gives them to discipline and punish. The following description of one police officer's way of dealing with 'hooliganism' was written in adulatory terms by a Magistrate for the Doncaster area. He is writing about a time in the thirties:

> One police Inspector, a tall, lithe, powerful man, had his own method, and a very effective one, of dealing with trouble makers. He used to sally forth after closing time, armed with a stout ash-plant, and dressed in plain clothes. Lying in wait at a strategic point, he would see and hear three or four members of the gang—drunk, shouting, cursing, and threatening all the passers-by—as they made their way home. Rushing out without warning, he used to set about the ruffians with his stick, beating them unmercifully until they fled in all directions, yelling with pain. The avenger, his work done, then returned to his station, by a quiet route, changed into uniform, and became again the representative of law and order!

This paragraph speaks volumes about the mentality of the police officer and the Magistrate; it shows clearly that as well as enacting state policy the constable acts out his own subjective moral and class view. This view is indistinguishable from the instruction which his job imposes on him. The moral disciplining of the working class is more frequent, brutal and open at times of social crisis when the working class appear to be making political gains.

In mid-September 1932 following fighting between unemployed marchers and the police in Birkenhead, the police mounted a series of night raids against the working class population. The following testimony was given to a Labour enquiry by the wife of an unemployed ex-serviceman:

> The worst night of all was Sunday night, about 1.30pm. September 18th. We were fast asleep in bed at Morpeth buildings, having had no sleep the two previous nights and my husband was very poorly. My old mother, 68 and paralysed, could not sleep, she was so terrified. I have five children aged six to nineteen. We were all wakened at the sound of heavy motor vehicles, which turned out to be black marias. Lights in the houses were lit, windows opened to see what was going on. Policemen bawled out 'Lights out!' and 'Pull those... windows'. Hordes of police came rushing

up the stairs, doors commenced to be smashed in, the screams of women and children were terrible. We could hear the thuds of the blows from the batons. Presently our doors were bashed by heavy instruments. My husband got out of bed without waiting to put his trousers on, and unlocked the door. As he did so, twelve police rushed into the room, knocking him to the floor, his poor head being split open, kicking him as he lay. We were all in our night clothes. The language of the police was terrible. I tried to prevent them hitting my husband. They then commenced to baton me all over the arms and body. As they hit me and my Jim, the children and I were screaming, and the police shouted 'Shut up, you parish-fed bastards!'

Over one hundred people needed hospital treatment after the police attack and there were forty-five arrests, mainly of unemployed organisers and Trade Unionists. In our time, we have seen the police acting in a similar way towards the inhabitants of Railton Road after the riots had ended. Police moved into houses and flats, wrecking them and throwing furniture out of the windows.

There can be little doubt that the British police force is primarily a public order force; its role in crime prevention and criminal apprehension is secondary. One unfortunate effect of the police's ceaseless propaganda is that many working class people have been convinced over the years that the police are in reality a force which protects *their* welfare and *their* property. The miners' strike however, is quickly educating people to what the state and the police establishment consider the real priorities of their time, money and deployment.

Riots and Community Defence

In the following section we look at the disturbances which have taken place in the pit villages. We will try to show that far from these disturbances being organised acts by working people against the state and their representatives, they usually occur when the community comes under attack from the police. The 'riots' are, in the simplest sense, the community resisting. There can be no doubt that the assults conducted by the police on the communities are acts of oppression that are inseparable from the state's strategy in the strike as a whole. It is time that Trade Unionists and their parliamentary representatives understood this and began to defend their communities instead of falling back upon police inspired propaganda about 'outside agitaters' and 'mob-rule'.

The use of the riot squad at Orgreave marked the authority of the militarised police upon the striking miners at the picket line, at least as far as the state was concerned. Under cover of this 'acceptable' and public violence, the police drove into the pit villages and tried to imprint their authority upon the inhabitants. This was a more difficult task for the police; whereas the picket is brought together from different areas, is not made up of family and does not have a network of community, the pit villages have all these things. Furthermore whereas the picket only has the police and NCB property to react against, there are within all communities those who do not have the interests of the great majority at heart and those who for reasons of their own gain are against the strike: there are then a number of targets and enemies.

Since the strike began, the police have been portrayed as coming under intense attack from striking miners. The truth is that the people always find it difficult to organise. The police know the ground, they are trained and organised and they have a monoploy of weaponry and techniques of violence. Whereas the state arms with ease against the people and holds human life in contempt, it takes an assualt of massive proportions for the people to arm against the state.

The following section details four separate conflicts in different pit villages. We begin by describing a relatively low-key assualt by the police on a small number of youths and then, by using other examples, show how serious disturbances are provoked by the police and how the community resists.

Just Another Friday Night

The first disturbance took place in Armthorpe in May. Since then, at the end of August, the riot police have conducted an all out attack on the village. They sealed if off and attacked striking miners in the streets, broke down house doors and smashed windows. Even in the small incident described below the embryonic signs of organised police violence can be seen.

At the centre of most pit communities is the 'Miners Welfare', a club financed by subscriptions from miners. Depending upon the size of the pit or the number of pits surrounding the village the Welfare can be anything from a rather barren meeting place to a fully equipped entertainments facility. On Friday and Saturday nights the Welfare is usually packed with people drinking, talking, listening to music and playing games. In the small villages the Welfare is a place for whole families and the atmosphere is one of community and familiarity.

Since the strike began the villages have been saturated with police officers, men who bring all the arrogance and uncontrolled power from the urban areas. Officers who do not understand the work which miners do, nor the way in which they live. Men who feel that their instructions for the policing of the strike have given them a blank cheque to assualt, ridicule and attack the community.

One Friday night in May,Jim, a face worker, left Armthorpe Welfare with his wife at closing time. They were about to follow their usual routine of crossing the road from the Welfare, going to the fish and chip shop, buying some supper and then walking home. Two weeks before that Friday evening Jim had broken his arm in four places; it was awkward and heavily plastered. They crossed the road and May, his wife, went into the chip shop. While she was inside, Jim saw a large group of police officers on the other side of the road near the Welfare; there were ten or twelve of them. They seemed to be trying to deal with an argument between a man and his wife. Jim thought it was absurd using that many officers to deal with an argument. He shouted acrosss the road to them: "Why don't you leave them alone and let them go home?". What followed would not have occurred before the strike:

> Two police officers immediately ran across the road and began shouting at me, 'Come here you'. The officers then grabbed both my arms and tried to push the broken one up my back. May tried to pull me out of the police grasp; she said, 'Leave him alone, leave him alone'. One officer knocked her supper out of her hand and pushed her away. Another officer who had hold of me said to her, 'he's under arrest'. I said, 'You're hurting my arm'; the officers said, 'It *will* be fucking broken when I've finished with it'.

While this violence was being acted out by the police, other young miners and their friends began to leave the Welfare. Seeing what was happening some of the younger ones tried to release Jim. In the struggle Jim managed to break free, but by this time other officers had joined the skirmish on the pavement. As Jim ran down the road, those young people who had tried to free him attempted to block their way, running in front of them. Jim managed to run about two hundred yards:

I got as far as the Post Office. A Rover 2000 came round the bend in the main road, in front of me. The car was travelling at about 60 or 70mph. There was no sign on the car. There were no other cars on the road. I was running in the direction of the oncoming traffic. The Rover appeared to go into a deliberate skid to block the road, it swerved and turned broadside. The car stopped about six inches away from me. I was frightened for my life, I honestly thought that I was going to be killed. The driver of the Rover ran from the car towards one of the other lads on the pavement and hit him in the throat. A white transit van came round the bend immediately after the Rover and stopped just in front of it. About eight officers ran from the van and 'jumped on me', they tried again to force my broken arm up my back and I was thrown in the van. After I was thrown in I saw a friend thrown in the front and punched repeatedly in the head and upper body by three officers.

After they had 'lifted' Jim, they mopped up the rest of the youths with much difficulty and a great deal of violence; four youths describe their experiences:

After they had got Jim and his brother, three or four officers came for me. One took me from behind around the chest. Others started punching and kicking me on the front and the back. It seemed to last for three or four minutes. I was then dragged by the hair into the front of the van. I was thrown through the van over the seats into the back.

I found myself trapped on the pavement between two groups of police officers. One officer came running from the direction of the fish and chip shop. He simply grabbed me by the collar with the words, "You'll do. Get him in the van".

I saw extra police arrive, and I saw Jim arrested. About eight officers ran from the van. They ran straight at us and dispersed us, I was struck and knocked to the floor. Two officers grabbed me and took me to the van. Those who had been arrested had to wait about ten minutes in the van before being driven to Doncaster police station. I was near the front of the van and overheard the driver shout out *that if any one was seen on the street after midnight, they should be arrested.* At the police station I was struck in the face while in the cell.

When I reached the group of four or five police officers who had hold of Jim, I saw that they were putting his broken arm up his back. I went up to them and said, 'Get off his arm'. I tried to help Jim release his arm. Four of five officers suddenly grabbed me. I didn't see where they came from. They pushed me up against the side of a white van with a blue stripe on it. They began punching me. I was punched repeatedly about the head and shoulders. They pulled my jacket over my head so that my arms were pinned to my sides. They handcuffed my wrists behind my back, the handcuffs hurt a great deal. During the journey to Doncaster in the van I was sworn at and told to shut up.

The five lads who were arrested were charged with assualt and threatening behaviour; one of the lads was a teenager and the others were in their early twenties. At the police station they all had their photographs and finger prints taken.

This 'minor' incident, was not a riot but it shows all the signs and possibilities of one. It occurred only a short time into the stike when many people in the villages were unaware and unaccustomed to the tactics being used by the police. It faced the NUM legal services with a problem because the four NUM members who were arrested were not on a picket line and had not been acting in pursuance of the strike. The fifth youth was unemployed, though the police who arrested him believed he was a miner. It was not until well into the strike that the NUM realised that it would have to defend those arrested in the community, because they were victims of a common police strategy.

At that time, the full implications of police training and their strategy during the strike was just beginning to dawn on people. The acting treasurer of the village NUM Branch gave us the following statement when we interviewed the arrested people. It is clear from his statement that he was beginning to piece together the provocative role that the police were playing in the villages: a role removed and seemingly distant from their more public one on the picket line:

> I returned from Doncaster to the village between 12.30 and 12.45 a.m. on the Friday evening. In the last mile before the Miners' Welfare I saw about six police cars, mainly Rovers. I would estimate that there were some 15 or 20 police officers at different points. I found out later that a number of miners had been arrested. On behalf of the NUM and as a resident of the village I feel the need to comment upon the police presence in this area on that night. Throughout my life in the village, I have never known there to be any serious policing problems. During the strike

however, myself and other members of the Branch Committee have become concerned about large numbers of police restricting peoples' movements. A large police presence in this village is leading to general intimidation of miners. We are fearful of the things that are happening in Nottinghamshire coming to this village. We are completely opposed to this kind of policing; it is uncalled for and unnecessary.

Assault on Eckington Precinct

There is an irony as well as a horror about the following story of a night of police violence in a small pit community. The centre of the village is dominated by an open precinct which contains some new shops and a few older ones. Some time before the miners' strike began, the local Parish Council broke off liaison with the police because they refused to provide an efficient policing service. It appears that at weekends particularly there was some noise and rowdyism in the precinct but the police claimed that they could not provide cover. When the strike began large numbers of officers flooded the village and one Friday night in June they carried out an attack on the community with the most terrible violence.

In a number of the reports which we received after there had been disturbances in the villages, we were told about acts of provocation by men who did not live in the villages or who were evidently plain clothes police officers. It appears that some of these attacks on the community were not entirely spontaneous. This is the only explanation for the large numbers of officers appearing so quickly at the scene and the consistent, sudden and unprovoked use of violence by many of the police who attended the disturbance. In this particular incident, agents provocateurs were identified by a number of people before the disturbance happened.

The disturbance began around 11.15 p.m. to 11.30 p.m. and centred upon a fish and chip shop and a Chinese take-away where people were congregating after a night out in various pubs and a disco. At first sight the incident appeared to have been sparked off by some of the youths shouting at the police. But statements from two men describe agents provocateurs at work:

> I left the Royal Hotel at about 11.15 p.m. and went to the Chinese take-away in the precinct. I was waiting with my wife in the queue

when four men came up and stood behind us. We overheard their conversation and they were discussing how they were going to sort out the police. One of them went to the door and he shouted, 'The bastards are here; there are four policemen here'. I did not have the impression that these men had been drinking. There was a commotion outside but I don't know what happened, I just wanted to go home. We went home. Much later when I was watching the events in the village from my door... a private car drew up and one of the men who I had seen in the take-away got out of the car and announced to the policemen standing around that he was going back to the station. I then realised that he was a police officer, and I consider that the men in the take-away were trying to pass themselves off as miners.

About 10.30 p.m. I was in the Angel Hotel; I had been downstairs and was on my way back up to the disco. Two plain clothed policemen followed me upstairs. I knew one of them through having dealings with him before. The one I knew said to me to keep my mouth shut about time being there otherwise there would be trouble for me. I left the Angel about 11.15 p.m. having said nothing to anyone. I walked up to the precinct and I saw that the police had got hold of a young lad.

Suddenly around 11.15 the centre of the pit village was turned into a battle ground. The precinct area was invaded by about thirty police officers; any striking miner or member of his family became vunerable to assualt. Within twenty minutes or so they had arrested eleven people, ten youths and an adult.

From the statements which we took, it is relatively easy to see that two young people were arrested first nearby the chip shop where a number of them had congregated. The police were obviously looking for trouble and were going to provoke it that night if nothing spontaneous happened.

I was standing eating my chips with three other lads when a police car pulled up outside the supermarket. Two police constables approached us and said, "Right, bastards, start shouting now'. We did not reply. One police constable took me by the arm and pulled me round the corner and invited me to have a fight with him. "Come on you little bastard, let's have you while you're on your own". I told him that I did not want to fight him. He and the other police constable began to walk away; someone, *not* me shouted 'bastards'. The police ran back and grabbed me; I tried to tell them that I hadn't said anything. My arms were forced up my back and I was put in the police car.

This arrest seems to have acted as a signal because the precinct was suddenly full of police officers who began to attack anyone in sight. The next lad to be arrested, or rather knocked unconscious and dragged away, was standing in the precinct with a girl friend:

> i was standing on the corner of the street at about 11.20 with a girl. The police arrived but I am not sure how many. There were a number of police cars near where I was standing. They didn't appear to have turned up in response to a situation. I was approached from the back and thrown down on to a police car. I then passed out. I was told later that four police officers had beaten me up. I had bruises on my arms and lumps on the back of my head.

We will return to the case of this twenty year old lad later; we will call him the 'second arrest'. It is really irrelevant how the arrests happened from that time onwards, or what the apparent justification was for them. The situation in the precinct can best be described by what the first arrested youth, an eighteen year old, saw from the back of the police car where he had been left by the arresting officers:

> I was left in the car. By this time, there were a lot of policemen on the precinct and they were hitting people and arresting them and people were becoming very angry. Some people, I don't know who, began kicking the police car. I was very frightened because the two police constables had got out of the car and I thought that it might be turned over. I opened the door and got out of the car. I started to walk away, looking over my shoulder, and I bumped into a police constable who grabbed me; two more police officers then grabbed me, one by the throat. As they dragged me towards a Range Rover, a police constable ran over and punched me in the mouth and broke my tooth, he stamped on my left foot and began kneeing and kicking me on the upper legs and thighs.

Obviously a number of people tried to stop the police indiscriminately attacking people. Some were met with obscenities, others got worse treatment. This particular man was charged with obstruction and abusive language:

> I approached the police and the young man they were arresting. I wanted to see what the trouble was and calm it down. The police pushed me away and told me to fuck off. I went towards them

again and was seized by a policeman. I struggled and released myself; I ran and was then apprehended by being pushed into a wall and held by the head and arms by two policemen. One policeman drew his truncheon and when I saw it, I said, "There's no need to use that" as I was in no position to cause any trouble. By this time there were several more police around us and I was lifted by the feet and slid to the ground. The policeman with the truncheon proceeded to strike me several times on the legs. I was then taken limping to the police vehicle. I was pushed up against the vehicle and handcuffed behind my back. I was then pushed violently into the police Range Rover where I discovered a friend, in a reclining position, having difficulty breathing as his nose and mouth were bleeding.

The following lad tried to get home when he saw what was happening; he had seen the 'second arrest' thrown against the car:

I saw that they had a young lad and they were banging his head on the windscreen of the police car; there were two or three police officers doing this. When I was pushed into the same car I could see the effect it had, there was saliva mixed with blood running down the windscreen. I took my girlfriend's hand and said to her, "Come on, we're going home". We walked past two police officers who pulled me away from my girlfriend. As I was taken, I could hear a police officer who stood in the road shouting, "*Make sure you get all them fucking miners*". I was handcuffed with my hands behind my back and thrown into a Metro. While we were going to Chesterfield police station, I asked an officer what I was being arrested for; he said, "Shut it sonny or I will fill it for you". When we got to the police station, the same officer got hold of me by the hair and pulled me out of the car. As he pulled me along he said, "You know what I would like to do to you, you little bastard, don't you", and with that he shoved me towards the wall. I just missed hitting it, but he kept his hold on my hair and kept kicking me at the back of my legs.

This seventeen year old lad ran to the ambulance station to get an ambulance for another lad who had been knocked unconscious. He left his jacket at the scene of the attack, and then returned to get it:

I ran back down to fetch my jacket and I held the ambulance door open while they took my mate in. I went up to another friend and asked him if he knew where my jacket was. A police officer turned me round by the shoulder and punched me in the mouth. I dropped on to the ground and two or three policemen were kicking and hitting me. I was pulled off the floor and dragged over to a police car. They threw me head down onto the bonnet, put handcuffs on behind my back and threw me in the back of the car.

The violence which the police indulged in was not reserved for men, or miners. The assault on this twenty-four year old woman graphically illustrates how wantonly violent the police can be:

I tried to impress upon the officer that the young man was hurt and in need of assistance but he just kept telling me to clear off. Out of fear and frustration I began shouting at him. He called two uniformed men over and told them, ''put her in the car''. I was forcibly taken to a Metro. The window was down, I stuck my head out of the window and began calling to my friend to let my parents know what had happened. A uniformed police officer pushed my head back inside the car. When I thought his attention was elsewhere I put my head back out of the window and tried to call my friend again. The uniformed police officer then punched me in the mouth with his right hand. This blow cut my lip on my teeth. My lip was bleeding heavily and became swollen. My dress was heavily stained with blood.

The worst violence was reserved for a father who came out to the precinct at around 11.30 to find out what had happened to his eldest son:

My youngest son came home crying and told me that my eldest son was being beaten by the police. I ran down to the precinct and approached two policemen and asked politely where my son was. They refused to tell me and told me to ''fuck off''. My youngest son pointed out one of the police officers who had been beating my eldest son. I asked this officer where my son was. He shoved me away telling me to ''fuck off''; he also tried to hit me but I grabbed hold of his wrist to stop him hitting me. Two more police officers arrived and the first one told them to arrest me. They handcuffed me and four officers gathered round me; then they shoved me to the floor and proceeded to bash my head against the floor also kicking and hitting me in the face with their fists. My left eye was swollen and black. They put me in a police car and took me to my house to inform my wife that I had been arrested. My wife pleaded with the police not to arrest me because I had only left the house to find my son. As we were pulling away from the house in the police car, my wife collapsed. The police allowed me to go to my wife and pick her up. We took her into the house and phoned for an ambulance; I asked the police if I could go to the hospital with her but they refused.

The violence from the police did not end with the rout of the community in the precinct; at Chesterfield police station and even in the local hospital the process of discipline and punishment continued:

> I was locked in a cell alone. I banged on the cell door and three officers came in; two grabbed me and one jumped on my chest. They handcuffed me with my hands behind my back; they said that the cuffs were not tight enough and tightened them. They went out and I rang on the bell and banged on the door because I wanted to get the handcuffs loosened. My hands were going numb. Then someone took me out of the cell and put me in an excercise yard which had no roof on it. It was raining heavily and they had taken my shoes away from me. I was there for about an hour and a half with the handcuffs on. My shirt was already ripped and I got soaked to the skin.

> When I got to the police station, I was put in a cell and later called out. I refused to tell them my name and so the policeman slapped me about the face. I still refused to give my name and the policeman threw me against a wall; this was followed up by me being thrown against the counter. I was then asked to take my jacket off, which I refused, so the policeman grabbed my jacket by the shoulders and ripped it off my back and threw it on the floor. I was still refusing to give my name so I was hit again across the face.

We will now return to the predicament of the twenty year old lad who was the 'second arrest'. He was taken unconscious to a local hospital and what happened to him there shows the manipulative authority which the police act out and take for granted in civic institutions:

> I was taken to hospital, and I regained consciousness in the ambulance. In the ambulance I was handcuffed to the bed. In the hospital, I was put into a bed and handcuffed to the side of it. A nurse requested that the handcuffs were taken off but the police officer refused. In hospital, I was sick a lot because I had been hit by the police at the back of my neck. My left eye wasn't focusing properly as a result of the blows. I had my temperature and blood pressure taken regularly.
>
> I was kept in hospital overnight. A police officer was present through the night and the morning. At this time, I had not been charged with any offence. In the morning I was discharged, though

I feel that the hospital was put under pressure to release me. I was taken to Chesterfield police station. I was charged with threatening behaviour. It was then Saturday morning and I was told that I was to be held until Monday when I would appear in court. I was given a letter at Chesterfield hospital from the doctor addresed to my general practitioner; it should have been delivered within twenty four hours. At the police station, this was taken from me and opened by the police.

One sees within this short story of a twenty year old miner just how criminal the police force are. This kind of violence, this type of terrorism, is without question more thuggish, more sadistic than anything which an isolated individual could practice against either a police officer or a citizen. It is calculated, organised, and cowardly; it is also institutionalised. The situation could not have developed as it did without senior officers being aware of what was taking place. It encapsulates the powerful contempt that the police have for working class people.

In both the disturbances so far explained there is little doubt that the intent and the objective as well as the physical 'victory' were on the side of the police. Both episodes could have developed into riots and in some senses it is alarming that they did not; sheer outrage should have been sufficient to inflame the whole community. However, certain things militated against there being riots to follow the police violence.

In the following two situations, people did fight back and took it upon themselves to defend their community and their values. Of course, the police held up their hands in mock outrage, MP's and some Union officials madly mediated, but the matter has to be looked at with a clear eye. If the state attacks the people as sure as night follows day they will fight back, they will organise and they will resist.

A Community Enraged

The town of Shirebrook has a pit on its doorstep. The streets which lead up to the pit are streets of dull red terraces with narrow back alleys running behind them. Shirebrook is a rough place; the Derbyshire people who live there are not like the people in Nottinghamshire or Yorkshire: they are more cautious with outsiders and almost hostile. The pit workers of Shirebrook live in the kind of working class conditions which are prevalant in the large urban centres of Manchester and

Liverpool before their ugly reconstruction in the late fifties and early sixties. Walls at the back of houses crumble, there is a bleak emptiness about the public houses; children play in the street and crowd round visitors.

The Shirebrook pit is a large one, drawing workers from many surrounding areas. In the town itself, there have only been five scabs during the strike. In July when the following statements were taken only one scab family remained, the others having, in the words of the locals, 'been flitted' by the NCB. This small number of families must have been a continual irritant to the rest of the community, many of whom were weathering a long strike and were short of food and clothes for their children.

The idea put forward by the government and NCB that the pressure put on working miners and their families amounts to a kind of terrorism is without rational foundation. All communities expel individuals. All communities have strict codes of conduct and punish those who transgress the morality of the majority. This is true of the most primitive and the most sophisticated societies.

Nowhere is it more true than in the closed and undemocratic societies of the police force and the private clubs of the ruling class. Any police recruit who puts up principled resistance against racism or, in certain squads corruption, is speedily and dreadfully dealt with. Officers who constantly stand out can expect to be harrassed, stopped and searched, even strip searched in front of other officers, their houses can be broken into, their phones tapped and their families intimidated. The police force is one of the most closed and undemocratic institutions in the country, its unity is based upon authority and punishment with the final sanction of expulsion for those who break ranks.

By the time that we went to Shirebrook in mid-July, working miners from outside Shirebrook were being bussed into work by the police. This exercise was accompanied at shift changes by a virtual curfew upon the striking miners and their families who lived near the pit. Half an hour before the buses were due to arrive, police officers would walk through the community commanding people to go indoors and stay there until the shift was through the gates. The rows of terraced houses which joined the road to the pit were blocked off at the end and free movement about that part of the town was prohibited.

This process, by which the majority of the community is placed in thrall to satisfy the self-seeking of a small minority, has nothing to do with the 'right to work' or the much vaunted 'freedom of the individual'. It smacks of the same value laden decision making which protected Martin Webster in his lone racist demonstration through

Manchester with the accompaniment of hundreds of police officers at great public expense. It smells of the same right wing bias which has banned meetings and demonstrations on Ireland in Trafalgar Square and tried to move anti-apartheid campaigners from the pavement outside the South African Embassy.

Where, after all, one might ask, is the police protection for the minority families in Nottinghamshire who wish to exercise their right to strike, picket and preserve jobs and communities for their children? Where is the police protection for the individual Asian and black families stranded on housing estates containing racists in the inner cities? For these minority families, or for white families who suffer intimidation from neighbours, there is never sufficient police cover or personnel. Minorities are driven off estates, have their windows broken and suffer physical attack every day yet police protection is never available. If you are a scab who wants to help break the NUM you are serviced by at least one District Support Unit each of whose ten or eleven officers are being paid three hundred pounds a week; they will do your shopping for you and drive you into work while mounting a twenty four hour guard on your house.

The answer to all these riddles is fairly simple. The police are happy to become involved in serious confrontation in the community whether it be generated by race or by class, *as long as they throw their institutional weight behind the state and its political values which are inherently conservative*. In Shirebrook as in all other mining communities the striking miners and their families have tried to impose their justice and their democracy upon those who offend the community. In doing this they have found themselves in continual confrontation with the police. This confrontation with the police helps the working class to identify the real enemy and determines a different consciousness about the state. Many striking miners will inevitably ask themselves whether physical attacks upon working miners might not be directing energy and organisation away from the state which prepares while looking on.

As the bias and political motivation of the police became evident to the community in Shirebrook, the attitude of striking miners towards them changed:

> The police came in large numbers to Shirebrook after four weeks or so. Originally the police seemed to turn out only for the picket, and there was little serious trouble there. The police at this stage did not patrol the village. As strikers became more conscious of who was scabbing they stepped up their action; there were five families working in our street but two of them have now flitted.

Their windows were broken and the women (strikers) used to stand on the street and shout at them. Individual scabs were escorted by large numbers of police, either walking or with a police van. During the period when workers go in or come out (12.40 a.m. to 1.30 p.m.) no one else in the community is allowed to move about. The police turn a blind eye to what the working miners do; on one occasion a working miner punched a woman on the picket line. It is after that kind of incident that the trouble begins in the community. At first, you had a bit of respect for the police but that has gone completely now. They provoke people on the picket line. Now there are groups of youths wandering around looking for police to attack; if there are isolated police officers around then they get chased.

The predicament of local police officers who would have to patrol the communities alone after the riot squads had left was a common theme in all the interviews which we did about riots. A couple of young strikers in different places went as far as to say that local officers were 'shit scared' of what would happen to them after the riot officers had left. These officers desperately try to convince the community that they are not playing a part in any violence. In some areas though, local officers have been identified leading attacks and provocation. It has always been the case that if the state wants violence inflicted against a community it brings troops or police from outside the community to do it. However, with the police force developing as it is presently, becoming more centralised and playing a more determined ideological role, to assume as some do that local officers are 'as good as gold' or 'come from mining families' and are therefore sympathetic, is naive. Local officers are indispensable to the riot force because they know the community and its personalities. They are an invaluable source of intelligence. Communities which have realised this have made efforts to expel the police from clubs or sporting facilities and to break off formal liaison with them during the strike.

Late one Saturday night in Shirebrook some lads threw stones at the windows of a working miner's house. The way in which the police dealt with this situation provoked a riot, or perhaps it is better explained by saying that the way the police tried to impose their military power on the community without regard for proper investigative processes ensured that the community resisted and attempted to expel them.

Michael is twenty. After an evening at the pub, he had argued with his wife Janet. It was nearly twelve o'clock when he walked home feeling slightly out of sorts. Janet had walked ahead of him and he expected to find her at the house when he reached it. They have a baby who was being minded by a fourteen year old girl while they were out. When David reached his front gate he found six police officers on the grass in the front garden and a number in the greenhouse by the side of the house. There were about six transit vans and somewhere in the region of a hundred officers round about the house. When he got indoors, through the wide open front door, he found the house empty:

> The police in the garden did not respond to me at all. I found out later that the police had called at the house, gone inside and searched it. The baby sitter had taken the baby off to someone else's house, and my wife had gone somewhere else. I went to get my wife, the baby and baby sitter and we were back indoors by 12.30. On Sunday morning at about 11 a.m. six police officers came to the house, one CID officer and five uniformed officers. They asked if they could come in and then they asked where Janet was. I told them that she was at the shops. My brother John was also staying at the house and as he entered the room they arrested him; they said, "As she's not here, we will take you two". We were taken out of the house and put in a car then taken to Chesterfield police station.

Unknown to Michael while he and his brother were in custody, the police had gone out again to take his wife and the fourteen year old baby sitter into custody. When the police took Janet and the baby sitter, Mary, they left the two babies aged two months and eighteen months in the house on their own. It was four o'clock before Michael was told that the two women had been taken into custody:

> I asked about the kids and the police told me that my parents had them; this was a lie because neighbours came in and looked after them. The police took me out of the cell and took me to an interview room. They told me that they knew that I had not broken the window. They were absolutely against the strike and they gave me a lecture about Arthur Scargill. I made a statement and signed it. They told me that two youths had smashed the window, they even told me their names and they said that one of them had blonde hair. John and I both have black hair. They told me that they were keeping my wife in overnight. They let me and my brother out at seven o'clock in the evening. When we got out, Mary had already been released.

Not only had fourteen year old Mary been released but she had told her story to relatives and friends; she had told them how she was held in custody without the presence of an adult and that she had been strip searched inside the police station. In a small community such as Shirebrook news travels fast and by late evening a large group of people had gathered in Mary's street to right the injustice by attacking both the property of the working miner whose window had been broken the evening before, and the police:

> That evening, I went to my parents for a meal. When I returned home at eleven forty five, I was with my dad and brother. I got into our street and saw a police car driving away; it had a door hanging off and all the windows were broken.

In the half darkness between the two rows of terraced houses, up and down the street, there was a battle of some proportion taking place:

> Further down the road there were sixty or seventy police, some with dogs on leashes. They didn't have riot equipment but they were shouting to each other about getting it. There was hand to hand fighting and the police had their truncheons drawn. There were some forty people: men, women and youths.

As in many of these disturbances which appear to be sparked off by one central incident, you only have to scratch the surface to find weeks of frustration and ill-feeling towards the police and the way in which they have abused the community during the strike. A twenty year old youth who saw what 'went off' on Sunday night articulates the atmosphere very well:

> There has been a lot of frustration in the area anyway, because the police keep telling us to get back into our houses between twelve and two. It has been like that for the last thirteen weeks. On the Friday before the Sunday, at about 2.30 a.m. in the morning the police were out in the road by our house. They arrested an unemployed man and searched him in the middle of the road. They took him to Shirebrook police station but released him about half an hour later.
>
> On Sunday night, I could hear noises from the road; it was about 11.30. I went out and saw a crowd of people on the side of the road and in the road. The police were pushing a man into a transit van. There were some fifty police, they were driving their vans at the people in the road and stopping dead in front of them. We tried to get the man released, we surrounded the

van and were banging on the sides of it. We were very angry because of the way the police have been policing the dispute. The van reversed and drove off. At one point we were hemmed in by police at both ends of the road and some people tried to drag an officer out of a car and take the car. A number of cars were smashed up.

Unlike the actions which take place on the picket lines, here in the community there is a solid class response to the police involving women and youths, people who are not necesarily miners but who can see that the provocation by the police is directed not just against the NUM:

I found out that the police had taken Janet and Mary into custody. I was told that Mary had been strip searched. When I got to the street at about 11.30 p.m., there were ten or twelve women and about ten men who where shouting at about forty police officers. There were black vans, cars and a dog van there. The women were standing at the gate ends shouting "Get back to where you belong", "Stop intimidating us", "Dirty bastards" and other things. I was standing by the side of a police van and I said to the police, "You should be ashamed of the damage that you have done in the village and what you did to this family". I was angry but I wasn't abusive. Two officers got out of the van and they began pushing me. I told them to be careful because they weren't messing with a fourteen year old.

I started pushing back and they backed off a bit. One went to get his truncheon. I told them to do what they wanted; I knew that we would get the blame anyway. As the police backed off, I could hear shouting and a woman screaming. I looked round and saw about twenty officers holding a man; one had hold of his head and they were thumping him and bashing his head against the van. His wife was trying to get the police off and she was getting thrown around. I tried to pull the police off and I got two off. I got very angry and then they started on me. There were about ten or twelve or them; they held my arms and pushed my head into the road. They managed to handcuff me. I was doubled over on my feet and as soon as I lifted my head up one of them hit me in the face with a torch. I was dragged to a van and thrown in head first. I could feel blows to my body and my head was bashed against the van. By the time I was in the van, everything had got noisier and more violent outside.

This affray did not last long. It ended with a couple of men and a youth being arrested and charged with assualt and criminal damage to police vehicles. Nevertheless, the community had, in a collective act, shown the police what they thought of their 'procedures'. They got more satisfaction from it than they would have done from a formal complaint.

A War against The People

Fitzwilliam and Hemsworth are two of six small pit villages clustered around three pits in West Yorkshire. In July these two villages were subjected to military style attacks by riot police. An examination of what happened in these two villages shows the division more clearly than in any other case between what has happened on the picket lines and what is now happening in the community. One older miner put it very succinctly:

> If you go on the picket line, you can expect some bother. But this was an assualt on the community, *a calculated attack on the community*.

Everything that happened in Fitzwilliam and Hemsworth would lead the observer to believe that the police carried out acts of warfare against the civilian population; it was 'teaching people a lesson' with a vengeance. In the late afternoon of July 9th two police constables called at the house of Michael Conner in Fitzwilliam and asked him to go with them to the police station to help them with enquiries. The police refused to tell the family what the enquiries involved, but later it was said that a local police constable in the village had had his porch window broken. Others imagined that the police might want to interview Michael as part of their enquiries into damage done weeks before at the Kinsley Drift mine. Some supported a more simple theory that Michael was being harassed because he was an active member of the Labour Party Young Socialists.

Michael refused to go with the police and they left: 'They would be back', they said. It was about an hour later when they did return and this time there were eight of them. They positioned themselves at the front and the back of the house and tried to threaten and cajole Michael out. The police did not have a warrant and he still refused to leave.

By the time that the police left empty handed a large crowd had gathered around the house and picket vans had been driven across the ends of the street to stop more police from entering. These particular villages are close knit communities and it is not surprising that from the beginning the acts of intimidation by the police were met with organised resistance from the community. Why the police chose to pursue their business in this manner we do not know; Michael could have been interviewed at home by a local officer or even an appointment could have been made for him to see the police with a solicitor. We do know from other eye witnesses that on this evening the roads around Fitzwilliam and Hemsworth were heavily policed by vans of riot officers.

Following the second visit to the Conner house, Michael's father, his brother and the crowd which had gathered went en masse to the police station in Hemsworth, with the local NUM Branch President. The crowd now numbered about 150. A deputation went into the police station and spoke to the officer on the desk; this officer claimed that he was alone in the station and knew nothing about the matter. After a time an Inspector came out and introduced himself; he too claimed to know nothing about the questioning of Michael Conner. The Inspector told the delegation that he was from Pontefract, that he did not know Michael Conner and didn't know why he was wanted.

Outside the police station the crowd was patient but becoming restless and two stones were thrown through one of the back windows of the station. In response to a demand from the delegation the Inspector agreed to go out in front of the police station and give the crowd an assurance that there would be no more attempts to take Michael Conner in for questioning.

If that promise had been honoured that would probably have been the end of the matter, but some thirty minutes after that assurance, the residents of Duke Street where Conner lived, were assailed by officers in two squad cars, driving up and down the road calling "We are coming to get you Michael". This intimidation lasted for about a quarter of an hour before the police cars withdrew.

Those who returned from the Hemsworth police station imagining that an honourable settlement had been achieved, made for the Fitzwilliam Hotel, a large and popular public house on the Wakefield Road in the middle of Fitzwilliam. After the incident in Duke Street the Conner household also made their way to the Fitzwilliam Hotel. By ten o'clock the pub was full and there were a large number of people outside standing on the pavement. At around this time, the police provocation began in earnest again as vans with officers shouting obscenities drove past time and again. It was possibly the intention of the police to attack the Fitzwilliam Hotel anyway, but as if waiting for a reason they did not mount the attack until one of the drinkers threw a beer glass at a D.S.U. van. For a short while there was a silence and the vans stopped passing, but it was only the lull before the storm. At 10.40 serials of police appeared marching from either end of Wakefield Road, converging on the Fitzwilliam Hotel.

What happened inside and outside the Fitzwilliam Hotel when the riot police reached it has been thoroughly documented by Tim Kaye, a Warwick University student, in his report 'A Village at War', written for the Yorkshire Area NUM. It is this report that we quote from below:

Around fifty police suddenly appeared. In charge was a big Inspector who had first been seen on the previous Tuesday. He shouted, "Get them in the pub!" Many of the crowd outside decided to keep out of the way by doing just that. The pub was already full to overflowing because most of those who had been to Hemsworth Police Station had come back to discuss the police behaviour over a pint. One witness described the pub inside before the police arrived as "a really family atmosphere with everyone enjoying themselves".

All the police had their truncheons drawn and some were in riot gear. As soon as they got to the Fitzwilliam car park they started running straight into the public bar. In their haste, they even smashed the pane of glass in the door which opens into the bar. Leading the raid was a 'snatch squad' of ten men in 'flying wedge' formation led by the big Inspector. Shouting "You!" they went straight for Michael Conner and pinned him to the pool table where he had been having a quiet game. Truncheon blows rained down on him, so that he was forced to curl up on the baize like a hedgehog in order to protect himself. Friends managed to pull the police off Michael and he escaped to the other end of the bar.

Meanwhile one constable had led a small detail into the lounge bar, where most of the Women's Support Group were drinking. There, he raised a white plastic chair above his head and threatened anyone who did not do as they were told; "Get out!"

The situation was far worse in the public bar. Police shouted to everyone: "If you don't want any fucking trouble, fuck off out!" They then proceeded to block both the front door and the fire exit, causing absolute panic. One frightened woman who attempted to escape into the lounge bar had a door shut on her arm by the police. Other customers tried to get away by climbing over the bar. Anyone in the way of the police was beaten with a truncheon. One man was hit on the side of the neck, another on the upper part of his left arm.

Some police officers started throwing pool balls and one of them struck a miner on the chin. Others told everyone to drink up, those who didn't had their drinks knocked onto the floor by police truncheons. One barmaid was so frightened that she suffered a severe asthma attack. As one miner put it, "All hell let loose. The police didn't care who they were laying into. It was completely indiscriminate". At least one person was hysterical with fear and had to be ushered into the toilets where several people hid until the police had left. When they came out, one of them described the scene: "It looked like a Western movie. Women and men were crying. The whole place was a complete mess, with tables turned over and glasses on the floor".

At one point the Inspector had shouted: "This fucking pub is closed". One miner was told amidst the tumult, "Fuck off you bastard" and when he protested, he was told: "You haven't got a fucking say in it. Fuck off home!"

But still worse incidents happened outside the pub. One man was attacked and arrested before the police got into the pub. Hearing shouting outside he came from the pub when a police officer addressed him by name and told him to "Stay where you are". He stood still with his hands up to show he intended no violence, but then two policemen grabbed him and another two knocked him to the ground. They proceeded to beat him up so badly that he had to spend the night in hospital. His brother tried to intervene and he too was handcuffed and beaten over the head; he was taken to a police van on his own where a police officer truncheoned him savagely on the knee several times.

When the police came out of the pub they began to herd the crowd down a terrace which leads to the Kinsley Drift Pit, Michael Conner was arrested in this push. Finally the people decided to fight back and began throwing bricks and stones at the police. As soon as this began Michael Conner was handcuffed to a telegraph pole between the police and the brick throwers to act as a human shield. Another miner was handcuffed to this same pole with Michael Conner; he had been knocked to the ground and then punched in the face by four police officers while running away down the terrace.

The last police van drove away at about 11.15 p.m. after an abortive attempt had been made by the police to rout the villagers in Railway Terrace had been repelled with bricks and stones. The end of that assault by the police was not however the end of the violence and intimidation acted out by the police in Fitzwilliam that night.

At about one-thirty in the morning when the last of those who had stayed around the vicinity of the pub were going home, some people who had remained by the railway bridge in Fitzwilliam saw about thirty or forty policemen marching up the railway line from Kinsley in full riot gear. These officers laid siege to a house where a young miner lived. They tried their best to provoke a situation which would lead to a riot by shouting obscenities at the occupants of the house, especially the elderly mother of the miner. These police retreated and disappeared only after the family had managed to contact the newsdesk of the *Daily Mirror* and told the police that the phone was off the hook and the line open.

The police arrested eight people that night and dealt injuries to the defendants which included: a hairline fracture of the shoulder; a badly bruised back littered with truncheon weals; a badly swollen knee caused by an accumulation of fluid and two split heads.

It would be absurd to expect the people of the pit villages around Kinsley Drift to have taken the attack on the Fitzwilliam Hotel on the Monday night lying down. Naturally the youth organised:

The villages are close and we needed a way of saying that the police were not going to do this to our friends and relatives. Everyone has to defend each other because many people have friends and relatives in the different villages. There was already bad feeling from what had happened on the picket lines and the new police brutality just made our blood boil. From Tuesday onwards there were police patrolling Hemsworth in groups on foot and there were cars and vans, more police than we had ever seen. It kept the feelings high but if they had gone it would have quietened down.

At about ten thirty on Tuesday night a group of villagers gathered outside the police station in Hemsworth. There were about forty youths aged between twenty and thirty; windows were broken in the police station and a patrol car was damaged as it drove out of the station. It could have been that the police forgave this incident, considering that the community had been provoked. In fact this seemed possible when Wednesday night and Thursday night passed without incident. But the small village of Hemsworth, only a mile and a half from Fitzwilliam, was now swamped with riot police and behind the scenes the police were making preparations which would show that they do not easily accept 'fair' settlements.

Friday the thirteenth was to be the night of a money-raising social for the soup kitchen in Hemsworth. The women's group had arranged to hold a 'sing song' in the tap room of the Blue Bell, a popular pub at the top of the village on the main road. The sing song was called off on Friday after one of the organisers had been told by a doctor friend that there could well be trouble with the police.

In Hemsworth on a weekend evening, hundreds of young people stand around the streets, talking and using the last part of drinking time. Hemsworth is like other pit villages; its community has to some extent a life of its own, unimpinged upon by that order which is imposed in urban centres like London. That Friday evening feelings ran high against the police and there was a great deal of tension. When, at ten-thirty or so, people began to congregate at the top of Hemsworth, they found that an arrest had taken place earlier in the evening. A man had been charged with assualting a police officer and taken to Hemsworth police station.

The crowd outside th Blue Bell public house was noisy and volatile; they were singing and shouting at groups of police scattered about. Probably the village was spoiling for a fight but even if they had not been the police were about to provoke one:

> At about 10.40 some twenty or so officers in partial riot gear walked up to the Blue Bell and went into the tap room. They went behind the bar and marched into the 'best end' where there were a lot of younger people. They came from behind the bar and marched through the room barging into people and knocking their drinks over. They went straight out through the front door.

This time, unlike in Fitzwilliam, the police appeared to want to make their attack in the street where they would have greater freedom of movement. Their behaviour in the Blue Bell was like a primitive ritual well known to bar room bullies and hooligans the world over. It was the whistle to kick off a riot, a pathetic macho call to 'come outside'.

> As the officers came out of the pub people began jeering and having a go at them. There were now a lot of people, young and old, male and female. Women were in the majority and overall there must have been about 130 people. The police were pushing and shoving people, ordering them off the streets and home. People began to push them back. There were groups of police officers all round and a line of them in the road immediately outside the pub. One man was grabbed and then rescued. The atmosphere was very tense. Then a scuffle started. People started

fighting the police. Then two police vans with reinforced mesh arrived and stopped just up the road from the Blue Bell. Officers got out, formed a squad and drew their truncheons. They started marching fast towards the Blue Bell, the people began to move away but as they did this the police broke into a jog and ran at them.

Hand to hand fighting went on for about twenty minutes while police vans arrived continuously and by the end of the battle there were some 150 police at the scene. A number of people were knocked unconscious and the police made twenty one arrests. About half an hour after provoking the battle the police withdrew. In the proper style of their counter-insurgency training, they did not withdraw completely but drove about the village making quick forays from their riot vans to drag off isolated individuals:

> On my way home at about 12.45 a.m. I met up with two other lads, my sister and brother in law and my mother and father. We stopped at the empty market in Hemsworth and were talking. The two lads were a little way in front of me. A police van passed me, slowed down and turned round just past them. It came back and four officers jumped out, grabbed one of the lads and threw him into the van. It set off again, got twenty yards or so away, slammed its brakes on, reversed and officers jumped out and threw the other lad in.

Violence and Resistance

Working class resistance to the process of continual and brutal disciplining by the police force is called 'violence'. The use of this word like many others in our language is carefully circumscribed with class connotations. One act by a constable, such as apprehension without reason, is called 'arrest', while the same act by a citizen to a servant of the state is called 'kidnap' or 'abduction'. While police brutality in pursuit of order is termed 'reasonable force', the defence of community against attack by the police is termed 'violence'. The use of the word 'violence' and its context is a good barometer of class positions in any conflict.

While male violence against women is a hidden quantity undisclosed within certain social norms, the violence of a wife or daughter against a husband or father is highlighted within legal and social institutions as an act of evil. While violence by racists against minorities is again sanctioned and institutionally normalised, violence acted out in self defence by the Asian community is deemed to be vigilanteism. While violence against state servants is viewed with wild alarm as subversion, the violence of the state, both hidden and overt, is legitimised.

In the miners' dispute constant media attention has been focused upon both the apparent violence conducted against scabs by striking miners and by striking miners against the police. But the *London Evening Standard* of August 22nd showed a picture of a working miner holding a shot gun which he had fired from his home; the headline read, 'Why a rebel needs a gun'. When acts of arson have taken place against the property of hauliers who have aided the government in their strike-breaking operations, there have been instant recriminations of the NUM and unproven allegations against its members. Yet the proposed raising to the ground of Dover port by foreign and British lorry drivers during the first dock strike, a promise which was certainly criminal, was met with glee and praise by the right wing press. "There is a certain satisfaction in seeing the mob-rule militants clobbered by their own weapons" (*Daily Express* July 21st 1984).

Each and every act of physical assertion by working people is put under intense scrutiny by the media; it is explained as if it were a regression from collective civilised behaviour back to a primitive state. The endemic violence of capitalism and imperialism is never questioned. The industrial vandalism which has laid waste whole areas and entire communities; the toll which it exacts in industrial injury, illness and disease; the violence of poverty and the inadequate welfare for those who produce all wealth; these acts of criminality are a part of the institutional normality of capitalism. Reason is turned upon its head to the point that the inhabitants of Newbury would, it seems, prefer a well ordered and 'clean' death by nuclear obliteration than a disorderly peace brought about by the women encamped at Greenham Common. And while these same sedentary inhabitants complain of the litter and vandalism, they raise not a murmur about the vandalism of a nuclear arms base which has destroyed the rural beauty of the common land.

It has been just this way with the disturbances in the pit villages, often provoked by well planned police actions; they have been described in the press as returns to some mediaeval past, outrages of vandalism and hooliganism beyond reason. Film coverage of the picket at Orgreave with its concentration upon burning barricades and rolling telegraph poles tried to implant in peoples' minds images of hooliganism, arson and vandalism. Since Orgreave, as the conflicts in the villages have escalated, the press has alluded to men in balacavas, and mob rule. Television shows film shot in the early morning, often badly defined, of threatening gangs marauding around the pit heads.

These images have two purposes; firstly to isolate and divide off from the rest of the mining community the radicals and the activists, to make them a 'small minority'. Secondly to further criminalise the striking miners, but rather than the straight forward criminalisation which has been practised from the start of the strike we now drift into a period where the striker becomes a terrorist. Beneath this canopy of distortion the police especially become more confident and more secure. The ground is prepared for the use of CS gas and plastic bullets.They attack with more violence and with greater regularity knowing that politicians of both left and right have created for them a climate where they are invulnerable to criticism.

Privatising Public Space

The disturbances in the pit villages have been provoked by attacks upon the working class community and the resistance which they show is directed almost entirely against the police. The collective culture of the working class represents a profound threat to the state. Culture is the common interest between people which makes a community cohesive; it is the cement of the community. For the middle class culture is formalised and enjoyed privately in the form of theatre, ballet, opera, museums and art galleries. Working class culture on the other hand revolves around public and social relationships, often out of doors; at the public meeting, in the workingmens club, at the Gala, in the fairground and most of all in the pub. It is within these circumstances that the working class come together.

Any observer who spends two weekend evenings in a coalfield village or town can see clearly who these streets belong to. The streets are full of noisy youths, moving from pub to pub, to cafés and fish and chip shops, while many young people unable to afford these things simply hang about in large groups. It is in these centres of social culture, in the village, that the police most commonly attack.

The object of police actions within the pit villages, as well as those already described , is to drive the working class back into the private areas of their flats, houses and estates. If working class culture is public then the desire of the state is to destroy it and put the public in fear of coming together collectively; to make each person private, isolated, and therefore more easily managed and controlled.

In this process of atomising the working class, control of the streets is crucial. One objective of the police in an authoritarian society is to control the public space, to own the streets and to take possession of the streets on behalf of the state. Why else is there such a concentration in recent law making upon 'stop and search', the use of road blocks and controlling public demonstrations and meetings? Why does the Notting Hill Carnival present such a serious threat to policing every year? In the inner cities of Birmingham, Manchester and Liverpool land space which previously used to be public and upon which there were crowded markets is now covered and locked during the evenings and at weekends; even while open they are often patrolled by security guards. The public space previously used by the working class to socialise is increasingly being taken from them and privatised on behalf of the state. Fascist societies have always made the point quite openly; a leading member of the third Reich said: 'Those who control the streets control the state'. Under fascism in Italy and Germany great symbolic significance was placed upon demonstrating the state's control of public space. In societies under martial law or states of emergency there is often a curfew, which stops people congregating, planning and acting collectively.

In London the Metropolitan police have become obsessed in recent years with the idea of controlling the streets. It was their determination to 'clean up' the streets in the face of a black community which uses the street much more than the indigenous white population, they started the Brixton 'riots'. In 1979, after the killing of Blair Peach by a police officer in Southall, the then Commissioner of the Metropolitan Police Sir David Macnee said: "If you keep off the streets of London and behave yourself you won't have the SPG to worry about". This statement alone gave a clear warning to people that the price of congregating on the streets could, in our society, be death.

All these complex matters have to be borne in mind when we look at the provocation which has led to the disturbances in the pit villages during the miners' strike. It is particularly important that Trade Union officials and their Members of parliament understand that in the pit villages working class culture thrives and that the people *do* own the streets. It is the police who are the outsiders, the alien influence, the trouble makers and the political extremists. The police have no natural right to invade the communities of the pit villages.

After nearly all the disturbances which have been described in this section, figures of 'authority' have wanted either to send statements and reports to the Home Secretary or ask for a police enquiry. There have also been calls for meetings between the police and local councillors, NUM officials, Members of Parliament and solicitors. These negotiations can result in only one thing: a defensive community and the increased confidence of the police. Negotiations or secret enquiries assume that the community are partly responsible for what has happened and they result in 'representatives' instructing the community to stay off the streets and to 'quieten down'. Any tribunals or enquiries into the police should be organised by the community and held in public without the police being present. Their objective should be to fight court cases and organise against any future attacks.

Although the great majority of working class people in the coalfields would not suggest it, it could be said that a community has every right to defend itself against the present policing presence. Some would say if the police have a role at all, it is only with the consent of the community, and only at the direction of the community, while being answerable to the community. When the community is forced to be answerable to the police, when their culture and collectivity is attacked, when their community is put on trial by a state police force, then the people are 'right to rebel'. Right is on their side if they try to expel the police by force from their commuities.

Imprisonment and the Spirit of Revolt

The assaults upon the pit village communities are not just acts of vengeance conducted collectively by police officers at 'the end of their tether'. As we have tried to explain in the last section they are planned operations which have as their objective the liquidation of community, the atomisation of collectivity and the beheading of community leadership. However, in this time of crisis, the state is unable to break the resolve of the working class or even separate the individuals within the class from their collective consciousness or their history. In this vital sense the state is fighting a loosing battle and it will inevitably be defeated. Struggle creates consciousness, defence creates community and solidarity. The political resolve of the working class is forged by the very attack which is intended to isolate its parts and break it up.

Nevertheless on the road to this newly organised community, the working class has to face all the impediments and strategies which its oppressors believe will break its collective resolve. From the first, the police who could not win in any all-out confrontation, use their power and their authority to drag people from their class and their peers. This act of violence itself can often frighten an individual into isolation but if it does not, the Courts are there to impose further discipline. To further debilitate and isolate the worker the Courts can impose temporary poverty through fines, threats of imprisonment, through suspended sentences, forms of self arrest through curfews and bail conditions. At the end of this ritual of punishment is prison, the final isolation and the ultimate end of community. Or perhaps, the end of one kind of community and the beginning of another.

Wherever people are oppressed they resist and the first act of resistance is to form bonds and relationships. This is no less true of prison than it is of the community at large. All working class people who consider serious resistance against the state have to be conscious of imprisonment as the final act of discipline and isolation which the state intends to impose upon them. Prison has to be prepared for, many misconceptions have to be explained and most of all it has to be understood that any conscious working class person takes their struggle with them into the prison system. To believe that the prison is an ultimate deterrent or to believe that those within the prison system are dregs left at the end of capitalist society's foul draft, is simply to believe that the state has ways of winning.

Although the Tolpuddle Martyrs have been on the lips of many leading members of the Labour Party and the Trade Union movement in this last year, the experience of prison by the industrial working class is not only historical. In 1972, Des Warren and Ricky Tomlinson were jailed for three years for conspiracy after a national building workers strike. While to anyone with an iota of class consciousness it was apparent that the state and the Tory government had organised the real conspiracy, Des Warren became a non-person to both the leaders of the parliamentary Labour Party and the Trade Union movement. No sooner had the judge deemed him a criminal than these respectable fellow travellers were grovelling in his wake. While inside, and then on his release after serving the full three years, Des Warren became an embarassment to leaders of the labour movement filled with the guilt of their own long betrayal. Unlike the Tolpuddle Martyrs he was expunged from labour history. As a matter of honour this must never happen again.

For those on the outside as well, the struggle of the working class movement has to be extended not only to a more intimate knowledge of police organisation, or ways of fighting back within the Courts, but to showing solidarity and supporting those in prison. Prison struggles are exceptionally difficult because undoubtedly the class fighter is isolated; he or she is disorientated and prison has such powers of isolation and separation that strength through unity is hard to forge. But with imprisonment we do not suddenly throw in the towel or recoil from conflict, we redouble our efforts on the outside to give support and help friends and comrades organise inside.

Early in the dispute five men were sent to Lincoln prison from one of the NUM Areas. They had arrived in prison after the Magistrate decided they had broken the conditions of their bail. Immediately other miners and family members picketed the prison. On the first day of the picket a senior union official was phoned by the Governor of Lincoln prison; his message was simple, withdraw the picket or your men will have their privileges withdrawn. We have to bear in mind that these prisoners were remand prisoners entitled not to 'privileges' but rights laid down in law. The Offical immediately ordered the picket withdrawn.

In all humanity it is easy to understand why he did this, yet it is this very attitude which has allowed imprisonment to sit unchallenged at the summit of the punitive measures used by our society against the working class. If we are courageous enough to face the state as it impoverishes us and damages our health by slowly withdrawing welfare facilities; if we are courageous enough to face the state on the picket line and in the community; to fight it in the police station and the Courts; we also have to find the courage to enter a new terrain and support our prisoners: more, fight to release them.

Prison is the antithesis of community and the regime within our present prisons was built upon the 'silent system' of the nineteenth century. This regime demanded absolute separation of the individuals within the building. Order and control was total and complete; during exercise, on the occasions when prisoners did not exercise alone within small high walled areas, they were forced to wear masks covering their eyes. They were allowed to look only at the ground, not to catch sight of any other individual. Communication of any kind was denied. This was the state's ultimate solution, a kind of living death, a life without relationships or conversation, or communion with any other individual. Today of course, overcrowding on the one hand and the development of phychotropic drugs and electronic surveillance on the other have modified the state's strategy.

Many working class people easily understand the condition of imprisonment as it exists now in the remand prisons, or dispersal prisons. They understand it perhaps more readily than middle class people because to a degree it replicates a condition that they have lived and worked with in the outside world: poor housing conditions and overcrowding, despotic overseers at work and a closeness and a collectivity which was described by one miner we interviewed as 'living in each other's pockets', while working down the pit. This is not to say that those miners who have been imprisoned have simply accepted their condition, it is to explain that the working class have a strength which their leaders sometimes do not show and they certainly have a power and an inner resource which those who impose imprisonment will never be able to understand.

> I had never been in prison before. I was in court without any representation because the police had brought me up on a Bank Holiday after telling my wife that I would come up the next day. I tried to plead my case and I was told by the Clerk of the Court to be quiet. When I was remanded in custody and I realised that I was going to prison, horror and shock went through my mind. It was the things that I had heard of that frightened me most, being beaten up or homosexually attacked.

This must be a common feeling, one generated by the propaganda of those who have established the prison system. Already within the court the victim is cowed and in fear. This particular miner is twenty three and he decided to impose his own kind of isolation upon himself; by retreating into himself he thought he would be safe: "I had decided not to talk to anyone in the prison. I was going to keep myself to myself".

Younger people obviously feel the fear more than older men who have more physical and intellectual confidence. But fear of imprisonment is not simply a physical fear or even a fear of the unknown, it is also dictated by political consciousness and attitudes to shame. One miner who spent a week in Lincoln was so shocked that it had happened to him that he tried to convince himself that he wasn't in prison:

> I felt sick inside when I was sent to prison, I was stunned, helpless. I said to myself, "No, this can't be happening". I only knew what I had seen on the telly. I was very frightened, I was frightened of what I was going into and not knowing what to expect. A fear of other people, not knowing who they were, being away from my family and home. I couldn't believe that I was in there all week.

Compare this view with that of a miner in his late forties who forced the police to arrest him after they had tried to stop him entering a public house alone, near a picket. From the time that he was taken into custody he refused to give the police his name and date of birth; he too was remanded for a week and documented as Mr. X.

I had so far made up my mind about resisting the police that I didn't have any worries about going to prison. As far as I was concerned, there was no shame attatched to it. I have never been in trouble with the police, if I had stolen something or anything else, I would have felt ashamed. I felt a sense of pride that I had stood up and been counted. I had no idea what prison would be like, I had an open mind about it, I wasn't frightened, I just saw it as a new experience.

When a person arrives at prison they are transferred from the custody of the police to the prison officers and then they go through 'reception'. In reception the prisoner is weighed and documented: this is the beginning of the pattern of order and discipline which will be imposed with varying severity upon the prisoners from that point. Reception is also the place where the screws first attempt to stamp their authority upon the frightened and impressionable prisoner:

In reception the screws shouted at me, I should imagine it's a standard technique, they tried to 'put the frightners on me'—*it worked*. They demanded that I take all my clothes off. I was standing naked. They gave me prison issue clothes which didn't fit me. I am six foot five and the the trousers hung over the ends of my feet; I had to keep my hands in my pockets to keep them up. I can't imagine how big the man was who the trousers were made for!

I was last to go through reception. I thought they may be rough with me, the police had told me that the prison would get any information from me. I was apprehensive. There were five screws in reception. The screw who was asking the questions was very aggressive and arrogant. I stood in front of him at a desk. I was told to stand up straight. He asked me my date of birth, I said, that as he knew, I hadn't given that information and I wasn't going to give it then. *He went up in the air*. He said, "Listen, I'm going to ask you again and all I want to hear, is the answer and woe-be-tide you if you don't give the right answer. I'm going to ask you again". He said, "date of birth?". I stood there and looked at him. He glanced at me for a moment and then shouted, "Throw him in number one".

There is something faintly ludicrous about these scenes, although they are not at all funny. Prison is a process which is meant to degrade and prison officers like police officers have real power, ultimately the power to kill inmates or inflict serious injury on them. What is ludicrous is that while politicians posture about great matters of state, while the economy of the western world plummets, while workers fight a life or death battle for their communities, here for one miner is the experience of the strike; the state with all its power cannot elicit his date of birth. For a Yorkshire miner of stuborn and proud disposition, this is an ideological battle of some proportion!

Very quickly after getting into prison, ordinary working people with no previous experience of imprisonment realise, as they have on the outside, who the real enemy is. Fears of other prisoners are quickly dissipated when they recognise their common heritage:

> After reception, they put me in a cell with two other blokes. They were lying on their bunks. One of the men, the older of the two, asked me what I was in for. I told him and he told me that there were five others on that landing and he introduced me to them as soon as the cell doors were open. When I went to slop out the next morning, once other prisoners knew that I was a miner, they couldn't talk enough to me. Some told me not to worry and that I would get bail, some advised me to go to the Judge in Chambers. I got on great with the two men I was banged up with. They were both on burglary charges. They kept my spirits up, the older one gave me his 'deps' (prosecution statements) to read, I read them three or four times. They were amazed at what was happening in the pit villages, they hadn't heard our side of the strike.

> I put my stuff on the bed and introduced myself. The other two men, Barry and Tom who had been burglars and done other things, couldn't believe that I was in prison for fighting for my job. Neither of them agreed with what the police were doing, even they didn't believe what was happening.

> I felt very sympathetic to the younger prisoners there, because they seemed so organised and skilled in their own way. They knew the system off by heart. They were also very sympathetic to the strike. They didn't believe that we should have been in prison, they thought that we didn't belong there.

There is no denying, of course, that many prisoners, especially those who are constantly imprisoned for small offences, have a conservative view of the world. The miners who were imprisoned soon realised however that this conservatism is not a hard ideological standpoint. While in prison the majority of prisoners realise that they have something in comon with many other prisoners and a determined opposition to the state, the governor and the screws. One prisoner who got a great deal of support from his cell mates knew that they didn't really "care one way or the other" about the strike but they did understand what he was fighting for and spent much of the time joking with him about the outcome:

> They often argued on the Government's side. They kept winding me up, they would say, "Maggie will win this one", "you won't have a job to go back to". They used to say in a really exaggerated tone, "You are telling us that you're in here and they're still working in Nottinghamshire!"

This same miner could say that when his wife came on visits and the visit went badly, he still felt fairly buoyant because "I was going back to my cell with lads who I trusted and they were good lads, so I felt all right".

Mr. X managed to get himself on the first rung of the punitive system of 'prison within a prison', when still refusing to give any information, he was put into solitary confinement. The fact that he was denied association, that he was made to wear prison clothes, that he was denied medical treatment and that he was placed in solitary, shows clearly how the prison conceives of itself as an institution which carries out the work of the state. While prison is only there to receive people consigned from the Courts and enact the sentence of the Court, in this case prison officers and the prison doctor continued the police role of interrogation until they obtained the man's name from him:

> My cell was different from everyone else's; I was put in a cell on my own and it had two doors. There was a door and a space and then the cell door, both doors were solid. Throughout the first day, I saw numerous screws who tried to find out who I was. I was told that I would get no visitors, no exercise, no medication and no food. In the evening I saw the Governor. He told me that it was in my own interest to give my name and address, that I would be kept in solitary and that I couldn't see a solicitor or have any letters or medication. I saw the doctor the next day, he told me that my blood pressure was up (this miner suffers from high blood pressure and knew what he was being prescribed outside for this condition) but that he wouldn't give me any medication. I was only let out of the cell to 'slop out' and go to the toilet; apart from that I was locked up all the time. I had a large number of evening visits from screws, but as soon as they mentioned Joe Gormley—favourably, or Arthur Scargill—

unfavourably, I said something and they walked off slamming the cell door. On the fourth morning I saw the doctor and the orderly told me that if I gave him the name of my G.P. I would get my tablets and they promised me that they wouldn't give my name to the police. I trusted him. I gave my name and that of my G.P.; he gave me a tablet. Half an hour later they took me to a room and asked if I would now co-operate; I said no. Then told me that they knew my name but I wouldn't get any privileges until I told them it myself. It all seemed silly then, so I told them. From then on I was treated like an ordinary prisoner, though I was still kept in solitary and I still didn't get any visitors.

Imprisonment has a different effect upon everyone and there is a difference in the degree of damage it inflicts upon people. For the ordinary working class person, especially those who have been in regular employment and not previously been in trouble with the police, three things seem to stay in the minds of those people we spoke to. The *atmosphere* of prison is something which is punitive in itself:

I knew that prisons were overcrowded but I didn't know about the smell, which was total and terrible. I also found the continual closeness of other prisoners irritating.

The smell was very bad, I was ill when I came out, I kept bringing up my food.

Secondly, however strongly people feel about the strike they will not have conditioned themselves to the enforced separation from their family. It is often said in criminal circles, especially by women, that being in prison is much easier than being left outside. While men who go to prison in a strike often do so because of principled decisions, they cannot always expect their relations who are sometimes over-burdened with responsibilities to 'do the time' so easily:

The loneliness affected me very badly, I couldn't see my grand-children. This upset me a lot. The time dragged.

The most upsetting thing was the fact that my wife had to go under the doctor for tranquilisers. The bottom fell out of her world. She stayed with my mam, she was very supportive and wanted to come and see me all the time. I found it difficult being left in the prison after the visits.

But perhaps the most lasting impression which imprisonment had on the men we talked to was the new insight which they got into yet another repressive arm of the state apparatus. Like many people within the organised working class they had entered prison feeling that it was a completely alien world populated by individuals who were truly beyond the pale. They came out with an understanding of what the state does to many working class people, in that secret world. Imprisonment gave them a new layer of consciousness about the working class condition and taught them a considerable sympathy for those for whom it has become a way of life:

> On the whole they were very sensitive blokes, their communication system was very good, their sense of community very strong. I am more sympathetic to prisoners now than I was.

> I understand now what prisoners go through, prisons are terribly overcrowded. The first night that I was in, the noise of the banging on the doors by the prisoners pleased me. It sounded good, going all round the prison.

When the mineworkers have won their strike, it is more than probable that there will still be NUM members in prison. Mr X had come to his own conclusion about how the leadership should respond to its prisoners:

> I don't think that it would be right to go back to work until our prisoners are released. Whatever the charges or the sentences are, the men have been forced into the situation. We shouldn't go back without people coming out of prison.

PART II
A Period of Change and Struggle

Industrial Gypsies

The 1984 miners strike was from the first a class strike. At its heart was one central question, 'Who should control labour and production'?. The strike of course did not begin with the ideological aim of defining an answer to that question, but it grew inevitably from the carelessness with which capitalists have always treated labour. To capitalists, labour is only necessary in any area or any industry for as long as *they* desire certain levels of production. They have created the right by power in different ways to shut a factory or a pit at the drop of a hat and sublimely expect workers to move home and family or to enter the identity-less void of unemployment.

Attempts by governments and capitalists to break up and destroy the unions which protect labour are obviously not restricted to the use of physical pressure from the police or the use of the criminal law. In the 'Iron Fist' we tried to show how right wing political initiatives had attempted for many years to divide and weaken the National Union of Mineworkers in Nottinghamshire. On the economic and financial front there is a constant erosion of the power of Trade Unions practised by both government and employers. In the following section we have tried to describe some of the complex manipulations which capital and the Government have tried to enact within the coal industry since the second world war.

The miners and the mining industry of 1984 bear little or no resemblance to their counterparts of twenty years ago. The difference has been produced by a series of changes of differing importance. Each of the changes, however small, have helped to shape the modern miner and his attitude to a variety of issues and thus to shape the con-sciousness behind the present strike.

Nationalisation held great promise for the miners, a promise that no sooner emerged than it was betrayed:

> I can recall that in 1947, when the NCB took over the coal industry, plaques were put up at the colliery stating that 'This mine has been taken over by the NCB on behalf of the people'. But it didn't take us long to realise that the deputies, overmen, undermanagers, group managers and area managers, were still the same people as before: company trained and company orientated. The old system still held sway, the role of the overmen and the managers was still to screw the men.

Some realised sooner than others that Nationalisation had not changed that much, but most trade unionists sincerely believed, in the beginning at least, that Nationalisation was a progressive step. In accepting Nationalisation, many also believed that certain sacrifices would have to be made in order that the industry should survive. Now, of course, they assumed that as Nationalisation gave the industry to the people, what the industry did would inevitably be in the best interests of the people who worked; a sacrifice was not so much a sacrifice but a contribution to the common good.

In the late nineteen fifties and early sixties, the National Coal Board (NCB) launched a programme to restructure the coal industry. Cheap, plentiful supplies of oil from the Middle East afforded the opportunity to slash output and manpower levels. In the twelve years from 1957 to 1969, 505 collieries closed with a loss of 378,000 jobs from the coal mining industry. The closure programme of the fifties and sixties, like the proposals for the nineteen eighties concentrated mainly in what is now termed the 'periphery' coalfields. That is, the coalfields of Wales, Durham and Scotland:

> I started work for the NCB in 1966 straight from school; by the time that the 1972 strike started, I was in my fourth pit. We would just be getting settled into a new pit when they would announce that it was closing. A familiar pattern was established, new men came to our pit from one that had closed even though there was no work for them. New, expensive and unneccessary equipment began to arrive at the pit, some of it not even going in the pit. Suddenly we were making a loss and had to close. Then, we moved to another pit where there were no jobs for us, then the equipment arrived and we were making a loss, and so on and so on.
>
> There were no transfer allowances or redundancy money in those days, if you wanted a job, you moved. Some poor buggers at the last pit that I worked at in Scotland, were having to get up

at about 3.30 am. to travel across Fife by bus begin work at 6.45 am. and then, they were not getting home again until about 4.30 pm. It was a bloody long day, but the only alternative was to uproot everyone in the family and move nearer the new pit, if you could get a house. Even if you could get a house, there was no guarantee that you would be in it for long. By the end of 1974, I had had enough of the uncertainties and moved to England. I was paid £100 by the NCB to assist with moving, it wasn't exactly a fortune.

Many miners from areas such as Scotland simply sought employment in other industries, some even emigrated. Others moved home across or within coalfield boundaries or travelled daily to and from pits in their own NCB areas. Some of these travelling men spent as much time on the move, to and from the pit, as they did in the pit itself. For the rest, who were either too old or unable to take advantage of a fresh start, there were the dole queues.

Only those left in the mining communities went on the dole. Britain was still going through an economic boom and those forced out of their work but willing to leave their towns and villages were quickly assimilated in new industry. There was little consciousness of and no struggle precipitated by the attack on the mining industry at this time. The closure programme in the mining industry still left 336,000 miners working in 317 NCB mines in 1969. But a great many mining communities had been devastated, even those not directly affected by closure were all affected in varying degrees by the general shift in employment patterns.

Those communities whose pits closed became virtual ghost towns with only the elderly and the disabled staying on. Businesses closed down or moved out. The coalfields of Scotland, Wales and Durham are littered with villages where the few houses still occupied stand out amongst the dereliction and decay.

Even those communities which did not suffer closures did not escape; some were expanded piecemeal to accomodate an influx of new families transferred after closures. In other instances, whole new villages were built to accomodate migrant miners and their families. Whole communities were restructured to take account of miners who had left for other employment, to suit the needs of capital and although in some places the bricks and mortar stayed the same, the complex family and community relations within the villages were artificial The older close knit communities were destroyed, expanded, reduced or diluted but they were no longer the same. With this restructuring died old traditions and consciousness.

High Wages and "Green" Labour

After years of accepting minimal wage increases, the miners struck in 1972 and again in 1974. These strikes led to substantial increases in wages and the Labour Government of 1975, fearful that they may meet the same fate as Heath's government in 1974, authorised a £12 per week increase in basic wages together with a consolidation of the £4.40 cost of living rises awarded under Heath. At this time, the miners were amongst the highest paid blue collar workers in Britain. This position had been reached with a strong union and a collective determination and it was this more than the wage rises which the employers resented. As always, there would be a price to pay for collective organisation and high wages.

Mick Carter, the NUM Delegate at Cortonwood was asked on Radio 4 recently, what a miner was; he replied, "My father always told me that you are not a miner until you have twenty years in'. Many miners would even not make that concession. As in many heavy industries, in mining, generation after generation of families have gone down the pit, sons following fathers, uncles, grandfathers and great grandfathers. Many older men would say that if you are the first in your family to work down the pit, you are not really a miner. Just as pit work was handed down from generation to generation so too was a fierce pride in, and loyalty to, the union. Young men entering the industry at 14 or 15 already knew about the union and its conflicts with the employers. Living in mining communities they had heard from an early age about the need for a strong union to defend jobs and conditions. While men might not necessarily agree with every particular agreement or decision it was considered a cardinal sin to go against the union or air greivances to anyone outside the union.

> I can't understand these people in Nottinghamshire and elsewhere who are scabbing. There can be absolutely no justification for their actions. The NUM is the NUM. It has built the strength of the miners. I can't understand either those people who take their own union to court.

The need for a strong union has never been doubted by those miners steeped in mining tradition; for many of these their earliest memories are of the Miners Galas in celebration of Trade Unionism.

The high wages won in the struggles of 1972 and 1974, combined with the drift away from mining by traditional mining families attracted new workers to the industry in the seventies. Peter Heathfield, the present General Secretary of the NUM, has often drawn attention to 'the butchers, bakers and candelstick makers' who have flocked to the pits and reaped the rewards of those two historic strikes. The mining industry was inundated with ex-police officers, ex-soldiers, Co-op Insurance men, people who in the past would not have come near mining or mining communities. Most essentially though,these people had never been in a trade union and their families had no history of trade unionism. These recruits had no idea what it was to confront an employer, to argue for rights, protect years of hard fought for welfare or show solidarity.

We only have to look briefly at those who are now making the running against the union to see how this influx of labour has it. Chris Butcher the *Daily Mail* Silver Birch from Nottinghamshire; an ex-barrow boy with only ten years in the coal industry. Robert Taylor, from Yorkshire; an ex-soldier with only eight years in the pits. Jim Pearson in Scotland; an ex-coal merchant with six years service for the NCB.

This influx of 'Green Labour' as the NCB labelled them, not only introduced 'outsiders' with no mining tradition, it also cut out job opportunities for miners' sons and therefore imperilled the mining communities at a time when the economy was going into crisis. Miners who had moved home with the promise of job security for themselves and job opportunities for their sons suddenly found their sons in the dole queues. Another promise had been broken. At Woolley Colliery in the Barnsley Area, almost 450 men left the pit under the redundancy scheme in the twelve months prior to the strike. In that same period, only fourteen school leavers were taken on:

> I am almost at retiring age, but I have refused to accept redundancy because it's not me that is made redundant, it's my job that is made redundant. If I was 29 instead of 59, or just starting in the pit, I wouldn't want to have to uproot myself and my family to go and work elsewhere. This is why I am supporting the strike, I wouldn't want it to happen to me and I will fight to stop it happening to others. I have lived in this community too long to be able to sit at home with my redundancy money and watch the kids hanging about the streets with no jobs. It's not my job, *it's theirs*, and I have no right to sell it. I don't care how long this strike lasts, we have to win. There can be no negotiated settle-ment, you can't negotiate the future of a community If we lose this strike, I've only lost money, the youth have lost everything.

Every Worker A Home Owner

It would be difficult to show clearly a link between home ownership and consciousness; however one of the factors which has evidently contributed to a disintegration on the fringe of the NUM is the higher rate of home ownership amongst younger miners. It is not simply that mortgage repayments create financial pressures but more centrally, it is the location of available private houses.

Before 1974 the miner who owned his own home was the exception rather than the rule, most miners lived in accomodation rented from the NCB or local Council or Housing Association property. Many of the new recruits under the Green Labour scheme were already home owners and those who were not tended not to live in the pit villages and commuted to work.

In 1978 the NCB began selling off their stock of houses either to the sitting tenants or the local council. Many sitting tenants availed themselves of the opportunity to buy their properties at reasonable prices. This however meant that those younger miners who could not afford to buy a house could no longer depend upon the provision of rented accommodation from the NCB. These workers were forced to rely upon the availability of Council housing or Housing Association stock; often this meant living some distance away from the pit and travelling to work.

The modern generation of miners and their families with better wages but limited rented accomodation opportunities are now buying their own houses. The possibility of family planning has enabled those women who can find work to continue working after marriage and contribute to a mortgage. More frequently now women will stop work to begin a family only when they and their partners have established a secure financial base. Again, it is not simply the reliance upon a mortgage, or the simple act of home ownership which has disrupted previous tradition, but the fact that the houses which such young married couples buy will tend to be outside the traditional pit villages.

All of these factors have contributed to the work force in many pits becoming more cosmopolitan. Although it may well be that this process has happened by historical accident the gain to the employers can be clearly seen in their plans for the super-pits. Now, when new pits are sunk or super-pits developed the NCB plans to scatter workers in areas distant from the pit. As the bond between community and work is broken so the reality of collectivity and consciousness based upon the union is destroyed. The new miner begins to resemble his industrial counterpart in the automobile industry or the container ports.

New Technology and a Changing Union

So far we have looked at the changes which have affected the lives of individual mineworkers and the identity of their communities but the changes in working practices and the different composition of the workforce has also affected the structure and the identity of the National Union of Mineworkers.

The NUM does not appoint officials; everyone, from the local Branch Committee member to the National President is elected by secret ballot at the workplace. Until recently, the majority of NUM officials and Committee members were drawn from the ranks of the faceworkers. Before 1966 all faceworkers were paid by piece-rate. This system of payment inevitably led to 'spot-bargaining' with the manager of the pit or his agents. The practice of spot-bargaining brought to the surface the best negotiators and those men who could be most resilient when confronted with intimidation from the management. Such men were quickly elevated from coal face leaders to Branch leaders. From this point, depending upon their ability, ambition and reputation they would progress up the union heirarchy.

In 1966 the system of piecework was abolished and a new 'daywage payment' system was introduced. Most men welcomed the ending of what was a divisive and unfair method of determining pay. In 1966 however, they were unable to understand the loss of local bargaining strength which would follow with the new system.

The NCB had been gradually eliminating old style coalfaces at which large numbers of men produced coal by shovel and sweat. Instead they introduced longer coalfaces worked by fewer men who operated machinery. As men moved onto these new mechanised coalfaces, they were payed a fixed wage. With spot bargaining gone the face workers were answerable to a new set of rules, the 'Conciliation Procedure for the Coal Mining Industry'. This document formalised the disputes procedure and laid out the step by step stages which a dispute must go through. The days of the table thumping trade union official who threatened stoppage were virtually at an end.

It was the 'National Power Loading Agreement' which was

responsible for ending piece work. This agreement also stipulated that wages could no longer be negotiated at local or district level and that function became the responsibility of the National Union. Inevitably, as well as the centralisation of wage bargaining and the new conditions at the face, the NPLA enforced new and different qualities on union officials. The old style candidates relied heavily upon bluff and bluster with more than a little helping of guile. The new trade unionist in the mining industry required a wide understanding of innumerable agreements, laws, regulations, local custom and practice, a nimble mind ever alert to management duplicity and of course the mental strength not to be intimidated by management. The new trade unionists have studied economics, Trade Union law and a number of other disciplines vital to the modern industrial world.

The possibility of obtaining the position of union official is now open to all categories of mineworkers and not just faceworkers as was the case before the NPLA. The rapid increase in mechanisation reduced the number of faceworkers and their proportionate strength within the union Branch. Now, it is very rarly the case that all the union officials and committee members are drawn from the single category of worker. In some union Areas the allotment and distribution of responsibility on the committee has now been formalised by the introduction of reserved places for certain categories of worker, for example, craftsmen, youth, surface workers.

The attendance at Branch meetings has suffered as a consequence of the standardising of rates of pay and the changes in the workforce which have been described in earlier parts of this section. With the ending of the ability to negotiate wages locally, many men lost the incentive to attend meetings. However, the greatly extended catch-ment of many pits has done the most damage to committee power and representative authority. Under the old social order when those at one pit lived in one village, the meetings were held in the Miners' Welfare or a local hall and it was easy for all those who wished to attend to do so.

The new more cosmopolitan workforces at many pits have forced many branches to rotate the venues for meetings in order to be as fair to as many members as possible. Being fair to one member though can often entail being unfair to another. Most men working at a pit are on a three shift rota which means that unless they are on dayshift, they cannot attend evening meetings. This difficulty is compounded by the distances involved or the availability of transport. Often, people who would otherwise wish to, are prevented from attending meetings.

The Bonus Scheme:
A Bonus for Who?

It had long been the aim of, first the Miners Federation of Great Britain and later the NUM, to instigate nationally the same rate for the job in every coalfield in Britain. The NCB, and the private coal owners before them, knew that as long as the miners were earning different rates of pay the union would find it more difficult to unite its membership on a national basis. The introduction of mechanisation caused the NCB to change its policy, not because they wanted an equitable wage structure but because they thought it would give management more control. Lord Robens, NCB Chairman at the time of mechanisation in 1966, said in his autobiography:

> We needed to do two things: first of all, to predict our wages costs (which were well over half our total costs) with more accuracy than we had done in the past: second with mechanisation, to secure an even greater degree of mobility from job to job within the pit and from hopelessly unprofitable, to potentially profitable pits, sometimes in other coalfields.

The NUM wanted equity; the NCB wanted more control over labour: both believed that the abolition of piecework would give them the result they desired. Initially, both were correct in their beliefs. Men got the same wage for doing the same job no matter which coalfield they worked in, and the NCB got the mobility of the workforce that it desired. However, in the long term the NCB was flying in the face of a basic employer's tenet: to divide and rule. The national wage united the miners; no longer could the Board point to differences between areas to pacify men in the higher paid areas.

The strike in 1972 quickly brought the NCB to the realisation that it had made a mistake; there were no longer any 'moderate' miners to temper the 'militants' and keep the union divided. Instead, every miner in Britain was affected equally by rises in the cost of living, now they were all 'militants'.

The Wilberforce Inquiry, set up by the Heath government to investigate and mediate the 1972 strike, recommended that the NUM and the NCB should agree a scheme which would reflect productivity. On the face of it, this recommendation was made because the NCB said in their evidence to the Inquiry, that they wished to introduce an incentive scheme because output per man-shift was declining; in other words, men were not working hard enough.

The Inquiry's recommendation took no account of Lawrence Daley's submission on behalf of the NUM. Daley told the Inquiry that consultants employed by the NUM had been unable to come up with an incentive scheme which would be fair and equitable. He also told the Inquiry that Lord Robens had studied twenty one different proposals for incentive schemes and had rejected them all.

The NUM and the NCB attempted to resolve an incentive scheme and failed. In 1973, the NCB proposed a scheme for each coal face making it absolutely clear that they were determined to return to the 'bad old days' of miner against miner. The NUM naturally rejected the proposals on the grounds that such a scheme would give rise to differences in earnings which reflected differences in geological conditions. After the 1974 strike, when 78% of the 'moderates' in Nottinghamshire voted to strike, the NCB appealed again for the introduction of a local incentive scheme. In November 1974, 61.5% of the NUM membership rejected a local incentive scheme in a secret ballot.

At the annual conference of the NUM in 1977 two proposals to introduce incentive schemes were rejected. However, the conference did pass a South Wales resolution opposing incentive schemes which contained the following wording:

> ...the reintroduction of the piecework system would destroy the unity in the union which the day wage system has created.

The right-wing dominated National Executive Committee (NEC) ignored the conference decision and in November 1977 balloted the membership on whether or not they wished to have an incentive scheme. Again the scheme was rejected by a 55.75% majority of miners. Joe Gormley, then the National NUM President, promised that he would never again attempt to introduce an incentive scheme. He kept his word for four weeks. In December 1977, the NEC voted to allow separate Areas to introduce incentive schemes. The vote was challenged in the High Court. Unsurprisingly, the court dismissed the challenge.

The schemes were due to take effect from the resumption of work after the New Year holidays. The NCB however, felt that the men in Nottinghamshire, South Derbyshire and Leicestershire had worked so hard to increase productivity that they paid them all an extra £30 in their Christmas wage packets. Coincidentally, the Areas which had promoted Area Schemes at the NEC were, Nottingham, South Derbyshire and Leicestershire.

Once the schemes were introduced in these three areas, it was only a matter of time before all resistance collapsed. Area leaders who had consistently argued against the schemes could not prevent their introduction and were forced to negotiate the best schemes they could for their own Areas.

It has long been suspected amongst mineworkers and now, there is strong evidence, compiled by the NUM, which suggests that the incentive scheme has been quite deliberately manipulated by the NCB. This manipulation has been undertaken to ensure that the old 'moderate' areas are well enough looked after to gain their continued moderation while sufficient miners in the 'militant' areas receive high enough bonus payments to dilute their militancy.

The NUM evidence would suggest that the NCB pays where it is politic to do so and doesn't pay where it doesn't want to. It would also seem that bonus payments in general increase for the few weeks preceding any ballot of NUM members without commensurate rises in productivity being recorded.

Creating Insecurity at a Time of Crisis

The miners of today are almost indistinguishable from other groups of industrial workers. They do not subject themselves to the control and influence of an employer from free choice, they work in order to earn money. How much they earn determines how well they live. As amongst other large groups of workers there exist varying degrees of consciousness; in many the consciousness is economistic. Consciousness is often limited to that of Trade Unionism and often does not extend to a political or class consciousness.

Many miners have come to believe that in the current struggle against Thatcherism and monetarism, that they are in the vanguard of a fight against the state. While they are happy to accept this role, they also argue that the role has been thrust upon them; that they did not actively push themselves to the front and take up the cudgel:

> Thatcher wanted us, she has been planning to repay us for 1974. We beat her to the punch in 1981 and because she was not ready, she gave us a body-swerve as Mick McGahey termed it. I also think that 1981 proved that we at least were not trying to make this a political strike. If we were, we would have gone on strike in 1981 when we had her and the rest of them in a corner. We

didn't, perhaps we should have done and cleared the matter up once and for all. If we lose this strike, Christ help the rest of the Trade Unions, we have to win, not just for the pits, but for all the unions.

Although, by virtue of their work, miners regard themselves as working class, many have gathered about them the trappings of what might be regarded as a middle class life style. An economic definition of class could quite easily place a considerable number of miners firmly in the middle class strata.

Working people, whatever their wage, do not readily go on strike, especially as many have heavy financial commitments. A great many miners have these commitments: mortgages, H.P. payments for cars, videos and stereos, as well as holidays booked abroad.

I have not been involved in a national strike before. I have been on strike for a few days or a week at most, on local issues. I am not militant at all, mainly because I can't afford to be.

When, within the surrounding society, one in every eight people are dependant upon state benefits it is unusual for miners or other workers not to know someone in this group. It is widely accepted that the existence of so many people dependant upon benefits has tempered wage claims; inevitably workers compare their wages with the scandalously low level of benefits. Of course, being employed in a society with such a high level of unemployment also develops a desire for self protection in people; male and female workers, however low their wages are so afraid of what they see awaiting them on the dole queue that they fight tooth and nail to make sure that they don't go there.

Thatcher and the Tories have done nothing to convice the miners that they do not intend to butcher the mining industry; all the signs endorse what the union leadership has consistently warned. The affected sincerity of Thatcher which seems to soothe the South of England cuts no ice in the de-industrialised North:

The Tories are geared to profit and loss and there is no room within that for the Trade Unions a having strong voice. The entire Tory policy is designed to weaken the unions and other organisations that are capable of protecting the workers. Margaret Thatcher *is* the Tory party. She is a strong woman, but she is vindictive too, she has no compassion and certainly no compassion for the working class.

The appointment of McGregor to the Chairmanship of the NCB confirmed everyone's suspicions. Miners already knew a good deal about the new 'gaffer' as most of them had been sent home at some time during the steel strike for refusing to use scab steel. His reputation for taking on the unions followed him from BSC where he had ridden rough shod over the unions, sacking 100,000 people. McGregor's reputation together with consistent rumours and leaks about job losses created an atmosphere of fear within the mining industry. The insecurity and fear was exacerbated by the fact that no one knew where the axe would fall first, or when it would stop falling. It was a re-run of the sixties; technological advances were threatening jobs instead of making them more secure and enjoyable.

After McGregor took over the Chair of the NCB miners began looking over their shoulders. If the new computerised systems were introduced at a pit they immediately worried about being made redundant. If the new systems were not introduced they were worried the pit was about to shut. It was Catch 22; instead of allaying fears the NCB and the Government fuelled them by frequent statements about 'uneconomic capacity' and the need for nationalised industries to 'break even'. If this creation of fear and insecurity was meant to split the men from the union, it failed miserably; the uncertainty pushed more people towards, rather than away from, the union.

The various Area ballot results would appear to contradict that conclusion, but the figures are understandable. In the privacy of a voting cubicle, many men were weighing their own chances of survival against someone else's. In the end in some areas, a majority convinced themselves that their own job was safe and they voted for someone else to get the sack. The hope was that a sacrifical offering would appease the beast.

However, in the year which preceded the overtime ban which started in November 1983, there was an upsurge of strikes and disputes. In every NCB area in Britain, small localised strikes sparked the atmosphere of fear and uncertainty deliberately created by the Tories and their agents, the NCB. The frustration of the men found expression in strikes which they themselves controlled. Seemingly trivial disputes produced strikes; overwhelming support would be given one day and the next day, or a few days later, without any change in circumstances, proposals to continue the action would be overwhelmingly defeated:

I think we all knew that sooner or later we would have to fight. Despite, or perhaps because of, the ballot results we knew that even if we wanted to avoid a strike, we would be forced into one. Management was getting too cocky, throwing their weight around, being bossy. We ragged up (went on strike) twice in a month over nought and came back to work the next day each time. To be honest, I think that we were all terrified of a national dispute, because we all knew it would be a long one and we couldn't go back to work just because the Road Tax or electric bill was due. We all knew that, but the pressure of waiting for it was hellish. In a back handed sort of way, it was almost a relief when it did come.

A domineering management became a recurrent theme. Unilateral decisions were taken where previously negotiations would have taken place. New practices were instigated without consultation. The threat of the sack was wielded at every opportunity, men's attendance records were scrutinised and warnings issued that unless attendance improved the sack would follow. Small favours were withdrawn if production targets were not reached. Although local management was 'responsible' for this more oppressive style of management, miners realised that these usually reasonable people were under enormous pressure themselves:

When Thatcher was elected, I knew the miners were in for a hard time because her and her kind don't care about such as us. When McGregor was appointed, we knew that he had been put there for one thing. At British Steel, he started by sacking gaffers first. It must be rough for them, stuck in the middle, but the bastards ought to get off the fence and we would all be safe.

PART III
The new
Community

Men of Coal

The people of the mining communities have, almost overnight, been forced into facing the political realities of the world in 1984. Suddenly lives are turned upside down and a question hangs over the legitimacy and morality of so much previously taken for granted. Those troubles and problems which previously belonged to others and even other countries, are brought home and connections are being made between what is happening to them and what happens or has happened to others.

Before the strike, it was perhaps, all too easy to divert attention from what was happening to other workers or what politicans were doing. As the strike continues people are coming to realise the true nature of the state and more particularly the ways in which the state uses its forces to protect the interests of capital.

When we first started picketing, we used to shout to the Notts. miners, that the police would not be there to ensure that they got into work when McGregor wanted to shut *their* pit. It wasn't a slogan, it happens to be true. I clearly remember police acting like commandoes and helicopters used to smash a workers' occupation in Manchester a few years ago—the Lawrence Scott occupation.

Nothing changes; my Grandfather used to tell me that the police were instruments of the state and tell me stories of how the police and the army were used by the government in the 1926 strike. The police are doing their own and the Army's job now. We haven't seen the Army out on the streets with rifles... yet. The government makes laws to stop people picketing, to stop effective picketing and if these laws don't work, they send the police or perhaps the Army in to prevent picketing being effective. The government does nothing to protect the workers; only the boss gets help from the law.

The courts always find in favour of the employer don't they? I can't recall the workers winning one single case. The most blatant example of the bias of the courts was when Joe Gormley and some others tried to introduce an incentive scheme in 1978. We had balloted and rejected the scheme earlier that year. Some Areas of the NUM went to the High Court for a ruling and the judge said that the National Ballot result didn't count!

I read somewhere once that very few judges have ever come from the working class. It's no wonder that the courts are always against us when all the judges are Tories.

Before the strike there was a certain ambivalence in the mining communities towards the police. The younger members were in no doubt that the police were not averse to meting out instant 'justice'. Tales of police duplicity and lying during the presentation of evidence in court are common in any mining community, as they are in most working class areas. The older more mature men in the community forget their own youth and see the police as an essential and useful part of the community. The strike has altered all of that. While both young and old blame Thatcher and her cabal for deploying them in the first place, both groups are also bitter in their condemnation of the police brutality and tactics used during the strike:

> I always thought that the police were there as servants of the public to protect people from criminals. They are not there as a para-military force to assault and intimidate people. It isn't their stated function, but they do it, they are not supposed to ride people down with horses, but they do that. Nor are they supposed to let dogs loose indiscriminately, which has also happened to miners.
>
> I had no complaints about the police before the strike. I had never been arrested so I didn't know what it was like. But after the way that the police have treated our lads on the picket line I have lost all respect for them. It makes me sick to see them wade into pickets with truncheons, riot shields and all that gear on. I will never be able to look at a policeman again without wondering how many heads he cracked with his truncheon during this strike. I remember Billy Connolley making jokes years ago about Govan—a district of Glasgow—he would say that the police were Glasgow's biggest street gang. I have since wondered if it was a joke after all; the way in which the police have behaved

during the strike would have done justice to any street gang.

I watched the news on the telly the other day; the main story was about a man in Ireland who was killed by a plastic bullet when the police attacked a Sinn Fein march and rally. As I watched, it came to me that the film could easily have come from a miners'picket or demonstration. The police tactics are the same, they charge straight in, fists, boots, batons flying.

I was at the NGA picket at Warrington, the police literally 'ran riot', they lashed out at anyone, men, women, young and old were all treated alike. The difference was, the attacks at Warrington took place in the dark miles away from anywhere. Now, against us, the police wade in in broad daylight and in the main streets of villages and towns. They don't even bother about the media filming them anymore.

Inevitably, the strike has brought the role of the media under the microscope for many miners. The leadership of the union had often criticised the media for misinterpretation and bias against unions in general. Those constant warnings seem to have gone unheeded by many miners; it has taken them a long time to realise that however eloquently they put their case, it doesn't come out the way they want it to. Despite this continuous education many are still seduced by the television or by the idea of seeing their names in print. It is a hard lesson for people to learn that the predominant view represented by the media is the middle class view of the world. The great majority of working people do not have the training to deal with the media and the fact that people need such a training is in itself an indictment of the way the media works. Not surprisingly anger and frustration results in blanket condemnations of the media and an inability to make distinctions between good and bad programmes or reporters. These contradictions prevent profitable relationships being struck up between striking miners and that small section of the media who are sympathetic to their cause.

This undoubted antagonism is not helped by the arrogance of many media representatives who consider that they have a divine right to appropriate then interpret what they hear or see. As Trade Unionists, representatives of the press have a particular duty to explain who they are, where they are from, and what they are looking for before they appropriate other peoples' experience':

The media make me sick, you stand on a picket line half the night and freeze. Just as it's time to go home, the media arrives, some posh car like a Range Rover pulls up about a hundered yards away; they all get out and set their gear up and then walk towards you with their cameras rolling. Then some smart-arsed reporter in a sheepskin coat shoves a microphone in your face and starts asking questions. Not a word of introduction, they don't ask if you want to be filmed, then they get all annoyed and self righteous when we tell them to go away—or words to that effect.

It's always the same; I know other people who have been interviewed, I've been on telly myself. I stood there trying to get it just right, big lorries were roaring past, I couldn't hear myself, so I kept saying "stop", and starting again. I thought very carefully before answering each question, looking for traps. I was there about ten minutes. When I put the telly on that night, I was on for about ten seconds and there was a great big lorry roaring past!

Even before the strike, I did not have a very high regard for the media, especially the tabloids; in particular, *The Sun, The Daily Star, The Daily Mail* and the *Express,* there isn't a good one amongst them. I object to the way that they have all personalised the strike as if it's between Arthur Scargill and MacGregor because that ignores all of us on strike and our views, along with the issues that we are striking for which are beginning to get lost.

There have been some really good documentaries on T.V. but they are few and far between. The papers are all owned by Tories, that's why they are all the way they are. The BBC is controlled by the government and ITV is owned by the Tories. What surprises me is that we don't seem able to realise that and are constantly angered when we are misrepresented.

The strike has really shown them up for what they are. They only ever show pickets throwing stones or hitting policemen, they never show it the other way. Someone must be afraid that the country will get to know what is really happening on the picket lines. Why else is the coverage so biased?

During the media clamour for a National Ballot, they insisted on saying that the ballot we had in Yorkshire in 1980—when about 86% of us voted for strike action if and when the NCB tried to close a Yorkshire Pit—was now irrelevant. What they did *not* say was that Thatcher's mandate was so long ago—when 43% of the people voted for her— most certainly that is now irrelevant.

Whatever else it achieves, the 1984 strike will be regarded by thousands of people as the catalyst which changed their lives. In particular, the role of women in the strike has caused most disruption to the well-established traditions upon which most men base their lives. It has called into question long held opinions and caused prejudices to be re-examined. Men who have been married to women for many years hardly recognise their partners as the same people they were before the strike:

> I'm really proud of our lass, she has been great, she supported me at the start of the strike as I knew she would. But I never expected her to get involved and certainly not to the extent that she has. She knows more about the industry, the facts and figures than I do. It's amazing what you learn about people you thought you knew.

> I think it's great that the women are involved to the extent that they are, it adds more strength to our cause. The women had a demonstration here in Barnsley and my heart was bursting with pride as I watched them march past. I must admit it, but don't tell our lass, I shed a few tears.

> I love it, we both come in from the picket and we spend hours comparing notes about our day or discussing politics in general, we never used to do that before. If I'm first in, I tidy up and prepare the supper or whatever, I never used to do that before either.

> When she said that she was joining Women Against Pit Closures, I thought 'here we go again' another womens' talking shop or that a bunch of loony lefties were going to con the women into attending meetings and get them to join some obscure political party with about ten members. I'm glad to say that I was wrong; those women have done a fantastic job, all power to their elbows.

It would be wrong to suggest that all the women have become active or that all the men in the lives of those who have approve. During the strike women have not only got to contend with the fact that mining is a male dominated industry but that they live within a patriarchal society; even, some would say in an area of the country renowned for its male chauvinism.

> Our lass hasn't joined the womens' group because I won't let her. I don't want to discuss it, it's between her and me.

> I've tried to encourage her but she won't go. She says that she supports the other women but she couldn't picket or march through the streets.

I must admit, I don't mind her going on a march or to meetings but she is not going picketing. I have enough on my plate worrying about myself without worrying about her too.

I hardly ever see my wife these days, if she isn't at a meeting, or picketing or demonstrating somewhere, she is working in the food kitchen. She is happy and I would not say anything to spoil it for her, but sometimes, I resent her because she seems to be more involved in the strike than I am.

Since the strike, the communities have been reactivated, the food kitchens have drawn people together and ended their isolation. Many families have had luxury goods re-possessed and although they have felt a loss at first, they quickly realise how easy it is to survive without them. Bourgeois notions of individualism and materialism which have slowly been woven into working class life have been pulled apart by the strike. Now, so much everyday experience revolving around food, money, friendships and support are shared experiences. Any personal difficulty now becomes public and no one goes without attention or support. Miners and their families from other communities who visit the picket line or attend meetings are welcomed with open arms and treated as comrades. Miners and their families are learning that there is life after video:

> Naturally, it's been hard, not having any money, having to send things back, but you get used to living without them, in fact, I don't know why we needed them in the first place. I was a bit dubious about the food kitchen at first because it seemed like charity. Now we go every day, the meals are great and have made life a lot easier. But it's more than that, everybody goes, you see your mates and their wives, have a chat; there is a good atmosphere.

I'm pleased we sent the video back, it was bad enough with just the telly before, we hardly spoke to each other. We would come in from work, have our tea, stick a video on and then it would be time for bed. We never used to go out or meet anyone. I don't eat at the food kitchen because my wife is still working, but I like to call in and just have a cup of tea after picketing, it's good still to see so many happy faces together after all this time.

The people who work in the kitchen ought to be given a medal as big as a dustbin lid each when the strike is over. The quality of the food is superb and on one four ringed cooker too. I don't know how they do it, but I do know that everybody appreciates it. It makes all the difference too to get some company. The food parcels are handy but I would much rather come here and see everyone, I like the way that people muck in together.

I remember in the 1972 and 1974 strikes, we didn't have food kitchens, but we did get social security so there wasn't so much demand for them. The same spirit of togetherness was there. My brother and I used to go poaching, for rabbits, pheasants, ducks and even a few sheep. We didn't keep it to ourselves, we gave it to the families that needed it most. We weren't the only ones, some lads used to get coal and some sawed logs but there was never any question of keeping anything to yourself. It's like that now, everyone helping each other, sharing things. My neighbour stopped me the other day and told me that he had dropped a bag of coke off in our coal shed. He had been given two bags by a relative, so he gave us one. It is that attitude that will see us through no matter how much Thatcher and her thugs punch, kick or threaten us, we will win because we have each other.

As the strike goes on, the will is strengthened and the resolve hardens. The strategies employed by the state and the NCB inevitably rebound; rather than weaken the men they make them more determined to see the strike through to a successful conclusion. It isn't simply a matter of pride or dogmatism, it is a carefully thought through class position:

I would rather see the pit close than go back now. After all we have come through there can be no compromise.

I voted for Arthur Scargill to be our leader because I knew that he would do as the men wanted. I firmly believe that he won't, but if he were to reach a compromise deal he would no longer represent the majority of the miners.

No matter how long it takes we will stay out. Nothing short of absolute victory will do. If we show any sign of weakness, the government and the NCB would smash us.

I haven't been picketing, or anything like that, but I don't believe we should go back until we have won.

Although the strike has polarised around the one basic issue of pit closures and communities, many men want more than just pledges on this matter. They are demanding a four day week, retirement at 55 and protection of earnings for those forced to take lower paid jobs through injury or age:

We have been out all this time, we must demand everything. Let's face it, there can't be a compromise, this strike won't, can't, end until one side or the other concedes. There is too much at stake. We will win, we must win, and when we do we must not go easy on them because if the situation were reversed they would show us no mercy, in fact the pits wouldn't be worth working in.

Coming of Age

I think that working miners are only thinking in the short term.
They think about a holiday this year, rather than starving in the
future. They make a lot of excuses but they know that they are
doing wrong. There are many influences, to do with class, people
move up the scale, they become deputies, they buy their houses,
their attitudes change completely.

To win, we have to win across the board, 100%. It's win or lose.

One day we sat in the Welfare of a small Yorkshire mining village.
I was interveiwing a tough squat miner in his fifties, who had been
mayor of the village. A lad of about sixteen was also in the Welfare,
who previously had been knocked unconscious in a police charge.
I asked the older miner how long the lad had been unconscious,
without any reference to me the miner beconed to the lad and shouted
across the Welfare "Tucker". It was a barked command rather than
a request. The lad walked quickly over, took off his cap and sat down
facing the miner. "How long were you unconscious for Tucker?"
"Quarter of an hour" the lad replied. The miner waved his hand
dismissing him; he got up from the bench and went to join his friends.
The join his friends. The older miner turned to me and said, "A
quarter of an hour" he paused for a moment, "of course his name
isn't Tucker, that's just what we call him".

This ritual of autocracy and patriarchy could have been seen in
many places, between the officer and the soldier, the teacher and the
pupil, the father and the son. Like women, male youths are not given
a life of their own, they are spoken for and their opinions are not
often noted. Unlike women, this period is for them only short; it is
a training for power, a disciplined introduction to adult life when they
will have a life of their own. Women on the other hand are denied
a separate existence and a life of their own for most of their life.

In the Union youth are a kind of underclass; much of the union's
business at branch level revolves around the highest paid and the most
powerful group of workers: the face workers. This attitude to youth
is common within all Trade Unions, especially craft Unions. It reflects
the society outside of work, where especially during a period of high
unemployment youth is marginalised. Only rarely will a young person
gain admittance quickly to face work. A few years ago it was possible
to travel up the hierarchy quickly but recently the NCB have cut back
on training courses and young people tend to stay for long periods

of time in the most menial jobs. This lack of work experience means
that their involvement in the Union is always peripheral:

> I think that the view is prevalant that Branch meetings are for
> older people. They used to say that we younger ones wouldn't
> fight, but the strike has proved them wrong. Younger people are
> very concerned about jobs and work and very knowledgeable
> about it.

> During disputes, I always felt that it was the older people who
> sorted out the problems. They never seemed to ask for your
> opinion. When you first join the union, no one tells you anything
> about it; you seem to have to learn as you go along. On the Branch
> Committee a teenager is voted on every year, but I think that
> this is just a token really. Since the strike, young peoples' views
> have been taken into account more because there are so many
> of them picketing.

> I haven't really been involved in the union until the strike. I went
> to a couple of meetings and found them boring. They were mainly
> meetings about face workers and the benefits that they get. You
> have to get involved yourself in the union; they don't involve
> you. The young people obviously have less experience and they
> don't ask your opinion.

Even though the young worker plays a full part in the community
of work from first starting down the pit, he is usually discriminated
against until he reaches an illusory point of adulthood. For working
class youth in the pit villages, this structural recognition of adulthood
is illusory because unlike middle class youth, the working class male
will often leave school and begin work in the most oppressive conditions without a break. Family pressures and convention determine
idleness or unemployment as a stigma and something which cannot
be economically tolerated:

> I began straight after school. My father and my step-father both
> worked down the pit. My father came from Ireland and my step-
> father from Scotland. I left school with seven CSE's. I would
> have liked to have done anything practical but 'moneywise' I
> didn't feel that any other jobs were available. I did look forward
> to working down the pit but I have never really liked it, I don't
> like the dust and the dead atmosphere.

The relationship of the young miner to his work is an ambivalent
one: work down the pit is greeted with a kind of grim fatalism and
even those who break with the family or village convention and start

work in other trades often drift back. Clearly though, working down the pit is not simply a job as are other means of earning money:

> The men down the pit talk a lot, they have to be close to each other because of the dangers and difficulties which might occur. I found that the best thing about the pit was comradeship. If you want something, someone is always there to help you. In factories, from what I have heard, it's boring work and everyone talks about each other. My father worked down the pit and my grandfather.

> I worked as a brick layer for three years after leaving school, but then I was thinking of getting married and I felt that the pit was more secure. Most of my friends worked down the pit. I knew that working down the pit I would be a part of the community.

Both the hard physical work down the pit and the surrounding working class condition in a society of high unemployment, demand that young miners learn, and understand their lives very quickly. For male youth both political consciousness and the understanding of work and the union, are transmitted through the medium of other men inside the family and at work. The strike has thrown youth to the forefront because they have the energy and the stamina and perhaps also the intemperance which is needed to join battle with the state. Surprisingly though the young miners do not slavishly follow the path of the adult males; the university of pit work gives even the most shallow youth a serious and learned understanding of what the coal industry means to the community and therefore what the strike is essentially about. Despite their marginalised position young people are also able to articulate what effect pit closures will have on the villages which have so far provided their security:

> My father did influence my attitudes, he worked down the pit for forty years before he was injured. He went through the '72 and '74 strikes. I know that eventually they would try to privatise the 'super-pits'. My father worked when the pits were in private hands; he says that safety standards and such things as pension schemes were very poor. If the Government wins this strike, they will move on, they have already had their way with steel. A privatised system would introduce complete control by the owners who could order you to do anything under threat of the sack.

> If the pits closed, the shops would close and it would be like a ghost town. I like working, I'd go barmy without work. I saw that programme on the television about child battering, it has gone

up with unemployment. It's bound to when people have no money and no work. The crime rate will also go up.

I don't see things any differently now we are on strike from the way I did before. I know now and knew then that she's (Thatcher) out to win. Nothing she would do could surprise me. I wasn't surprised to see all the police. She wants to show that she can break the unions, she doesn't want any unions.

We are striking to stop pit closures, it means saving my job and other peoples' jobs. If there were no unions, they could tell us to do whatever they wanted. The sole purpose of shutting down the pits is so that they can increase their profits. I am aware of what happened in the steel industry, thousands of jobs being lost and only a few factories staying open.

I could see that none of the pits are safe, we had to stop and fight now. If they shut a pit they shut a community, the community goes to ruin and falls apart. Shops go bankrupt, folk drift into the cities and a way of life goes. You get unemployment and a rising crime rate.What is loss and profit to a community, money doesn't buy you a community.

Naturally young people can be articulate and serious when faced with an interviewer. But youth can also be volatile and unreasoning when in a large group.The emancipation of male youth during the strike has brought problems of discipline for the union and local officers. In trying to develop social responsibility in the youths, the union faces the same problem as other radical organisations which are pitched into battle with the state; how is it possible on the one hand to harness the energy and aggression of youth in confrontation, while developing within them a more sensitive approach to people in their everyday lives? In resolving this problem, again, the union turns to the old community and the hierarchy of respect which has developed amongst older miners. Discipline is best exerted by those who are respected for their length of service and their years of activity within the union.

For the vast majority of young strikers though, the strike is the most serious aspect of their lives, it is the anvil upon which their attitudes are being re-shaped. Many of them realise that in some strange way they are on trial within the union. They believe that the eyes of both older miners and the media are upon them; they are conscious that many people thought the strike would stand or fall on the basis of the actions of the younger miners. Would the relatively high wages and the high spending power of young married miners turn their heads and their consciousness, after all they had a great deal to lose:

> I am twenty one now. I left school when I was sixteen without any qualifications and I went to work down the pit. I was living with my father and brother, my mother left three years ago because of my father and she now lives with a miner who is on strike. My brother is sixteen; he has only been at the pit three months. He has been under constant pressure from my father to scab, my father is scabbing himself. I persuaded my brother to strike but he went back. I have been able to stay out because I left home some time ago. I am married and live with my wife in a caravan. I wanted an NCB house and I was sixth on the list then I was suddenly taken off it during the overtime ban. Now, we have no hot water, no gas, and no electricity. My wife has had pneumonia, pleurisy and bronchitis, from living in damp conditions in the caravan. My wife's dad and grandfather worked down the pit. She supports the strike and my choice to strike.

Young miners have adapted as quickly to the strike as they were forced to adapt to conditions of work down the pit straight after leaving school. They have learned most quickly about the police and the role which they have had in the strike and about the hypocrisy of a government which on the one hand pursues a political aim to liquidate the unions while smiling benignly to the world and lying about its involvement:

> She (Thatcher) should be out because as long as she's in, the rich will get richer and the poor poorer. Of course she's intervening. It's bound to be a political strike because she's pulling McGregor's strings. She doesn't want unions because they fight for peoples' rights. The police are a political tool of Thatcher. If they weren't taking sides, there wouldn't have been the arrests.

> Before the strike, I felt that the police were there to do a job. The majority were normal and there were a few bad ones. I realised at the same time, that there seemed to be rules for us and different ones for the upper class. Now, I can't think of any situation where I would help the police. I used to think that the police were individuals, now I think that the orders come from higher up to be rough with people.

> As far as I was concerned before, the police were just doing a job, I thought that there were a few bad ones. Now, I wouldn't talk to them, I don't like seeing them, I hate what they are doing.

Their purpose is to break the strike. As far as I can see, the Government is running them.

Young miners have come very quickly to realise the different facets of the enemy which they are fighting. Along with their inplacable hatred of a hireling police force, they now see clearly the role that television and the newspapers have played:

> You go picketing and you see what really goes on, then you come home and see it differently on the television. Before the strike, I might have had more confidence in the media, now I know that they cover things up.

If they have managed to identify the enemy more clearly, in striking they have also come to a deeper understanding of the position of those who they now stand compared with in the eyes of the middle class:

> I used to have a very immature attitude to black people. When the riots went off in Brixton, I thought that black people were to blame. My view has definitely changed on that: I now know that it had to do with the policing. No doubt people up and down the country are thinking that we are responsible for all the violence.

> I don't agree with policies in South Africa. If I went as a white person, I would just be controlling cheap labour. They have a very strong police and army and people get killed even in industrial disputes like this one.

> I don't think that Thatcher should have seen Botha, or put out the red carpet for him. If we went over there as miners, we would live like kings, while they treat the black people like slaves.

> It could well get like South Africa over here, but it wouldn't just be the blacks who are oppressed, it would be the trade unions and the working class. Thatcher hates the unions. She was on about 'Solidarity', not because she supports unions but because she is anti-communist.

It is not only the strike which has changed people; in fact in the abstract the strike has done little except pauperise the participants. The positive spin off from the strike has been incalculable. New insights into the world have been gained, and what were previously only loose ideas have been joined up. This change in consciousness stretches far beyond the staid acceptance of party politics and though many young people gravitate in this time of new consciousness to the Labour party they are developing a class view which will find no place to rest within the new realism of Neil Kinnock.

The new consciousness is an understanding of basic class values and older forms of working class organisation. It is also a consciousness which matures people quickly and makes them see the benefits in solidarity and collectivity. One twenty year old lad pointed out what the working miners had missed; it was as if he saw not only a strike but a new richness in his life and that of the community:

> We have stuck together. Those who have gone into work haven't seen what has happened in the soup kitchen, it's a massive gain, we have got to know each other. We have survived and it has been possible because of the community of support well outside the pit areas.

There is a rare tolerance amongst the young which is not found with the older, harder miners. This shows itself in relation to scabs; whereas older men talk with an angry edge to their voice, young strikers talk with an almost sad wisdom, often expressed by saying "They know that they are wrong" and as if that moral judgement inevitably brought guilt to the man who contradicted it. In expressing this sadness one lad again pointed to the gains he felt he had made:

> Just starting the strike centre was important. You thought that the Labour council was all for you but they wouldn't let us have a strike centre. Even bad things that happen teach you lessons, you learn by struggling to overcome problems. In the soup kitchen so many people who didn't know each other in the past have grown together. I just wish that we had been solid like those in Yorkshire, then we could have grown together in large numbers.

For many the organisation and the administration of a new community has begun to replace the tired image of waged work, which even down the pit does not leave space for proper relationships and which reinforces the divisions between white and black and men and women. New bonds and new relationships have been formed without the old hierarchies and with a new sense of power; one lad described it simply by saying 'The community has come into being'.

Nowhere is this changing attitude more noticeable than in the view that young male strikers have of the work which the women are now doing inside the strike. Unlike some of the older men the growing autonomy of the womens' groups seem to present very little threat to the younger lads, many of whom seem openly proud of their female contemporaries:

> We are all in the same boat. The women are well organised and we have had wonderful support. It's their lives as well that will

be affected. I think things will carry on afterwards, we could see a team at Greenham Common.

The women go off to other areas and speak and organise. It's always good that people help each other. I think that it would be good if womens' organisations carried on after the strike.

For the young and the old, the men and the women, the strike is a vortex of changing attitudes, a truly regenerating experience out of which comes a new and remarkable even class conciousness. Most spectacular of all is the confidence which it generates, women who have been confined within the home now feel capable of speaking to mass audiences, men who argued carefully even within the field of their own labour now feel able to discuss the future of the coal industry and the place of nuclear power. For some of the youth this emerging confidence points the way to a new organisation of life and the possibility of controlling the life of the community:

The pits would be better run if the people controlled them themselves. If the men organised themselves things would be done better. There was a face at our pit, the gaffers said we had to do it their way, it took twelve months to get the face working and still it isn't working well. At another face nearby, the men went to see the gaffer and told them how it should be done, it was done in six months. You see, the conditions are different at each pit. Gaffers only know from school or they see it as a technical problem; it's not really like that.

Women: Holding Up
Half The Sky

Women's involvement in the miners' strike is one of its most crucial aspects. For the first time during a miner's dispute women have played an important role from the very start, a central role which has enabled the men to stay out and ultimately will enable them to win the strike.

All over the country, women's support groups have been set up and are flourishing. Women who have never been directly involved in political activity before are joining these groups and are creating their own future, and the future of their communities, through their involvement.

The part that women have played is, at least, two-fold. Firstly, by giving their moral support to the aims of the strike, women have thrown their weight behind the struggle for the mining industry and for jobs in the future; for the NUM itself and for the preservation of their communitites. Secondly, the women have organised to give support on a practical level: on picket lines; by raising funds and providing food.

The extent of the women's involvement in the strike could never have been anticipated—either by the women themselves, or the miners and certainly not by the state. Women have always taken part in political and trade union activities but this has been hidden and trivialised. Their role in this strike cannot be hidden and is radical because of the level of their involvement; because they are not themselves the workforce and because the strike could not continue without them.

Women's activities as political beings have always been overshadowed by the traditional view that women belong, first and foremost, in the family. This is how women are 'placed' in society: men are 'people' but women are wives, housewives or mothers. This removes a woman's identity of herself as an individual, since she is always identified in relation to someone else i.e. another member of the family. The strike has enabled women to create an identity *for themselves:*

> I feel I've changed a lot during the strike. Before, I was a quiet housewife, staying at home and looking after the children. It's opened my eyes and I've found I am a person and I'm not just a housewife and a mum. You get into a rut—you just feel like an object and not a person. Now I feel I can have a say in what happens in the community.

Within the family, women have primary responsibility for housework and childcare; employment for women is seen as being of secondary importance to their domestic duties. Housework is not seen as 'real work' despite the time, effort and energy expended by all women daily in carrying it out. Even when a man does 'his share' of the housework, it is still ultimately seen as a woman's responsibility, whether she works outside of the home or not.

Housework is also very isolating—it is something carried out in private and on an individual basis. As a result, women are removed from most forms of collective activity, and in particular trade union and political action arising from working outside of the home. Even where women do work away from the home, and most do at some time in their lives, it is often in non-unionised industries, or where the union is inactive, or run by men. Neither are women 'allowed' the same type of collective friendship networks that men, particularly in the working class, enjoy—playing football, going down to the pub for a drink with the mates and a game of darts etc. This is not to say that women don't ever do these things, but that women's relationships with other women are often on an individual basis—a next-door neighbour or a relation.

There are few opportunities for women to organise together outside of the confines of the home. The strike offered women the chance to take part in a collective political struggle, and they grasped it eagerly with both hands. New links have been forged and new ways of organising created, pulling together all of the forces in the community for a common end: to win the strike. The women are the means by which this end is being achieved.

The implications of women's activities during the strike go far beyond the immediate level of practical support, both for the women themselves and for all women. For themselves, women have learned how to organise as a body and have adapted quickly and effectively to the task they set themselves. More than this, women's consciousness of themselves, of their capabilities and strengths, and of their role in political activity has changed. They no longer identify themselves as 'just' housewives and mothers, but as political beings. They have experienced, through struggle, a part of themselves they never realised existed and they will never turn back from this.

The women's organisation during the strike has also brought into stark relief the separation of roles between women and men both inside and outside of the family. This has entailed some degree of role reversal, with the men staying at home and the women going out organising fundraising activities, working in the kitchens and so on. While re-assessments and changes to life-style are being worked out individually in separate families, the women's activities as a collective group represent a sharp and sudden challenge to the dominance of men in working class culture. The taking over by women of areas of public space in the centre of pit villages has brought them to the very heart of the village's social and political activities. They have created the kitchens for all to use; but for the women this space represents the carving out of their legitimate right to a place in the centre of the community and a recognition that all women should be seen, heard and respected for their contributions to the very life and soul of that community. In this way, women in mining communities have also been fighting to give *all* women a voice in a society where traditionally women are silenced by men.

From the very start of the strike, women realised the importance of the struggle and learned very quickly what they needed to do in order to sustain and win that struggle. In their recent booklet about women's involvement in the strike, Barnsley Women Against Pit Closures point out that traditionally women married to miners are portrayed as being against strikes.* Their main concern is held to be a financial one—and as a result they are seen as pushing the men back to work. This is, in fact, an extension of the myth that women are, at best, 'apolitical', and at worse, a very conservative element in the working class. There is no doubt that the state relied on the women encouraging men not to strike in order to defeat the NUM more quickly.

In reality, of course, the exact opposite is true: women in some cases have been responsible for bringing their husbands out on strike and financial commitments were seen as being of secondary importance to the struggle being fought:

> My husband was on strike from day one. We discussed it and there was never any doubt in my mind.

> My husband came out on strike, then went back to work for a week. Then he came out again and has been out ever since. My young son is ill and we had to keep going to the hospital with him and I was worried about the money. At first I thought it would be a waste of time him coming out on strike, but I never forced him to go in. Then I realised if he didn't go on strike, there'd be no jobs and he'd be out of work.

Barnsley Women Against Pit Closures, 1984, published by the women themselves.

My husband went along with the vote to work, becuase I think he was worried about the money. I could see he wasn't happy going through picket lines. I said, if you want to come out then I'll back you to the hilt. If I hadn't said that he wouldn't have come out.

My husband was worried about maintenance payments for his ex-wife and didn't come out at first. He's a very strong union man and he crossed a picket line twice and he felt sick about it. One night we went out for a drink and he spent the whole evening talking to a scab. I was very annoyed about it and we had a big row. For 2 or 3 weeks he just went in on odd days. I said to him—you're either on strike or you're not, and he came out for good then.

There was never any doubt in the women's minds that their first step was to give the men practical support and help. For most women, this was generally on the picket line at first, despite some resistance from the men themselves:

The first day that my husband was on strike, he wanted to go on the picket line at his pit. So did I. He said he'd drag me into a police car himself rather than let me go picketing. I did anyway, and met other women who I knew. The men say that violence on the picket line is a problem, and that's why we shouldn't go. But we won't let them dictate to us. Now they say—what you're doing is fantastic and it's keeping us together.

My husband told me that some of the women were going picketing, so I went up with my friend. The men reckoned we did a better job with turning the cars back than the men.

Women have a different effect on the picket line because the men going in know the women don't have any money and they feel guilty, especially when they see our kids on the picket line as well. With men (pickets) the scabs just get angry.

From our house at night we could hear pickets shouting; it sounded exciting and we wanted to get involved. You just couldn't help yourself.

Despite threats, violence and intimidation by the police on picket lines from day one of the strike, the women did not hold back and refused to allow themselves to be intimidated. Neither would they allow the police to fit them into the traditional women's passive role of being the quiet, gentle woman who should really be at home and not out in the rough and tumble of the real world:

> At first the police talked to us on the picket line and were very
> nice, but that was probably only to get information out of us.
> One policeman tried to talk to me—he said I should be ashamed
> of myself.

The initial view of the police was, presumably, one of
ambivalence: not knowing how to take the women, but certainly not
taking them seriously. However, when they saw the strength of the
women's resolve, their views changed and they soon began to treat
women violently and with contempt. In Shirebrook, Derbyshire, the
women claim they are 'flashed' at by police officers who expose
themselves as the vans escort scabs through the picket line. This is
not something that the police have been doing to the men, and
expresses the contempt the police feel for women not conforming to
their notion of the 'ideal' woman.

For women, being directly involved in violent situations has a
very different significance than it has for men, and it is important
to realise the extent of the women's bravery on picket lines. Men are
brought up to believe that they should be strong, aggressive,
'masculine' and ultimately protective of women who, on the other
hand, are taught to be weak and reliant on men's superior strength.
Violence plays a part in men's lives from an early age: in games they
play or toys they are given; while for women violent behaviour is
seen as unacceptable. Men are steeped in a culture of fighting and
learn skills both to attack others and protect themselves. Women are
taught to fear violence, but not how to defend ourselves, and indeed
this is an important way of controlling women, both inside and outside
the home: we must keep off the streets at night; we mustn't go out
alone and so on. This threat is a way of confining women to the home
and preventing us from carrying out an independent existence,
although of course for many women the home can be more violent
than the streets.

However, the women from mining communities were completely
undaunted by the threat of violence, and forced themselves to learn
quickly how to react to the police. They were fearless in their pursuit
of the right to picket; one woman described her arrest:

> I never really thought about the police before: I just had an image
> of the traditional British bobby. Now after all I've seen, I think
> they're Maggie Thatcher's paid thugs. I was arrested at a women's
> picket at Calverton colliery. We were standing on a corner and
> the police tried to move us on. We said no, and we started

shouting and singing. Then more police came and they surrounded us and pushed and kneed us into the middle of the road. I got pushed over a small fence and fell down. I got arrested for obstruction.The police questioned me about the soup kitchen— who runs it, how much money have we got. They asked me for names of NUM officials and who worked at the soup kitchen. They said that they knew me and Sandra went out picketing. They said they knew all about me. They were trying to frighten me but I wasn't frightened.The police were really abusive and kept making jokes about cunts and things, but I just ignored them. I won't have anything to do with the police now, I feel so strongly about it. They're not even human, half of them.

This was often the women's first contact with the police at all, and they found themselves in direct conflict. All of the women's views on the police were changed and, as a consequence, their ideas about the strike. They saw how the police were being used by the Government to break the strike, protect the scabs, and the way in which the police themselves made the law on the picket lines. For the women, picketing broadened the strike out beyond the immediacy of their attempts to stop scabs getting into work. It brought them into direct confrontation with the forces of the state. It focussed their ideas, through struggle, on the manipulations of the Government and the NCB, designed to break the NUM and destroy their communities. They also saw the strength of the media as the reality of their lives was trampled on and destroyed by propaganda which bore no relation to the daily battles on picket lines and their struggles to survive:

Before the strike I'd never had any problems with the police and didn't think about them very much—I just thought they did their job alright. Now I wouldn't give tuppence a bucket for them.

Before the strike I had respect for the police. I thought the police were there to help the people. I thought they were totally unbiased and I was proved wrong. On the picket line they are bastards— they are very hostile. At the beginning they were friendly. We saw what they were doing to the pickets yet the scabs can do what they want.

I don't speak to the police now. I think they're bigger scabs than the men going into work. They've made it clear that they're there to get the scabs into work and not to protect us.

The women have expressed grave doubts about the policing of their communities ever returning to 'normal' after the strike. Having

seen miners and their families beaten on picket lines; arrested indis-
criminantly; experienced violence themselves and seen intimidation
in their own homes and communities, they have seen the 'strong arm
of the state'; they have struggled against it and will not accept it's
potentially brutalising effects. This represents the women's changing
consciousness about the nature of policing, and it can be seen as a
positive and healthy disrespect for the police and the whole legal
process. The police are never going to protect *them*, only attempt to
contain them; their job will be made doubly difficult now.

For many women the crucial issues of the unaccountability of
the police had been raised, and the way in which the police are not
independent but are acting in a politically biased way against striking
miners:

> I don't think the police are independent. How can they detach
> themselves? It seems to me it's the beginnings of fascism—and
> the way they treat black people too—all the powers they've got.
> Even the powers they haven't got—they play a lot on people's
> ignorance of the law. I think to some degree they've learned a
> lot from Northern Ireland.

> I'd like to see the police made more accountable. Like the com-
> plaints system—it should be dealt with like a normal criminal case.
> They shouldn't be left to deal with it themselves. I think they
> should dismantle the riot force. If you have a good police force,
> which is under control, the people wouldn't need to riot. I think
> more control should be given to the local Councils.

> The police here are doing the same sort of things they've been
> doing in London, but we didn't realise it before. The police are
> only doing what Thatcher's told them to do, and no-one will
> respect them anymore. I think the Police Bill's absolutely
> atrocious. You're going to be frightened to move. They've been
> doing body searches of the Greenham Common women, and
> they'd do that even more. The police are here to do a job for
> the people and not treat us like this.

> I hadn't realised that the police were like this, or that there was
> a riot force. Changes are going to have to be made. The police
> are used more and more against sections of the working class.
> More people are realising and the people will have to insist that
> something's done about it.

Picketing has been of primary importance in establishing women's
role in the strike. However, it has only been one part of women's

activities. Providing food and raising money was clearly essential for the strike to continue at all. Women's solid commitment to the strike was quickly translated into activities to keep families fed and enable them to have the basic necessities of living.

Most of the women's families were surviving on very small amounts of money, with help from friends and relatives, and the donations provided by people from all over the country. This also enabled the women to organise food parcels and soup kitchens. Pressure was put on families from an early stage by the DHSS who based all payments to miners on the 'assumption' that they were all receiving £15 a week in strike pay from the NUM. The men have never received anything of the kind and are lucky even to get travelling expenses for going out picketing. Many of them get a maximum of £1 for petrol no matter how far they are going to picket. The hardship caused by the strike was exacerbated by the overtime ban which had been in operation since November 1983, and some of the families had been struggling before the strike began. It was clear that commonly-held views about miners' bulging wage-packets were untrue; any job that relies on working regular overtime to make a living wage is obviously paying insufficient money:

> The overtime was a problem not so much in itself, but it was never knowing whether there'd be a full week's wages in his pay packet. It made a real difference to his weekly wage, and so the overtime ban used to get me a bit. Now I think about it, it's not a big wage. He can't work on the face any more because of his angina. Without overtime he used to bring home £80 a week.

> During the strike, money's been really bad. I get £15 a week for me, my husband and the lad, plus £2 a day family allowance. My sister gives us breakfast and dinner. Since the soup kitchen opened, we go to that. I haven't been out for the evening since New Year's Eve.

It is important to realise that women's creation of soup kitchens and the provision of food is not 'merely' an extension of their role as housewives. Within their organisation, domestic tasks once carried out individually have now been collectivised. Women are not cooking individual meals at home for their families, but are spending their days preparing, cooking and serving meals for the community, in addition to speaking at meetings and raising money. Childcare has also become communal and removed from the 'private' sphere of the home:

> All the children are here but any woman can shout at any other woman's kids if they do something wrong and no offence is taken.

This might have been one of the reasons we could have fallen out, and so it's good that it's working.

Bringing the servicing of individual men in the home out into the public arena has made women understand more clearly their own roles as housewives and how women's lives are privatized:

> Being here, I see what women have to put up with. We're just unpaid bottle washers and cooks. I won't go back to just staying in the home after the strike—it'll be different. I feel as though I want something totally separate from the home.

It was on the picket line that women met together and planned future actions to raise funds and start the soup kitchens:

> I went on the picket line straight after my husband came out on strike. One of my friends and several other women I knew were there and said they were glad I'd come. My friend and I decided that we ought to try and get something else together and a couple of women suggested opening a centre of some sort. We wanted to use the local youth club but we had a real battle to get it, and in the end we had to have a sit-in. The Labour Party members and a scab tried to keep us out of the club and in the end the Pit Manager offered us a hall, which is good for our needs. We went out speaking and got support, food and money. We brought in kitchen equipment from home and started a soup kitchen, and doing food parcels.

> I'd been out picketing twice and then I started going up to the soup kitchen. They weren't really properly organised—they'd started with just £9. A few days after I'd started going there, we decided to set up a Committee and elect a Chairman. I'd been on the picket line that day and had a battle with the police which they'd seen. Someone suggested my name and all the hands shot up and I was in. I said then that I wasn't sure what I was letting myself in for.

The soup kitchens are all organised on similar lines, and in most of them the tasks are shared out so that some women do most of the public speaking, some do the driving etc. They elect Committees of Chair, Secretary, Treasurer and so on, and have regular weekly meetings to discuss their work, and organise fund-raising events and holidays for the children. The soup kitchens provide hundreds of meals every day with food and money donated from trade unions, individuals and local businesses. Some of the local businesses and restaurants which donate food are genuinely sympathetic; others know they must show support in order to regain custom when the strike is over. Local traders who have shown hositlity to the dispute are boycotted.

The women go to the soup kitchens at about 8.30 am and food is prepared for dinner which is served from 12.00 onwards. Some kitchens also provide breakfast. Because they've had to get the kitchens ready very quickly they often don't have the equipment or facilities they need: one kitchen uses a baby's bath to do the washing up. Since many of the halls are used for other purposes, the women have to put everything away and out of sight at the end of the day and bring it all out again the following morning. The men and some families are served with a 2 course meal, a cup of tea and endless supplies of bread and butter. The number of men using the soup kitchens varies—from about 180 to 350 a day. The atmoshpere is always hectic but they are run on a tight schedule and always serve meals on time:

> There are about 20 women involved in our soup kitchen. Now we've got it running properly we get about £500-600 a week and food in donations. We also make up food parcels—they take a lot of money.

> I normally get up at 5.00 am and take my husband down to the strike centre. If I have a lot to do I stop up, but sometimes I go back to bed till 7.30. I get down to the soup kitchen at 8.30 and leave at about 2.30-3.00. It's hard work but I enjoy it. I then go to work at 4.30 and get home at 10.00.

For the whole community, the soup kitchens are more than just places where miners and their families are fed, essential though that is. They are places to meet, discuss the strike, organise other activities and share problems. The kitchen keep up morale, particularly for those men who can't go picketing because of their bail conditions. Being at home can mean being isolated and dejected.

The response of the women's families and friends to their activities has been varied. For some it has caused bitterness and splits:

> When I was at work I had a lot of friends who were my workmates, but then the strike started and most of their husbands were working. The women used to go on about what they spent their money on and how they thought our husbands were mad to be on strike. It was made impossible for us—the women didn't talk to us and it made it very difficult. I wanted to work full-time on the strike anyway, so I left.

> My husband's mother has cut him off since the strike began. She

watched Orgreave on the TV and said after that she only has 2 sons, not 3. She sees it all as hooliganism. All of his family are against it—they don't understand the implications.

Women sometimes felt that the tensions created living in communities with working miners would go on well after the strike:

All of Ollerton is tense with what's happening. It's like a time-bomb really. I think the slightest thing could cause trouble. I'd like to think that everything will be OK after the strike, but the scars are going to go very, very deep. My husband says he'll never work with a scab, and you can't blame him.

Women's husbands, too have responded in different ways to their activities. The new voice that women have found during the strike has taken men by surprise, making them sit up and take notice. Initially, some men responded with hostility, some with contempt and many with indifference. But the women proved themselves so successfully that the men were forced to recognise the importance of their activities:

I don't think the lads up there (at the strike centre) were behind us at first. When we wanted to set up the soup kitchen, we went to the local Miners' Welfare club and all the lads said was 'Hey up, what thee want here?' They said there was no way they could let us have it for a kitchen. A couple of the women's husbands who were in there started shouting things like—'I want my dinner ready when I come home' and they were just sitting there boozing.

I don't know whether or not now they're fully behind us. I think they might have been frightened that the men wouldn't go picketing (if they came to the soup kitchen) or that we'd start and then not have enough money to carry on. But there is more support now—they're realising what a good thing it is.

Women had on occasion been turned away from meetings and denied seats on coaches to demonstrations. The latter is now rare, as women's commitment has been demonstrated and the men are beginning to understand the central role that women are playing in keeping the strike going. However, the problem still remains that women are excluded from all decision-making processes in the NUM. Women are organising fairly independently of the men and although this reflects a positive choice to work with women, the extent of their separation is also partly as a result of the attitudes of individual men, and branch officials, and the structure of the NUM itself.

Women have not been actively invited to take part in any union meetings or discussions despite their crucial involvement. Men are incredibly reluctant to open their doors that far to women, and hand out any of their power as officials, as trade unionists or simply as men. Women need to be strong in their demands for a share in that power, and men will have to learn to provide it.

The strike has resulted in many changes in women's lives, and in their consciouness. It has shown them their strenghts and capabilities; it has extended their lives beyond the home where traditionally women are confined. Their political consciousness has developed radically. Quite clearly the women were not as uninterested in 'politics' before the strike as they claim, since they became involved so quickly and organised so effectively. In fact, the strike has been for the women the spark for activating their political ideals, and extending their view of the 'political':

> Sometimes it frightens me a bit because I didn't realise I was so strong in what I felt and I didn't realise I'd be able to survive all this intimidation. What it's done is made me feel strong and the more kicks we get, the more I want to fight back.

> Before the strike, I wasn't involved in politics. It's changed me—now I know a lot more people and it's made me more aware of things. The Greenham Common women came to see us. I'd supported them before, but now I support them even more. I hadn't considered what they were doing as political, now I do.

It was the picket line that was the starting point for the women's organisation, and this worked in two ways. It allowed them to meet other women, talk about the strike, and what they could do. But it also allowed them a taste of their own political strength—they were standing on the picket lines *as women,* not as their husband's wives, not playing second fiddle; and they were immediately having a direct effect on the strike, with their success at stopping men going into work.

The women went from strength to strength. Throughout the course of the interviews, women would often state that they didn't really have any particular skills or knowledge, whilst sitting in the midst of a bustling organisation they themselves had created! The women drew on their own organising abilities to start the soup kitchens and the fund-raising; and what they didn't know they were prepared to learn: whether it was keeping books as the treasurer of a committee, speaking at public meetings or planning how many potatoes to peel for 300 dinners:

> I hadn't been involved in anything directly political before. I've been out fund-raising and on the picket-lines during the strike

with the women. I work in the soup kitchen and I'm the Treasurer.
I've had to learn as I go along.

I've only spoken at one meeting about the strike and I was really
nervous, but I'd do it again if I was pushed. When men start talking at meetings I sit back—I know it's wrong to do that , but
it's with not knowing things about trade unionism or politics. With
women I feel able to talk a lot more easily.

This sort of political activity is not like any other. One of the (many)
myths about women workers is that they don't take part in trade union
activities and by inference, are not interested in 'politics'. Apart from
the fact that women in their thousands are heavily involved in political
organisations of all kinds, the women's support groups show all trade
unions and political parties the narrowness of what they consider to
be 'politics'.

At first I was frightened to speak at meetings, but now I've spoken
to a rally at Barnsley with 10,000 people. Before the strike I didn't
get involved in politics. After we'd started to speak at meetings,
people used to come up to us and ask us to get involved in their
political parties. I said no, because I was Labour. I said I wasn't
involved in politics, and people said to me, but you're a socialist.
It frightened me at first because I didn't know I was talking politics
until someone told me. I never realised I was politically involved
until this. Now it cuts deep and I feel I have to voice my opinion
about Thatcher's dictatorship. We've met so many people and
we need never be in trouble again. Sometimes I think it's a dream.
It's unbelievable.

Another aspect of some women's non-involvement in traditional
political organisations is their incredibly bureaucratic structures. Trade
unions in particular, organise in very complex ways which remain
shrouded in a mystique of jargon. Men can learn about the union while
they're going for a drink with their work-mates, and get involved that
way. There's little training for women in trade unionism, no
encouragement to take part and therefore exclusion:

I've been in the Communist Party for 3 years. I went to the
meetings and I didn't get too involved. I'm still learning, and
I don't know a lot. I keep my feelings to myself because I feel
like I can't say some things in case they're things I shouldn't be
saying. I haven't got much confidence but it's getting better.

Men use to exclude us—they all thought we should be at home
and now men think we can do all sorts of things. They've found

that women can raise money better than men.

Many political organisations exclude women. This may be a fairly direct exclusion, or a lack of encouragement, but it's also related to other factors: a lack of understanding of women or a commitment to the aspects of working life which affect women. Quite simply, women get the worst and the lowest paid jobs but how many trade unionists take these issues up unless the women themselves take the initiative? Women feel that trade unions and other political organisations don't really have anything to do with them; and most of them don't:

> I work in a clothing factory, 5 days a week and 5½ hours a day on evening shifts. I've always liked working. I think women are discriminated against in jobs. When I applied for this job they asked me if I had children. They don't care now, as long as I can fulfill my hours. They (the employers) say that they get more work out of married women than out of the younger ones. They just do that to keep friction going between the two groups. I'm in the T.& G. but it's a poor union. You don't pay union dues in the first month of work in case you're not kept on. It's a few people who run the union and you don't get to know what's going on.

For the women, organising the soup kitchens and the fund-raising did not require the difficult process of being accepted by and working within a ready-made male structure. The women created a basic structure for themselves and, because all the women have taken part in this, individuals are able to change it if they wish. This kind of political organisation, born out of necessity and from women's own resources, has nothing to do with the traditional male politics which had previously touched women's lives. It remains a tribute to women's strength and political commitments.

The effect of the women's activities caused an immediate change in their domestic circumstances and a partial reversal of roles within the family; the men have had to accept that while their wives are out at meetings, working in soup kitchens and organising fund-raising activities, they have to stay at home. As a result, men have had to face up to the reality of domestic responsibilities: housework, cooking and childcare, probably for the first time in their lives at such a level. It is possible to detect an underlying current of resentment from some of the men on an individual basis, to the upheaval caused by their wife's removal from the domestic scene. This is rarely stated overtly; and in fact many men express their appreciation wholeheartely.

It is likely that the men hope all will return to 'normal' after the strike within their families, but for the women there will no returning to the rigid separation of roles within the family, which is particularly marked within the working class, though is a feature of all families:

> My husband is deep down amazed at what I'm doing. At first he said he wouldn't come to meetings where I was speaking, but now he will. He'll never say to me—you're doing a good job, but he'll tell other people. I think he feels a bit left out but it won't hurt him.

Women want to continue their political activities well beyond the boundaries of the strike. For some, this is a matter of working on local issues; for others going to Greenham Common and a host of other activities. The women were very definite about wanting to change things and saw more clearly the way to do it. They were very critical of male ways of organising politically and felt strongly that they wanted to work with women:

> There's always trouble working with men! There are men involved in the soup kitchen, but at first it was just women and we enjoyed that. After the strike, I think I'll probably work just with women. Men feel threatened by us. I think they appreciate what we're doing but they're a bit resentful.

> I'd rather work with women than with men, because I get on better with women. I don't feel comfortable with men, especially ones I don't know. I never know how to take them and I don't like their attitudes much. There's one lad at work who's a real pain— he's always making comments and doing stupid things. I think they're all a pain, men. I want to carry on working in a women's group. I'd like to do some work on apartheid, or CND. There's no doubt theat women have got the power and ability to organise. It's been proved with what's happening now. It's just a matter of time before all women realise the potential they've got.

> There are some men on the committee. I'm not prejudiced against men but I think there's a place for women to work together because it adds to their strength. For so long I think women have been seen as second class citizens. I feel now that I want to go out and fight with women to get them a better place in society so that we can have an equal place. Women are just as capable to get to the top. If you don't fight you won't get anywhere.

Women had gained strength from other women's political struggles throughout the country, and particularly Greenham Common. Now they wanted to share their experiences with all the women who had helped them during the strike, and support them in their organisations:

> I've always known that women had organised at Greenham Common and I've admired them, but I never thought I'd have the gumption to join them. Now I'd love to stand with them in their struggle. One thing that's really impressed me is the amount of support we're getting from women all over the country.

> I think the Greenham Common women have helped us a lot to see how strong we are. I like Greenham because it's just women; I'd love to go down there.

The links made with other women's organisations are strong; the Greenham women have made many visits to strike-bound areas and the women from mining communities are making trips down there. For other women, their energies are directed towards the Labour Party; however, the main opinion of this was very low and the women wanted to form a Women's section to organise within it. In one small village in Nottinghamshire, 28 women had joined a reactionary local Labour Party Branch en masse, determined to force a radical change:

> There's not enough women involved in the Labour Party. Men have kept women out and not taken up women's issues. I think we could have some influence and there's enough of us. We weren't very pleased at the first meeting we went to—they were't for any changes and they weren't happy to see us.

> When it's all over, we'll meet once a week and form a Labour Party Women's Section. At the moment I think the Labour Party's a load of rubbish, but it's important instead of just sitting back to try and change it. All of the women can meet and discuss what the Labour Party's about and other issues—welfare rights, policing. The majority of women here feel the same as I do—they can discuss things in a group, but outside of that it's different. They feel just as strong, but find it difficult to talk about things in groups with men.

Political struggle always involves gains and defeats, and the experiences of both women and men during the strike have sometimes been very painful. For the women, though, the positive aspects of the dramatic changes in their lives resulting from the strike are over-whelming. Women's activities have turned the communities on their heads and *new* communities have been created which for the first time give women the political space to organise for themselves. Women have established themselves as a powerful political force for the

present and for the future, a force which is fired with the enthusiasm
born out of injustice and which, now created, will never be defeated:

In my opinion, Thatcher's done me a favour. It's all backfired
on her because of the women. She thought when this started that
the women would be pushing the men back to work. The women
are behind the men and are backing them—they're 100%, the
women. The women are there now, it's opened our eyes. They're
not going to sit back and wash pots—they're going to get out and
fight. It's the best thing that's ever happened.

References

1. Applegate, Rex. 'Riot Control, Material and Techniques'; London. Stackpole Books 1969. Quoted by Jill Box-Granger in 'The State and Repression: Law and Order in a Capitalist Society'.
2. WEA/Cobden Trust. 'The Police', August 1974. Quoted by Jill Box-Granger.
3. Report of the Commissioner of the Police for the Metropolis. 1965.
4. T.V. Eye programme 3rd May 1984.
5. This paragraph is taken in great part from an article by T. Bunyan and L. Bridges in 'Journal of Law and Society'. Vol.X No.1 Summer 1983.

Appendices

Appendix 1
Special Patrol Groups in the UK
State Research Bulletin (Vol 2) No. 13/August September 1979.

Force	Name of Group	Date established	Size*
England			
Avon & Somerset	Task Force	1973	55
City of London	Special Operations Group	1977	16
Derbyshire	Special Operations Unit	1970	11 (1976)
Essex	Force Support Unit	1973	32 (1974)
Gloucestershire	Task Force	—	—
Greater Manchester	Tactical Aid Group	1976	70 (1977)
Hertfordshire	Tactical Patrol Group	1965	28
Humberside	Support Group	1978	47
Lancashire	Police Support Unit	1978	—
Merseyside	Task Force	1974 — 76	68 (1975)
Metropolitan Police	Operational Support Division	1976	—
	Special Patrol Group	1965	204
Norfolk	Police Support Unit	—	—
Northumbria	Special Patrol Group	1974	46 (1977)
North Yorkshire	Task Force	1974	—
Nottinghamshire	Special Operations Unit	—	34 (1976)
Staffordshire	Force Support Unit	1976	23
Thames Valley	Support Group	1969	41
West Midlands	Special Patrol Group	1970	85
West Yorkshire	Task Forces	1974	—
Wales			
Gwent	Support Group	1972	20
South Wales	Special Patrol Group	1975	54
Scotland			
Central Scotland	Support Group	—	—
Strathclyde	Support Units	1973	145 (1975)
N. Ireland			
Royal Ulster Constabulary	Special Patrol Group	1970	368

* 1978 figures except where stated

Appendix 2
Statement given to Gerald Kaufman by the Yorkshire NUM for his information in the Debate in the Commons.

1. *Detention of Vehicles*
Vehicles are being impounded on all major and most minor roads going into Nottingham from South Yorkshire and Derbyshire. Keys are being seized and men made to walk home. In some cases vehicles are being damaged where men are asking to be allowed to continue and insisting on their rights to use the highway e.g. F S—Maltby Branch.

2. No explanation is being given as to why vehicles are being impounded. Drivers are also being arrested and taken into custody. Those who are, seem to be held on the charge of obstructing a Police Officer in the execution of his duty.

3. Questioning of detained men is taking a political line. A number of men are being interviewed by plainclothes Officers and questioned about political affiliation and membership. The questioning appears to have nothing to do with the enquiry, which in the main should confine itself to the minor charges being brought against the man e.g. obstruction. There are also instances of interviewing officers having background information on the political activity of detainees—e.g. P., D., S., and J.—Woolley Branch, held at Mansfield Police Station on 27.3.84. Also R., Darfield Branch, held at Hucknall Police Station on 26.3.84.

4. There seems to be evidence that Officers are searching through belongings held at the Station whilst the men are in custody e.g. R., Darfield Branch.

5. Aggressive police activity is also leading to complaints from men travelling home and/or being present on a picket line. On 27.3.84 at Newstead Colliery D.—Woolley Branch, suffered the effects of an angina attack and needed medical treatment. The Police Officer refused him access to the Medical Centre at the Colliery, despite requests from local Union Officials in Nottingham and also from the pit Manager. B.— Newstead Branch Secretary and the nursing sister at the Colliery can give evidence to this effect. He was only allowed into the Medical Centre after repeated requests from the pit Manager.

6. On 29.3.84 we received a complaint from B.—Bentley Branch, that he had been arrested outside a pub near Clipstone, Nottingham, where he had stopped having been turned back by the Police outside the village. He had gone to the pub to use the telephone. He was ordered out by the Police Officers and on trying to leave was arrested and charged with a breach of the peace. On making a formal complaint at the Police Station he was subsequently released. It would appear that this arrest had been carried out by an outside Police Force i.e. Hertfordshire. Mark Herbert has a full statement on this matter.

7. Aggressive police activities appear to have led to the unfortunate incident at Junction 30 on the M1 on the night of 27/28th March. In this incident, one of our members, R. of Manvers, appears to have been quite badly beaten by a group of four Police Officers, equipped with full riot gear. Men are now being detained in relation to this incident and being taken from their homes in South Yorkshire. To date we have knowledge of eight arrests relating to this particular incident.

On 29.3.84 in the early hours we were informed that a member of the Barrow Branch had been detained, fingerprinted and photographed and subsequently released. No charges had been made and he could not get an assurance from the Police Officer that the prints and photographs would be destroyed, being told they would be destroyed as and when the Police decided it was necessary. (name is in log book in Strike Centre).

Appendix 3
A. Content of letter from Tony Smythe of NCCL to James Callaghan Home Secretary at the time of the anti-Vietnamese war demonstrations in 1968.

9. We have received many complaints from demonstrators and members of the public who had no connection with the demonstration about the searching of vehicles in and around London, including the motorways, on the 26th and 27th October. These indiscriminate and widespread searches appear to us to represent the major defect in the police handling of the situation. We would like to know:

a. what statutory authorities were used to conduct these searches.
b. how many vehicles were searched and how many individuals were involved.
c. how many prosecutions resulted. (We realise that some cases may not have been dealt with yet by the courts but we would like to see the final figures.)
d. what instructions were given to police officers on the searching of vehicles; what were they looking for, and what criteria were involved in chosing which vehicles to stop.
e. is it true that provincial police forces brought pressure on coach companies not to bring parties of demonstrators to London that weekend. (The allegation has been made in Hull and in Preston, Lancs). On what statutory powers could these approaches have been based.

10. You will see from some reports that disquiet was expressed about

the activities of individuals thought to be plain-clothes police officers. It is confusing for the public if men who are not directly identifiable as police officers intervene in the course of a demonstration, for example, by making an arrest. We would therefore like to know how many plain-clothes officers were on duty and whether or not their brief was restricted to observations rather than direct involvement.

11. One issue remains which causes us some concern. Four NCCL observers were harassed when identified. The harrassment included anything from tearing their notebooks to direct assault. We would hope that the allegations made by Mr Saunders (report no.44) could be investigated under the 1964 Police Act complaints procedure.

Mr Saunders, like some other observers, had identified himself visibly as an NCCL observer by pinning the blue badge we issued and a credential card to his coat. In fact we had intended the badge to be used to enable observers to identify each other and had expected them to retain the cards in their pockets. We protest most strongly about the way in which Mr Saunders was handled and do not consider that visible identification should have provoked such a reaction on the part of the police officers.

The case of Mr Haedley Griggs (report no.48) is even more serious and we must refrain from commenting further as we understand Mr Griggs will be taking civil procedures against the Commissioner of Metropolitan Police.

In future we would appreciate an instruction to police officers assuring them that observers do not attend demonstrations to make the work of the police more difficult but to protect the rights of assembly and free speech and the rights of all individuals including police officers who are involved in such occasions. Attacks on NCCL observers are most serious although to get the matter into proper perspective only four observers suffered this treatment out of 200 and that by constrast many observers found individual police officers most co-operative.

B. Commons questions and answers on this subject.

Hansard 28th November 1968, written answers.

Demonstration, Central London (Police Searches)

Mr. Peter M Jackson asked the Secretary of State for the Home Department what criteria were used by the Metropolitan Police on Sunday, 27th October to search selected vehicles at the junction of the M1 and A5.

Mr Callaghan: Judgement, based on experience, of the likelihood that offensive weapons were being carried.

Mr Peter M. Jackson asked the Secretary of State for the Home Department how many offensive weapons were found by the Metropolitan Police on vehicles travelling to London on Sunday, 27th October; how many persons were charged; and how many convicted.

Sir Ian Orr-Ewing asked the Secretary of State for the Home Department if he will publish a list of offensive weapons taken from those who took part, or intended to take part, in the demonstration in London on 27th October.

Mr. Callaghan: The number of offensive weapons seized is not available. The following items were found in the possession of those arrested on 27th October for possessing an offensive weapon:

> Bags of flour; bottles; dyes, firework, gas pistols and ammunition; knives; marbles; razor blades; sticks; weighted chain.

Five persons were arrested as a result of articles found in vehicles. Two of them were convicted.

Mr. Peter M. Jackson asked the Secretary of State for the Home Department under what authority vehicles were stopped by the Metropolitan Police at Toddington Service Station on the M1 on Sunday, 27th October.

Mr Callaghan: Toddington Service Station is in the area of the Bedfordshire and Luton police force. The Chief Constable informs me that members of his force were acting in pursuance of their duty to prevent breaches of the peace.

Mr. Peter M Jackson asked the Secretary of State for the Home Department what were the grounds on which the Metropolitan Police stopped and searched the hon. Member for High Peak and his wife at 12.25 p.m. on Sunday, 27th October.

Mr Callaghan: The Commissioner of Police has not been able to trace the incident involving my hon. friend. The Metropolitan and other police forces stopped several hundred vehicles on 27th October to search for offensive weapons which might be used to cause a breach of the peace at the demonstration arranged for that day.

Appendix 4
'Out of Court' Article from the Guardian April 4th, 1984. by Richard de Friend and Ian Griggs-Spall

Comment on the nationally coordinated anti-picketing operation mounted by the police has tended to concentrate on its legality. It has clearly had a serious impact on fundamental civil liberties and, notwithstanding assurances to the contrary given by the Attorney General and the Home Secretary, and by some senior police officers, the operation's basis 'in' law is indeed dubious. After all, in Hubbard v Pitt (1976) Lord Denning stated that ''picketing is lawful so long as it is done merely to obtain or communicate information or peacefully to persuade''. And in

Piddington v Bates (1960) Lord Parker, whilst acknowledging that a police officer could place restrictions on picketing to prevent a breach of the peace, nevertheless made clear that "there must exist proved facts from which a constable could reasonably anticipate such a breach". He further emphasised that "it is not enough that his contemplation is that there is a remote possibility; there must be a real possibility" of a breach materialising.

Applied to the present dispute, these dicta could justify preventative measures being adopted around pits themselves, but hardly action taken at the Kent or even at the Nottinghamshire County borders. We certainly had these considerations in mind when, on Sunday, 18 March we were informed by local NUM officials that throughout that day a number of their members had been stopped at the Dartford Tunnel and threatened with arrest if they proceeded further. We contacted Kent Police Headquarters at Maidstone to enquire about the legal bases for that action, and later we agreed to accompany two Kent miners on a trip from Deal to a pit in Warwickshire where they intended to mount a picket in time for Monday morning's shift.'

However, our experiences led us to conclude that the significance of this national operation derives not from whether it was lawful and whether the Kent NUM might eventually have succeeded in its action against the County's Chief Constable, but rather from the fact that police officers with whom we had contact seemed largely—and confidently— indifferent to their apparent lack of legal powers.

Thus Kent Police Headquarters did not at first deny that miners had been threatened with arrest at the Dartford Tunnel, but simply claimed that such action was based upon the secondary picketing legislation. Only after being told that this was a matter of civil not criminal law did an officer subsequently inform us that there had in fact been no threats of arrest, and that police at the Tunnel had merely advised those they identified as NUM pickets that they would waste petrol if they drove on. We were ourselves offered such advice by an inspector when we reached the Dartford Tunnel shortly before midnight. However he also invoked the law on secondary picketing when we challenged his authority for stopping and interrogating us, and then conjured up the Road Traffic Act to justify inspecting and recording the details of our driver's licence.

At about 4.00 am we were stopped by a road block, one mile from the Dawmill pit in Warwickshire, and were told we could not proceed any further except on foot. Our car was searched by an officer who on being asked for his authority, said 'I'm not getting into that. I have my orders and that's enough.' Finally we were confronted by a three deep line of police stretched across the road about 150 yards from the pit entrance itself. In front of the line were four Kent miners who had been held there for six hours and prevented from mounting what, in the circumstances, could only have been a limited and peaceful picket at the colliery gates.

When we pointed this out to the officer in charge, he simply referred us to what he termed the 'prohibition' against secondary picketing and although he eventually conceded that this was indeed a civil matter over which the police had no jurisdiction, he nevertheless categorically refused on at least 10 further occasions to allow the miners through to the gates. Eventually, having been ordered to do so by his Deputy Chief Constable, he did allow a maximum of six 'official pickets' (a term he never defined) through the line but only after each of them had had their names and credentials thoroughly checked and recorded, and only on condition that they made no attempt actually to speak to anyone going into work.

The police then, did not seriously maintain that their actions had much—if any—basis in law and, interestingly, never once mentioned their common law 'preventative' powers to which so much reference has been made by politicians and in the press. Rather, we suspect they knew that being part of the most extensive police operation since the General Strike, organised on a national basis and sanctioned, as it must have been, by the Home Secretary and the Cabinet, would immunise them from any effective legal or political challenge. Authority for individual actions and decisions stemmed from the bureaucratic chain of command itself, and legitimacy from whatever popular perceptions a generally sympathetic media could be relied upon to create or exploit. For these reasons alone this operation must be seen as more characteristic of an, albeit efficient and developed, police state than of one founded upon the rule of law.

Richard de Friend and Ian Grigg-Spall are lecturers in law at the University of Kent.

Appendix 5
A letter from the Doncaster Central Branch of the NUR to its London Headquarters; given to the South Yorkshire Police Authority Enquiry by the NUR.

re: Mineworkers Dispute: Police Action

With reference to the above, this Branch reports the following occurence.

Tuesday 3rd. April, 1984 at 08.15 hours, a British Rail Road Vehicle of the Signal & Telegraph Department Doncaster conveying some eight of our members to a site of work were travelling southbound from Doncaster and were stopped by a Police Road Block at Bawtry where the boundary between South Yorkshire and Nottinghamshire meets. They were questioned as to who they were, and to where they were travelling, and means of identification were demanded.

This Branch is very concerned that our members who were merely going about their legitimate business are being subjected to his high handed action by the Police.

The Branch therefore requests that you make the strongest possible protest to the appropriate authorities, and demand that persons legitimate freedom of movements be respected at all times, and that such actions cannot be tolerated in a democratic society.

Appendix 6
Photograph of the police taking a polaroid picture of an arrested man. The Guardian April 21st 1984.

POLICE hold a man while another officer photographs him, during the eviction of a group of hippies from their camp near Stone henge. There were 25 arrests in an operation involving 400 police

Appendix 7
Article by Nick Davies on phone tapping from the Guardian April 18th, 1984.

British citizens can have their telephones tapped and their mail opened by the Security Service, the Special Branch, Customs and Excise and regular police units. The raw material which is gathered from the taps is known in MI5's office jargon as Source Towrope. The mail intercepts are called Source Phidias.

There is no sound legal basis for Towrope or Phidias—a fact which has been underlined in judgements by the High Court and the European Commission and which has now forced the Government to draft new laws. Those who believe they have been targetted have no right to confirm their suspicions and no right of appeal. Both operations are supposed to be controlled by the issue of Home Office warrants. But there is evidence which suggests that warrants may be issued too often and that some interception takes place without any warrant at all.

According to the warrant system, outlined in Government White Papers, an intelligence officer in MI5 who wanted to use Towrope or Phidias has to submit a written request which is filtered through his section chief, his branch director, the Deputy Director General, up to the Home Office where it would be vetted by the Permanent Under Secretary before finally being signed or rejected by the Home Secretary. Special Branch has a similar procedure.

A warrant is not supposed to be issued to MI5, according to a 1980 white paper unless there is 'a major subversive, terrorist or espionage activity that is likely to injure the national interest'. For a Special Branch warrant, there must be 'a really serious offence' a term which used to mean 'punishable with at least three years in prison' but which now includes 'an offence of lesser gravity in which either a larger number of people is involved or there is good reason to apprehend the use of violence.'

The participants in the warrant process to whom we have spoken—throughout the Home Office—all betray a striking nervousness about the consequences of someone being caught intercepting without a warrant or using a warrant for a 'soft' target. They add that taps absorb such a lot of time and labour that they are not worth the risk. 'Taps are not misused,' said one senior political source. 'No way.'

But there are problems with this view. Firstly, there are those who say they are profoundly worried about the 'effortless ease' with which old warrants are renewed and new warrants issued on the basis of information which is not objectively tested at any point in the procedure.

They also point to loopholes, particularly in Towrope: tapping a whole organisation by getting a warrant for one particularly militant member; tapping all members of an organisation by getting a warrant for its headquarters; planting a listening device—which requires no warrant at all; using the satellites run by GCHQ to eavesdrop on international calls; getting an 'any name' warrant to open all mail posted to an organisation.

Unless such loopholes are being exploited it is hard to understand how many of Britain's intercepts can legally take place.

● Greenpeace, the environmental group, planned last September to row across the Thames, climb Big Ben and unfurl a banner at the top. They arranged the protest at short notice over the phone and arrived at the river to find police everywhere. Two months later, their diver tried to block the discharge pipe at Sellafield nuclear plant, only to find that the pipe's end had been reshaped to stop them.

● The El Salvador Human Rights Campaign discovered at one o'clock one day that Henry Kissinger was due to pay a flying visit to London. At three o'clock they decided to organise a picket by phone. At five o'clock they turned up to find the police waiting for them.

● Repeated signs of tapping—from police fore-knowledge of plans and unofficial tip-offs to the sound of their own voices being played back—have been experienced by numerous CND activists, Plaid Cymru, Women for Life on Earth, Trades Councils, the local, district, and national offices of trade unions, left-wing groups, right-wing groups. The Operation Countryman inquiry into police corruption, and the National Council of Civil Liberties.

● David Norman, general treasurer of the POEU whose members execute the tapping said: 'To our certain knowledge, the process of tapping telephones is systematic and widespread, far more widespread than we are led to believe by official statements.'

Towrope is provided by Post Office workers in a system disclosed by Duncan Campbell in the New Statesman in 1980: the headquarters in Ebury Bridge Road, Chelsea, known as Tinkerbell, with the capacity to monitor 1,000 lines at once; the British Telecom vans—distinguished by having no home area marked on their door—which visit exchanges at night to place the taps.

Towrope is relayed on to MI5's Curzon Street office where A Branch has its own transcribers to handle the material. Then it is passed on—the Russian material to K Branch, the domestic material to F Branch—for analysis and logging. An MI5 warrant lasts for up to two months, but is renewable.

Police material is similarly passed to the 'client unit' for transcription. Their warrants are also issued for two months: they are supposed to be renewed for up to a month, but Special Branch is known to be granted longer renewals on request.

Letters are taken from sorting offices to the local Post Office Investigation Branch—Union House in St Martin's-le-Grand near St Paul's in London's case—where specialists still use a hot needle in the steam from a kettle to ease them open, cutting them only as a last resort.

They are trained to take special care to replace any loose hairs under the envelope flaps and generally to watch for other traps set to reveal their work. The contents are photocopied and passed to the clients.

Appendix 8
Articles on the involvement of the army in the miners' strike

1. News Line April 21st 1984

Army Already in Coalfields

The army is already in the coalfields, miner John Bishop of the Bargoed surface lodge, South Wales, told a meeting organised by the Bristol trades council.

Bishop described an incident at Birch Coppice colliery in the Midlands where one of his colleagues came face to face with his Welsh Guardsman son, dressed in a police uniform.

'There were a lot of policemen there when we arrived, but after a while, they marched them off and a new group of about 100 were marched into their place. They had no numbers on their shoulders.

I said to one of them, 'Where's your number then?' He answered: 'It was nicked this morning.' I said, 'Whoever it was, he must have been busy then', because none of them had numbers.

'Then I heard one of our members say out loud, "Good grief. What are you doing here son". It was to his son, who was dressed in police uniform. The son replied: "Well, dad, you know I am in the army and we have to do what we are told".'

He went on to outline the actions of the police at the picket line at Port Talbot steelworks.

They are putting policemen in plainclothes into the pickets. The miners are not causing the trouble. Now we have proved that they are doing it.

Bishop called for maximum support for the miners who 'are doing a good job'. We are stopping all the coal and carbon dioxide going into the power stations. You have got to understand that MacGregor has had time to put this together. He called the strike, not the miners.

'He has gone into the Midlands and said to the boys there. "This is a long-life pit. We'll give you a bonus of £60 to £80 a week to work it.'

'It's those boys who want the ballot, but we can say today there there is no ballot. There will never be a ballot.'

He explained the devastation that the government's plans would mean to Wales. 'You are talking about 20,000 jobs. Not just miners. The local bus company for instance does most of its work carrying miners. We are talking about all those jobs too.

'People ask, "Can they do a 1926 on us?" They are going to have a bloody good go. But with the support of the community and financial help, we will fight.

'We'll fight to the bitter end. We'll never give up. If we lose, whose job is safe? Stand together with us now, and this fight will be won.'

2. Brighton Voice, April 1984

Were paras used against pickets!

Disturbing evidence has come to light that soldiers from the parachute regiment may have been amongst a police contingent travelling from Sussex to miners' picket lines in the Midlands. Together with other indications that military personnel have been involved in the miners dispute, and the recently announced strengthening of the territorial army, this shows that the government is increasingly ready to impose a military solution on problems of industrial and social unrest.

In parliament on March 20, Tony Benn asked the Leader of the House, John Biffen, whether he could give a categorical assurance 'that the Government have not put the armed forces on the alert' in connection with the picketing of Midlands coalfields by the National Union of Mineworkers.

There was laughter in the House, then Mr. Biffen replied that he could indeed give such an assurance. It all seemed to confirm Benn's image as an extremist much given to fantasising about right-wing plots.

But now it seems that the question—while it may have been wrongly phrased—was not as ludicrous as it appeared. Evidence has been accumulating about the involvement of at least one army unit and of RAF police in the operation to stop miners from Kent and Yorkshire from travelling to the Midlands.

According to the Evening Argus (March 26), in the first week of police action 400 officers from Sussex were transported to the Midlands coalfields. On Sunday March 18 three coachlaods of police were driven up from Gatwick by southdown drivers based at Brighton.

The drivers thought it odd that during the whole of the 150-mile trip to Nottinghamshire the policemen on the coaches remained absolutely silent. It was assumed that they were under strict instructions not to say anything that might be overheard by the drivers (all TGWU members) and passed on to the NUM.

When the police officers' gear was being unloaded, two drivers noticed something unusual: many of the 'police' kit bags and some first-aid boxes were marked '1st. Battalion, Parachute Regiment.' It appeared that soldiers were being sent on anti-picket duty dressed as policemen.

When the drivers reported this back to their TGWU branch, the matter was taken up by the Union's Fleet Chairman, John Jays. The Paras' presence was of course flatly denied.

But this incident was followed by other signs of military involvment in the coalfields. Jim Colgan, Midlands NUM secretary, said on March 20 that miners at Dawmill Colliery in Warwickshire had spoken to police with no numbers on their uniforms. The officers told them that they were RAF police from Oxfordshire who had been brought in to assist the civilian police.

On March 26 Defence Secretary Michael Heseltine announced that the Territorial Army is to be strengthened by six new battalions, including a 140-strong company at Brighton's Preston Barracks, to increase its numbers from 75,000 to 86,000 over the next six years.

He was asked by Labour MP David Young to assure the House that the TA units would not be used politically as 'forces that can be commanded by departments to enforce political dogma'. According to both the *Financial Times* and *The Guardian*, Heseltine made *no* direct denial, but merely said that 'the whole House would reject Mr Young's assertion that the maintenance of law and order amounted to the imposition of political dogma'.

So, are the new TA units designed more to combat internal social unrest than to 'strengthen NATO's conventional forces' as the government claims? The evidence from the NUM dispute, Heseltine's evasiveness on the TA question, and the increasing level of police violence against pickets (shown for instance at Warrington last December) suggest that the lessons learned by the armed forces and the police in Northern Ireland are being applied on the UK mainland much sooner than anybody had thought.

Appendix 9
Police Support Units

In volume one we said that we believed that the Instant Response Units which have now been incorporated into a National Riot Force had originally been set up for use in a nuclear war. We have now seen the 'Police Manual of Home Defence' which was first published as 'Police War Duties Manual' in 1965 and we can confirm that this was the original 'excuse' for them being brought into being.

1. The formation of PSU's has been mentioned in the previous chapter at paragraph 11. Some of the many special and urgent tasks which would fall to the police in a war crisis are listed in Chapter 7. These special tasks coupled with day to day work impose big demands on all forces. At the same time police manpower would, as far as possible, have to be conserved for the vital law and order tasks which would follow a nuclear attack (see Chapter 9).

2. Accordingly the flexibility necessary to meet situations before and after attack is created by the formation of PSU's comprising about 20% of the regular male police strength of each force.

Establishment

3. A PSU will consist of 35 regular male police officers and a civilian driver. Alternatively under local arrangements a police officer could replace the civilian driver. The establishment of personnel and vehicles is shown at Appendix D. It will be seen that the units rely largely on existing resources of police transport.

4. PSU's would be established on a divisional basis, the actual number of units being proportional to manpower strengths. Each division would provide, at minimum, one PSU.

Administration

5. The important feature of a PSU is that it will remain as an integrated unit under the administrative and operational control of the pai‿nt force up to and beyond the attack. Each force will be responsible for all matters connected with their units's efficiency, i.e. transport, accommodation, food, petrol, oil, communications and vehicle replacements. Resupply and support when operating away from their own base will be the responsibility of divisional headquarters in whose area they are deployed.

Communications

6. Units will rely on existing radio and line facilities within their own forces are not always straightforward, but many police vehicles have ten-channel sets crystalled to operate on at least two neighbouring force channels. If required the number of channels would be increased by installing additional crystals.

Mobilisation

7. Chief Constables on receipt of a message from the Home Office would take steps to form Police Support Units in accordance with pre-arranged plans. *At the Chief Constable's discretion* some units may have already been formed up to deal with local situations.

8. Those units in potential target areas would as far as practicable be deployed and housed at a nearby divisional headquarters with a good protective factor. The point in time when such deployment is ordered will be a matter for the Chief Constable's judgement in the light of guidance from central government sources and the needs of the local situation.

Command and control

9. If units were deployed before attack on tasks outside their own force areas, the existing peacetime arrangements for control of mutual aid reinforcements would apply.

10. Units would be deployed on a divisional basis under the operational control of the divisional commander. The unit commander would be responsible for orders to his men to ensure that tasks are carried out.

11. Individual support units would not be amalgamated to make regional formations, but circumstances could arise when several units were required for a major incident. In such circumstances the Chief Constables would appoint a more senior officer to command the whole operation.

Appendix 10
The Association of Chief Police Officers.

In volume one on the policing of the first six weeks of the miners' strike, we considered the role of the Association of Chief Police Officers (ACPO). Through the National Reporting Centre (NRC) at Scotland Yard, ACPO are organising the deployment of specially trained riot force units to police the strike on a national basis. One of the questions we asked was: how had ACPO been able to override the statutory regulations for the organisation of local police forces? We can now address ourselves more fully to this issue; this information comes mainly from Brogden (1982).

ACPO arose from the County Chief Constables Club, dating from 1858, and the Chief Constables Association, formed in 1896. Both were distinctly different organisations, the former being more concerned with social functions; and both were independent from the Home Office. In 1908 the Home Office set up an annual Central Conference for both organisations, and the Inspectors of Constabulary (HMI), under Home Office supervision. The aims of these meetings were to increase the co-operation between local forces and central Government; and to allow for an exchange of ideas between different forces. As a direct result, in 1922, the two Chief Constables' organisations set up a meeting prior to the annual conference in order to present a united force to the Home Office, and increase the autonomy of senior police officers from Home Office interference.

ACPO was formally constituted in 1948 with the following aims: to promote the welfare and efficiency of the police service; to safeguard the interests of members; to provide opportunities for internal discussions of matters affecting policing; to give advice to other bodies such as the Home Office, the local Watch Committees and Royal Commissions on subjects related to the police service; and to provide social amenities for members. By 1968 it had a full-time secretariat. It is state-funded, but has always defended its voluntary status, and through that, its independence and right to confidenitiality. Brogden points out that: "ACPO has all the trimmings of a powerful secret society—financed through the central state but not directly beholden to the paymaster."

Since its formal constitution, ACPO had developed as a major political force in the arena of policing and law enforcement. In the immediate years following its formation, overtly political statements were limited, but gradually more and more political interventions were made. Individually, senior police officers were making contributions to political debates about forms of law enforcement, the Courts and public order on the one hand, in addition to their 'managerial' responsibilities on the other: the allocation of resources etc. But individual statements take on a new significance when stated *collectively* by an organised body. ACPO established that senior police officers had the right to contribute to political debates and, over time, a wide range of social isssues.

This has been achieved in four particular ways. Firstly, by establishing themselves at the forefront of *all* debates about policing policies and law enforcement. Senior Home Office ministers, and the Home Secretary, appear at ACPO conferences each year to justify their new or existing policies and guage the response of senior police officers.

Secondly, by increasing professionalism and acting as a source of expertise. ACPO have given advice to Royal Commissions, Select Committees and other public bodies on issues not directly related to policing, including mental illness, civil liberty and the Constitution. This general trend has, over a number of years, allowed them increasing latitude in their contributions, which have strayed well away from issues of policing to the directly political. In 1978, for example, in giving evidence to a Parliamentary Select Committee on disorder at an election meeting, ACPO proposed that the level of Parliamentary deposit should be raised to reduce the number of candidates who were 'unjustifiably' contesting seats. Their lobbying in the wake of the Royal Commission on Criminal Procedure, which led to the new Police and Criminal Evidence Bill, resulted in the dropping of the few safeguards for suspects proposed by the Commission and the increasing of repressive police powers. In some cases their political lobbying is dressed up as moral concern: for example on the breakdown of law and order in an increasingly uncivilized society; which of course requires more police powers and resources. Disguised as moralistic, such pleas are far more acceptable to the public.

Thirdly, ACPO acts as an innovator of new techniques and policing methods. These interventions vary from the introduction of new technology to the creation of specialised units to deal with picketing. We have already seen that ACPO are controlling the policing of the miners' strike. In the face of a gread deal of evidence of their direct political interventions, their continued denial of their involvement, most recently at a conference in Torquay, carries no weight at all.

Fourthly, ACPO provides a unity of policing policies and methods amongst all Chief Constables. This allows individual Chief Constables less discretion and gives ACPO control over policing methods on a *national* basis. Decisions are taken with reference to ACPO, who also provide public support for any officer who has handled a situation badly.

ACPO are now the major policing force in the country. They have played a large part in the growth of police autonomy. ACPO have established for themselves a power base which, at this stage, would be very difficult to destroy. This has been achieved by making interventions into an increasingly wide range of social, moral and political debates, and by providing initiatives in areas which are problematic for the state, such as industrial disputes. They have established their absolute *right* to make such interventions, and have acted completely unchallenged by all Governments and Police Authorities, thus bypassing any formal chains of accountability. Their increasing concern with the preservation of social order has established the police firmly as acting in defence of the State, and against the interests of working people and other groups which are identified as 'enemies'.

Appendix 11
The National Reporting Centre

In volume one we described the role and the function of the National Reporting Centre. Nick Davies, a journalist, has provided us with this short article which give us a little more information about how the Centre operates.

The National Reporting Centre was conceived at a meeting of the Association of Chief Police Officers with senior Home Office officials on April 4 1972. Its aim was specifically to prevent Arthur Scargill ever repeating the victory he had scored two months earlier on February 9 at the Saltley coke depot.

The picketing of Saltley traumatised the police by exposing a basic strategic weakness in their organisation: while the trade union movement was organised nationally and could sweep pickets across the county to converge on one target, the 43 police forces in England and Wales were trapped by the tradition of local policing into a fragmented reply.

The 1964 Police Act, which recognised the essentially local character of British police forces, allowed in Section 14 (1) for a Chief Constable to call on another Chief Constable for aid. But that was all, and, after Saltley, that was not enough.

The meeting at the Home Office in April 1972 attempted to extend national police liaison beyond what the Police Act stipulated without actually breaking the law. The device which they chose was the NRC, portrayed simply as an administrative link between Chief Constables to make mutual aid more efficient.

In practice, it has taken 12 years for the potential of the NRC to become apparent—largely because the Centre has been so little used in the intervening years.

It was first activated on February 10th 1974—again to deal with the NUM—and operated for 25 days. It then lay dormant for six years— through the Wilson and Callaghan governments—until October 21st 1980 when it was activated for a week during the prison officers' dispute to organise the overflow of prisoners into available cells. Over an eight week period in the summer of 1981, the NRC intermittently came on stream; on May 27th 1982, it was activated for five days to deal with the Pope's visit.

The current operation is easily the biggest action it has engaged in.

Since March 17th, ten officers have been working in shifts around the clock on the 13th floor of Scotland Yard, welding the 43 forces into a united response to the miners.

All sides agree that the centre is a clearing house for resources and information, using a microcomputer to record the number of officers, vehicles, dogs and horses available around the country and matching that against an array of wall charts showing the current disposition of police and miners and their expected movements over the next 24 hours.

There are three definable areas of concern about the NRC. The first is that it is distributing not just resources and information but also orders; that it is, in other words, the central command for an undeclared national police force. There is some evidence to justify the concern.

The Police Authorities, for example, who represent the local part of police management have been totally excluded from the planning, funding and running of the NRC. From those points of view, it is a national operation. Police tactics across the country have shown a striking uniformity—arrests at road blocks far from the scene of picketing, the imposition of bail conditions of an unusually severe character, the use of guidelines for civil law as the basis for criminal charges.

On a visit to the NRC control room in the second week of the strike, I heard an officer on the phone to a Midlands force, passing on the registration numbers of pickets' coaches. "They have been stopped and spoken to," he said. "Could you just monitor them until they get to the Notts. border where they'll turn them back?" It sounded very much like an order.

David Hall, the Chief Constable of Humberside and current President of ACPO, is in charge of the NRC. He denies that such orders are given. "You couldn't have heard that," he said. "There are no central directions from here."

The second concern is that the NRC is a tool which the Home Office can use to direct the police operation, thus breaking the taboo that the police should be free of political control. Mr Hall denies the charge very strongly.

He agrees that each day he travels to the Home Office to meet with civil servants from F4 department, which is responsible for public order, and he agrees that he has 'informally discussed' the dispute with the Home Secretary, but he insists that this is a one-way traffic in which he reports on progress without receiving any instructions or requests for action.

The third concern is the more specific one that the NRC marks a new intensity in the gathering of intelligence on trade unionists. The control room on the 13th floor of Scotland Yard is four floors away from the headquarters of the Special Branch on the 17th floor. The civil servants in F4 who Mr. Hall meets each morning are also responsible for 'security liaison'—dealing with the demands of MI5, particularly for phone tapping warrants.

MI5 is known to have a special interest in the miners and the thrusting young executive who is now in charge of MI5's anti-subversion branch is considered a specialist on the NUM. Mr. Hall says that he has had no help from the Special Branch and no intelligence from F4.

Appendix 12
The arrest of Mr. S.

On 22nd March 1984 I was on the picket line at Thoresby Colliery, Notts. I left it and travelled as far as Ollerton roundabout in my car with three others. I intended to go to the garage at the roundabout for petrol and cigarettes. When we got there the garage was closed. I went round it to go back to Thoresby on the same road but just as I was leaving the roundabout the car stalled and flooded. I waved down the car that was follwing me—its occupants were pickets who had come with us to the garage—because I thought it might need a push off the roundabout. Before I could explain to them what had happened, a police officer came over from a car that had been parked over the other side of the roundabout. He started shouting and swearing at us. I tried to explain what had happened and he walked off. We all got back into the car and I put my foot right down on the accelerator to clear the carburettor of excess fuel. The car started but was backfiring and spluttering. I drove off steadily and as the car picked up speed and ran more smoothly, I put my foot on the accelerator to clear the carburettor again. I then went back towards the picket line at Thoresby. Just before we reached the pit, I saw in the mirror a police car passing several cars behind me. It went past me at high speed with it's lights flashing. It pulled in to a lay-by about 200-350 yards in front and stopped. I continued to drive towards the pit and indicated to go into the lay by, opposite the colliery. I was stopped from going in by police officers who surrounded the car in lines of 2 or 3 deep. There were about 20-30 police officers and they started banging on the roof of the car. When the pickets realised what was happening they pushed forward from the picket line to get a better view. At this stage I thought the car was going to turn over. The same police officer who was at the roundabout came up and asked us to get out of the car. I advised all the occupants to lock the car doors and remain inside, as I was concerned for their safety. I thought that if we got out we would be trapped between the car door and car body and be injured. There was a lot of abuse from the police and banging and shouting. I took out a camera from the glove compartment and took several photos. Without any warning as I was finally unlocking my car door when things had calmed down a bit, I saw a police officer wielding a 2' 6" iron bar straight towards my face. I ducked my head, closed my eyes and the next thing I knew I was being showered with glass. The officer had hit the front windscreen. Before this had happened, I had asked the police officer to give us 2 minutes to allow the situation to calm down and agreed to get out of the car if they did this. This was ignored.

I was dragged out of the car, as were the others. We were taken to Mansfield police station and charged with obstructing the highway, obstructing a police officer and failing to stop. (Me.) The others were charged with obstructing a police officer.